Introduction to Cobol Programming

Maxwell Vector

Contents

3

4

Chapter 1

Structure of a COBOL Program

Overview of Program Organization

A COBOL program is architected as a meticulously partitioned construct in which each division addresses a distinct facet of program specification and execution. The organization is governed by a rigid structure that delineates the program into sections, each contributing to an overall clarity of design and execution. Every division is embedded with a precise syntactical framework that ensures the translation of procedural intent into a form amenable to both human inspection and machine processing. This architectural paradigm reinforces an environment in which administrative metadata, environmental parameters, data definitions, and executable logic are clearly segregated and individually expounded upon.

Identification Division

The Identification Division represents the formal declaration of program metadata and intrinsic identity. This division encapsulates administrative descriptors such as the program name, version identifiers, and authorship details within an austere yet unambiguous format. The delineation provided by this division imposes a disciplined method for associating a unique identity with the program, thereby serving as the foundational descriptor upon which further specifications are layered. The inherent structure of this division adheres to strict fixed-format rules, ensuring that each element related to program identification is positioned in a manner that alludes both to its functional role and its contextual relevance.

Environment Division

The Environment Division is dedicated to specifying the external conditions and interfacing requirements of the program. In this division, the configuration of file systems, input-output devices, and various system-dependent attributes is articulated with precision. The division is organized to encapsulate the characteristics of the execution platform, defining parameters that govern how the program interacts with its operational milieu. Its syntactical structure is designed to comply with fixed-format mandates, thereby ensuring that elements such as file-control descriptors and device assignments are presented in a uniform and predictable layout. This structural consistency is instrumental in maintaining the integrity of external interconnections and in enabling reliable data handling.

Data Division

Central to the data management paradigm of a COBOL program, the Data Division is tasked with the definition and organization of all data entities and variables. It adopts a hierarchical approach through the use of level numbers, which demarcate parent-child relationships among data items and records. This systematic hierarchy facilitates a natural mapping between the logical structure of information and its physical storage representation. Detailed specifications of data types, such as alphanumeric and numeric representations, are given explicit form through the use of picture clauses and other declarative statements. The resulting structure not only underpins data integrity but also optimizes the clarity and manageability of variable definitions throughout the program's lifecycle.

Procedure Division

The Procedure Division constitutes the operational core wherein executable logic is delineated and sequential processes are defined. It organizes the flow of computational instructions into distinct paragraphs and statements that collectively describe the dynamics of data manipulation and control flow. Within this division, operations ranging from simple data transfers to complex arithmetic expressions are articulated in a form that emphasizes explicit procedural semantics. The organization of the Procedure Division is inherently systematic; it enforces a disciplined layering of control constructs that govern sequential, conditional, and iterative processing without ambiguity. This methodical segmentation of logic into comprehensible blocks is emblematic of COBOL's overarching commitment to clarity and rigorous syntactical discipline.

Cobol Code Snippet

```
IDENTIFICATION DIVISION.
PROGRAM-ID. CALCULATION-DEMO.
AUTHOR. Maxwell_Vector.

ENVIRONMENT DIVISION.
INPUT-OUTPUT SECTION.
FILE-CONTROL.  * No files are used in this demonstration.

DATA DIVISION.
WORKING-STORAGE SECTION.
* Numeric Variables for Basic Arithmetic Operations
01 WS-FIRST-NUMBER    PIC 9(4) VALUE 12.
01 WS-SECOND-NUMBER   PIC 9(4) VALUE 4.
01 WS-SUM             PIC 9(5) VALUE ZEROS.
01 WS-PRODUCT         PIC 9(7) VALUE ZEROS.
01 WS-DIFFERENCE      PIC 9(4) VALUE ZEROS.
01 WS-QUOTIENT        PIC 9(5)V99 VALUE ZEROS.

* Variables for an Illustrative Algorithm: Factorial Calculation
01 WS-FACTORIAL       PIC 9(10) VALUE 1.
01 WS-COUNTER         PIC 9(4) VALUE 1.

* Message storage for error handling or info display.
01 WS-MESSAGE         PIC X(50).

PROCEDURE DIVISION.
MAIN-PROCEDURE.
    DISPLAY "COBOL Calculations and Algorithm Demonstration".

    PERFORM CALCULATE-SUM.
    PERFORM CALCULATE-PRODUCT.
    PERFORM CALCULATE-DIFFERENCE.
    PERFORM CALCULATE-QUOTIENT.
    PERFORM CALCULATE-FACTORIAL.
```

```
        PERFORM DISPLAY-RESULTS.
        STOP RUN.

    CALCULATE-SUM.
        ADD WS-FIRST-NUMBER TO WS-SECOND-NUMBER GIVING WS-SUM.
        DISPLAY "Computed Sum:" WS-FIRST-NUMBER " + " WS-SECOND-NUMBER "
    ↪    = " WS-SUM.
        .

    CALCULATE-PRODUCT.
        MULTIPLY WS-FIRST-NUMBER BY WS-SECOND-NUMBER GIVING WS-PRODUCT.
        DISPLAY "Computed Product:" WS-FIRST-NUMBER " * "
    ↪    WS-SECOND-NUMBER " = " WS-PRODUCT.
        .

    CALCULATE-DIFFERENCE.
        SUBTRACT WS-SECOND-NUMBER FROM WS-FIRST-NUMBER GIVING
    ↪    WS-DIFFERENCE.
        DISPLAY "Computed Difference:" WS-FIRST-NUMBER " - "
    ↪    WS-SECOND-NUMBER " = " WS-DIFFERENCE.
        .

    CALCULATE-QUOTIENT.
        IF WS-SECOND-NUMBER NOT = 0
            DIVIDE WS-FIRST-NUMBER BY WS-SECOND-NUMBER GIVING WS-QUOTIENT
        ELSE
            MOVE "Error: Division by Zero" TO WS-MESSAGE
            DISPLAY WS-MESSAGE
        END-IF.
        .

    CALCULATE-FACTORIAL.
        * Compute factorial of WS-SECOND-NUMBER using an iterative loop.
        MOVE 1 TO WS-FACTORIAL.
        MOVE 1 TO WS-COUNTER.
        PERFORM UNTIL WS-COUNTER > WS-SECOND-NUMBER
            MULTIPLY WS-FACTORIAL BY WS-COUNTER GIVING WS-FACTORIAL
            ADD 1 TO WS-COUNTER
        END-PERFORM.
        DISPLAY "Computed Factorial:" WS-SECOND-NUMBER "! = "
    ↪    WS-FACTORIAL.
        .

    DISPLAY-RESULTS.
        DISPLAY "-----------------------------".
        DISPLAY "Final Computation Results:".
        DISPLAY "Sum        : " WS-SUM.
        DISPLAY "Product    : " WS-PRODUCT.
        DISPLAY "Difference : " WS-DIFFERENCE.
        DISPLAY "Quotient   : " WS-QUOTIENT.
        DISPLAY "Factorial  : " WS-FACTORIAL.
        DISPLAY "-----------------------------".
```

Chapter 2

COBOL Syntax and Format

Fixed-format Rules

COBOL adheres to a fixed-format layout that is an inheritance of early computing practices, where physical media imposed stringent spatial delimitations on source code. Every source line is structured to conform to predetermined column boundaries. Columns 1 through 6 are allocated for sequence numbering, which historically facilitated tracking and error detection in batch processing environments. Column 7 functions as an indicator field where special notations—such as comment flags or continuation markers—are unambiguously signified. The substantive portion of each line is confined to columns 8 through 72, a delineation that ensures the core syntactical elements occupy a consistent and predictable space. This rigor in spatial allocation is not a mere relic of documentation practices; it enforces a discipline that precludes ambiguous interpretations during both the lexical and syntactic analysis performed by the compiler.

Column Significance in Source Code

An intrinsic element of COBOL's design is the semantic assignment of meaning to specific columns within each line. In this paradigm, the significance of a column is inextricably linked to its position.

Zone A, defined by columns 8 to 11, typically houses division headers, section identifiers, and level numbers, thus establishing the hierarchical structure within the program. Zone B, which spans columns 12 to 72, is reserved for the detailed statements, continuations, and operational instructions that define the behavior of the program. The precise subdivision of these zones contributes to the language's inherent resistance to syntactical ambiguity. Any deviation from these prescribed boundaries can disrupt the compiler's interpretation of the code and lead to errors that are challenging to diagnose, given that the spatial context directly informs the processor of the intended structure and sequence of the instructions.

General Syntax Conventions

The syntactical rules of COBOL extend beyond mere spatial formatting, encompassing a comprehensive set of conventions that orchestrate the overall structure and clarity of the language. COBOL's verbosity is a deliberate design choice, intended to enhance readability by delineating program structure through explicit keyword usage and systematic naming conventions. Critical divisions of a program—such as the IDENTIFICATION, ENVIRONMENT, DATA, and PROCEDURE divisions—are each signaled by keywords that serve as unambiguous markers of different functional areas. Within these divisions, the structure is further refined by the use of level numbers, which establish a clear parent-child relationship among data elements and program sections. This lexical discipline is supplemented by strict rules governing delimiters, separators, and continuation markers, which collectively ensure that each syntactical component is parsed in a precise and deterministic manner. The interplay of these fixed-format rules and general syntactical conventions underpins the robustness of COBOL, contributing to its enduring capacity to support large-scale, error-resistant applications.

Cobol Code Snippet

```
IDENTIFICATION DIVISION.
PROGRAM-ID. COMPUTATION-EXAMPLES.

ENVIRONMENT DIVISION.
```

19

```
DATA DIVISION.
WORKING-STORAGE SECTION.
*---------------------------------------------------
* Variables for Circle Calculations
    77  RADIUS       PIC 9(4)V99 VALUE 5.00.
    77  PI           PIC 9(3).99  VALUE 3.14.
    77  AREA       .  PIC 9(6)V99 VALUE ZEROS.
    77  PERIMETER    PIC 9(6)V99 VALUE ZEROS.
*---------------------------------------------------
* Variables for Factorial Calculation (Algorithm Example)
    77  FACT-NUM     PIC 9(2)   VALUE 6.
    77  FACTORIAL    PIC 9(8)   VALUE 1.
    77  FACT-COUNT   PIC 9(2)   VALUE 6.
*---------------------------------------------------


PROCEDURE DIVISION.
    MAIN-PARAGRAPH.
        DISPLAY "COBOL Computation Examples".
        PERFORM CALCULATE-CIRCLE.
        PERFORM CALCULATE-FACTORIAL.
        PERFORM DISPLAY-RESULTS.
        STOP RUN.

    CALCULATE-CIRCLE.
        * Compute the area of a circle using AREA = PI *
        ↪  RADIUS^2
        COMPUTE AREA = PI * RADIUS * RADIUS.
        * Compute the perimeter of a circle using PERIMETER =
        ↪  2 * PI * RADIUS
        COMPUTE PERIMETER = 2 * PI * RADIUS.
        EXIT.

    CALCULATE-FACTORIAL.
        * Compute the factorial of FACT-NUM using a
        ↪  descending loop
        PERFORM UNTIL FACT-COUNT < 1
            COMPUTE FACTORIAL = FACTORIAL * FACT-COUNT
            SUBTRACT 1 FROM FACT-COUNT
        END-PERFORM.
        EXIT.

    DISPLAY-RESULTS.
        DISPLAY "Circle Calculations:".
        DISPLAY "  Radius    : " RADIUS.
        DISPLAY "  Area      : " AREA.
        DISPLAY "  Perimeter : " PERIMETER.
        DISPLAY " "  .
        DISPLAY "Factorial Calculation:".
        DISPLAY "  Factorial of " FACT-NUM " is: " FACTORIAL.
        EXIT.
```

Chapter 3

IDENTIFICATION Division Essentials

Purpose and Role of the IDENTIFICA-TION Division

The IDENTIFICATION Division serves as the foundational meta-data repository for a COBOL program, providing a delineated header that encapsulates essential descriptive attributes. This division occupies a critical segment in the overall structure, ensuring that the program is unequivocally distinguished within multi-faceted software environments. Its structured declaration is integral for both the compiler's parsing mechanisms and the archival practices that maintain software integrity over time.

Central to its role is the establishment of a precise identity for the program module. The division is crafted under rigorous fixed-format constraints that guarantee the consistent placement and recognition of its components. This meticulous arrangement permits the systematic management of legacy and modern systems alike, serving to facilitate maintenance and verification processes through an explicit account of the program's provenance.

Mandatory Elements and Their Semantics

At the core of the IDENTIFICATION Division lies the PROGRAM-ID clause, the principal element that uniquely designates the program. The syntax of the PROGRAM-ID clause is governed by strict formatting conventions inherent in COBOL, ensuring that the program is immediately identifiable by both automated processes and human reviewers. This clause serves as an unambiguous marker that aligns the source file with its intended functionality and system role.

In addition to the PROGRAM-ID clause, the division conventionally includes elements that detail the authorship and origin of the program. The author's identification, typically expressed through a dedicated clause, contributes critical information pertaining to the individual or entity responsible for the program's design and implementation. The precise articulation of these metadata elements not only supports accountability and traceability but also reinforces organizational standards within software development. Each component is embedded with a clear semantic function, collectively delivering a robust description that underpins the systematic management of the code throughout its lifecycle.

Cobol Code Snippet

```
IDENTIFICATION DIVISION.
PROGRAM-ID. CALCULATE-INTEREST.
AUTHOR. Maxwell_Vector.
DATE-WRITTEN. "2024-10-12".

ENVIRONMENT DIVISION.
CONFIGURATION SECTION.
* No file-control entries are necessary for this example

DATA DIVISION.
WORKING-STORAGE SECTION.
01 WS-PRINCIPAL    PIC 9(7)V99 VALUE 10000.00.
01 WS-RATE         PIC 99V99    VALUE 05.50.
01 WS-TIME         PIC 99       VALUE 03.
01 WS-INTEREST     PIC 9(7)V99 VALUE ZERO.
01 WS-COMPOUND     PIC 9(7)V99 VALUE ZERO.
01 WS-COUNT        PIC 99       VALUE 1.

PROCEDURE DIVISION.
```

```cobol
MAIN-PROCEDURE.
    *------------------------------------------------------
    * Compute Simple Interest using the formula:
    *     Interest = (Principal * Rate * Time) / 100
    *------------------------------------------------------
    COMPUTE WS-INTEREST = (WS-PRINCIPAL * WS-RATE * WS-TIME)
    ↪  / 100.

    *------------------------------------------------------
    * Compute Compound Amount iteratively for each period.
    * The algorithm multiplies the current amount by
    * (1 + Rate/100) for each time period.
    *------------------------------------------------------
    MOVE WS-PRINCIPAL TO WS-COMPOUND.
    PERFORM UNTIL WS-COUNT > WS-TIME
        COMPUTE WS-COMPOUND = WS-COMPOUND * (1 + WS-RATE /
        ↪  100)
        ADD 1 TO WS-COUNT
    END-PERFORM.

    *------------------------------------------------------
    * Display the results on the console.
    *------------------------------------------------------
    DISPLAY "Simple Interest: " WS-INTEREST.
    DISPLAY "Compound Amount: " WS-COMPOUND.

    STOP RUN.
```

Chapter 4

PROGRAM-ID Clause Fundamentals

Defining Program Identity Through PROGRAM-ID

The PROGRAM-ID clause serves as the definitive marker for a COBOL program, establishing a unique identifier that distinguishes the module within complex systems. This clause resides within the IDENTIFICATION Division and is the principal mechanism by which the program's name is declared. In formalizing program identity, the clause not only provides a label but also embeds semantic information that is subsequently utilized during the compilation and linking phases. The value specified by this clause is incorporated into the metadata, ensuring that the program is unambiguously mapped to its corresponding functionalities within the software ecosystem. By strictly adhering to the syntactic and formatting rules prescribed by COBOL, the PROGRAM-ID clause guarantees that the identifier is both recognizable to automated parsing tools and interpretable by system-level processes.

Structural and Syntactical Characteristics

The construction of the PROGRAM-ID clause is governed by stringent structural constraints inherent to COBOL's fixed-format style.

The clause is typically positioned at the commencement of the IDENTIFICATION Division, where the strict layout demands that keywords such as `PROGRAM-ID` appear in a fixed column range. Each constituent element—the clause name, the program identifier, and the trailing punctuation—must occupy designated positions to ensure accurate parsing by the compiler. The identifier itself is subject to formal naming conventions, often limited to an alphanumeric sequence interspersed with hyphens, and must be delimited by periods in accordance with the language specification. Such rigor in syntax and format facilitates consistency across diverse programming environments and minimizes ambiguities during the translation of source code into executable form. The careful preservation of fixed-format constraints maintains a high degree of predictability and reliability within the compilation process.

Semantic Significance in Compilation and Linking

Beyond its role as a nominal identifier, the PROGRAM-ID clause carries substantial semantic weight that influences several phases of program processing. During compilation, the unique identifier declared by this clause is incorporated into the global symbol table and used as a reference point for inter-module communication. The precise naming provided through PROGRAM-ID is critical when resolving subprogram calls or establishing links between discrete units of functionality. Furthermore, the identifier facilitates runtime diagnostics by serving as a key reference in error reporting and performance monitoring systems. The semantic embedding of program identity thus ensures that system-level operations, such as debugging and memory management, can rely on consistent naming across various stages of program execution. In this way, the PROGRAM-ID clause acts as a cornerstone in maintaining the integrity and coherence of the overall software structure.

Cobol Code Snippet

```
**************************************************************
*   Example COBOL Program: FORMULA-CALCULATOR
*   Demonstrates the use of the PROGRAM-ID clause along with
*   various arithmetic operations and a looping algorithm to
*   compute important equations and formulas.
```

```
*************************************************************

IDENTIFICATION DIVISION.
PROGRAM-ID. FORMULA-CALCULATOR.

ENVIRONMENT DIVISION.
CONFIGURATION SECTION.
SOURCE-COMPUTER. IBM-370.
OBJECT-COMPUTER. IBM-370.

DATA DIVISION.
WORKING-STORAGE SECTION.
* Define numeric variables for various computations
01 WS-NUM1        PIC 9(5)V99 VALUE 12345.67.
01 WS-NUM2        PIC 9(5)V99 VALUE   89.01.
01 WS-SUM         PIC 9(6)V99 VALUE ZERO.
01 WS-DIFF        PIC 9(6)V99 VALUE ZERO.
01 WS-PROD        PIC 9(10)V99 VALUE ZERO.
01 WS-QUOT        PIC 9(5)V99 VALUE ZERO.
01 WS-RESULT      PIC 9(10)V99 VALUE ZERO.
01 WS-ITER        PIC 9(3)     VALUE ZERO.
01 WS-TOTAL       PIC 9(10)V99 VALUE ZERO.

PROCEDURE DIVISION.
MAIN-PARA.
    DISPLAY "COBOL FORMULA CALCULATOR STARTED".
    DISPLAY "------------------------------------".

    * Basic Arithmetic Operations
    ADD WS-NUM1 TO WS-NUM2 GIVING WS-SUM.
    DISPLAY "SUM OF WS-NUM1 AND WS-NUM2: " WS-SUM.

    SUBTRACT WS-NUM2 FROM WS-NUM1 GIVING WS-DIFF.
    DISPLAY "DIFFERENCE BETWEEN WS-NUM1 AND WS-NUM2: "
    ↪  WS-DIFF.

    MULTIPLY WS-NUM1 BY WS-NUM2 GIVING WS-PROD.
    DISPLAY "PRODUCT OF WS-NUM1 AND WS-NUM2: " WS-PROD.

    IF WS-NUM2 NOT = ZERO
        DIVIDE WS-NUM1 BY WS-NUM2 GIVING WS-QUOT
    ELSE
        DISPLAY "ERROR: Division by zero."
    END-IF.
    DISPLAY "QUOTIENT OF WS-NUM1 DIVIDED BY WS-NUM2: "
    ↪  WS-QUOT.

    * Complex Equation: Difference of Squares Calculation
    COMPUTE WS-RESULT = (WS-NUM1 + WS-NUM2) * (WS-NUM1 -
    ↪  WS-NUM2).
    DISPLAY "RESULT OF DIFFERENCE OF SQUARES: " WS-RESULT.

    * Looping Algorithm: Sum of First 10 Multiples of WS-NUM2
```

26

```cobol
MOVE ZERO TO WS-TOTAL.
PERFORM VARYING WS-ITER FROM 1 BY 1 UNTIL WS-ITER > 10
    COMPUTE WS-TOTAL = WS-TOTAL + (WS-NUM2 * WS-ITER)
END-PERFORM.
DISPLAY "SUM OF FIRST 10 MULTIPLES OF WS-NUM2: "
↪   WS-TOTAL.

* Final Complex Computation using a Combination of
↪   Operations
COMPUTE WS-RESULT = ((WS-NUM1 * 2) + (WS-NUM2 / 2)) -
↪   WS-SUM.
DISPLAY "FINAL COMPUTATION RESULT: " WS-RESULT.

DISPLAY "COBOL FORMULA CALCULATOR COMPLETED".
STOP RUN.
```

Chapter 5

ENVIRONMENT Division Overview

Structural Overview of the ENVIRONMENT Division

The ENVIRONMENT Division occupies a distinct role in the architecture of a COBOL program by delineating the operational context in which the application executes. This division is carefully structured to isolate environment-specific definitions from the computational and data manipulation aspects handled in other divisions. Its design establishes a framework where file-control directives and system interfacing constructs are declared according to rigorous syntactic conventions. The spatial organization of this division, with its predetermined placement of keywords and identifiers, facilitates an unambiguous association between the logical program elements and their corresponding external resources. Such a clearly defined structure contributes to a consistent mapping during compilation and runtime execution, ensuring that the program's file manipulation and peripheral interactions are reliably maintained.

File-Control Entries and Specifications

A fundamental element within the ENVIRONMENT Division is the specification of file-control entries, which function as the formal mechanism to associate logical file identifiers with external data sources. Each file-control entry adheres to a prescribed syntax that dictates the placement and formatting of its components, including attributes that describe file organization, access modalities, and data alignment. These entries establish vital links between the file definitions found in the DATA DIVISION and the actual entities accessed during program execution. The precision involved in formulating file-control specifications is instrumental for guaranteeing consistency in file-based operations. By providing a disciplined mapping between the logical and the physical, these entries support robust mechanisms for data input and output, error trapping, and resource scheduling. This layer of abstraction enables the program to maintain a high level of portability and modularity, whereby file-related operations are insulated from variations in the underlying operational environment.

Interfacing with System-Level Software

Beyond the establishment of file-control directives, the ENVIRON-MENT Division encapsulates detailed specifications that facilitate interfacing with the broader system-level software infrastructure. This interfacing is achieved through declarative constructs that define resource allocation strategies, file status codes, and operational parameters without delving into particulars related to system hardware. The constructs within this division serve to harmonize the COBOL program with the operating system's management routines, ensuring that resource access and process scheduling are coordinated efficiently. Notably, the mechanisms for system interfacing provide symbolic representations of system resources that are reconciled at runtime with actual allocation data available via the operating environment. The careful abstraction employed here guarantees that variations across deployment platforms are managed systematically, thereby enabling reliable error detection, recovery operations, and performance optimizations. The interplay between these interfaces and the program's file-control entries underscores the importance of an integrated approach to environment management within COBOL, where software-defined protocols dictate the behavior of external interactions while remaining agnostic to the underlying hardware specifics.

Cobol Code Snippet

```
IDENTIFICATION DIVISION.
PROGRAM-ID. ENVIRONMENT-ALG.

*-------------------------------------------------------------
* This program demonstrates key COBOL constructs from the
* ENVIRONMENT Division along with file-control handling,
* and includes two important algorithms:
*    1. Calculating the average of numeric values read
*       from an external data file.
*    2. Computing compound interest using the formula:
*         Compound Interest = Principal * ((1 + Rate) ** Time)
*-------------------------------------------------------------

ENVIRONMENT DIVISION.
INPUT-OUTPUT SECTION.
FILE-CONTROL.
    SELECT NUMBER-FILE ASSIGN TO "DATA.DAT"
        ORGANIZATION IS SEQUENTIAL
        ACCESS MODE IS SEQUENTIAL
        FILE STATUS IS WS-FILE-STATUS.

DATA DIVISION.
FILE SECTION.
FD  NUMBER-FILE
    RECORD CONTAINS 80 CHARACTERS.
01  NUMBER-RECORD.
    05 FILLER       PIC X(2).
    05 NUM-VALUE    PIC 9(5)V99.

WORKING-STORAGE SECTION.
01 WS-FILE-STATUS        PIC XX.
01 WS-END-OF-FILE        PIC X     VALUE 'N'.
01 WS-SUM                PIC 9(7)V99 VALUE ZERO.
01 WS-COUNT              PIC 9(5)    VALUE ZERO.
01 WS-AVERAGE            PIC 9(7)V99 VALUE ZERO.
01 WS-NUMBER             PIC 9(5)V99.

* Variables for compound interest calculation
01 WS-PRINCIPAL          PIC 9(7)V99 VALUE 1000.00.
01 WS-INTEREST-RATE      PIC 9(2)V99 VALUE 0.05.
01 WS-TIME               PIC 9(2)    VALUE 10.
01 WS-COMPOUND-INTEREST  PIC 9(7)V99 VALUE ZERO.

PROCEDURE DIVISION.
MAIN-PROGRAM.
    OPEN INPUT NUMBER-FILE.
    PERFORM UNTIL WS-END-OF-FILE = 'Y'
        READ NUMBER-FILE
            AT END
                MOVE 'Y' TO WS-END-OF-FILE
```

```
            NOT AT END
                MOVE NUM-VALUE TO WS-NUMBER
                ADD WS-NUMBER TO WS-SUM
                ADD 1 TO WS-COUNT
        END-READ
END-PERFORM.
CLOSE NUMBER-FILE.

IF WS-COUNT > 0
    COMPUTE WS-AVERAGE = WS-SUM / WS-COUNT
    DISPLAY "Calculated Average: " WS-AVERAGE
ELSE
    DISPLAY "No data records found."
END-IF.

* Compute compound interest using the formula:
* Compound Interest = Principal * ((1 + Interest Rate) ** Time)
COMPUTE WS-COMPOUND-INTEREST = WS-PRINCIPAL * ((1 +
↪   WS-INTEREST-RATE) ** WS-TIME).
DISPLAY "Compound Interest after " WS-TIME " years: "
↪   WS-COMPOUND-INTEREST.

STOP RUN.
```

Chapter 6

DATA DIVISION
Overview

Conceptual Framework of Data Definitions

The DATA DIVISION serves as the central repository for all declarations pertaining to the program's data elements. This division systematically delineates every variable, record, and structure that will be employed throughout the computational process. The formalism adopted in these declarations establishes a rigorous mapping between logical data models and their physical memory representations. A hierarchy of level numbers is employed to impose order and nesting upon data items, thereby affording a clear and unambiguous structure. The precision inherent in specifying data definitions, including character strings, numeric values, and composite groupings, underpins the reliability of data manipulation and ensures that the attendant memory allocation is both predictable and efficient.

Variable Declaration and Memory Configuration

Declarations within the DATA DIVISION articulate the characteristics of individual data items with meticulous syntactic detail.

Each variable is declared with a precise definition, often articulated through picture clauses that constrain both the format and the range of permissible values. The explicit assignment of level numbers to these data items governs their hierarchical relationships, thereby facilitating the grouping of subordinate variables within larger, logically coherent structures. This systematic approach not only fosters clarity in the declaration process but also directly influences the configuration of memory. The stratification of variables into elementary and group items enables a robust memory model wherein each data element can be precisely addressed and manipulated in accordance with its defined constraints.

Record Structures and Hierarchical Organization

The organization of records within the DATA DIVISION is achieved through a deliberate hierarchical framework that leverages the ordered structure of level numbers. Records are conceptualized as collections of logically related variables, each positioned within a structured hierarchy that delineates parent–child relationships. Group items, which encapsulate several subordinate fields, are defined in a manner that inherently supports the segmentation and aggregation of complex data constructs. This hierarchical methodology ensures that each record is decomposed into well-defined substructures, where the integrity of data types and the prescribed formats are maintained. The interplay between level-based organization and picture clause constraints results in a coherent blueprint for data representation, effectively bridging the abstract formulation of data items with their concrete realization in memory.

Cobol Code Snippet

```
IDENTIFICATION DIVISION.
PROGRAM-ID. EquationAlgorithmDemo.

ENVIRONMENT DIVISION.
* For this demonstration, no specific hardware configuration is
↪    required.

DATA DIVISION.
WORKING-STORAGE SECTION.
```

33

```
* Define numeric variables with explicit PIC clauses and initial
↪  values.
01 WS-VARS.
   05 WS-A       PIC 9(5)V99 VALUE 0123.45.
   05 WS-B       PIC 9(5)V99 VALUE 0678.90.
   05 WS-C       PIC 9(4)V99 VALUE 0010.00.
   05 WS-D       PIC 9(3)V99 VALUE 0005.00.
   05 WS-E       PIC 9(5)V99 VALUE 0050.00.
   05 WS-TOTAL   PIC 9(7)V99 VALUE ZERO.

* Define a record structure to illustrate hierarchical grouping.
01 WS-RECORD.
   05 WS-HEADER.
      10 WS-PROG-NAME  PIC A(20) VALUE 'COBOL DEMO PROGRAM'.
      10 WS-DATE       PIC X(10) VALUE '01-01-2024'.
   05 WS-DATA.
      10 WS-NUM1       PIC 9(5)V99 VALUE ZERO.
      10 WS-NUM2       PIC 9(5)V99 VALUE ZERO.

PROCEDURE DIVISION.
MAIN-LOGIC.
   DISPLAY 'Starting Equation and Algorithm Demo'.

   * Perform calculation using an important formula:
   *   WS-TOTAL = ((WS-A + WS-B) * WS-C / WS-D) - WS-E
   IF WS-D NOT = ZERO
      COMPUTE WS-TOTAL = ((WS-A + WS-B) * WS-C / WS-D) - WS-E
   ELSE
      DISPLAY 'Error: Division by Zero encountered in calculation'
   END-IF.

   * Update record structure with sample values.
   MOVE WS-A TO WS-NUM1.
   MOVE WS-B TO WS-NUM2.

   DISPLAY 'Computed Total: ' WS-TOTAL.
   DISPLAY 'Program Name: ' WS-PROG-NAME ' | Date: ' WS-DATE.
   DISPLAY 'Record Data - Num1: ' WS-NUM1 ', Num2: ' WS-NUM2.

   STOP RUN.
```

Chapter 7

WORKING-STORAGE Section Fundamentals

Persistent Data Storage and Lifetime Management

The WORKING-STORAGE section in COBOL embodies a fundamental design artifact responsible for preserving variables that persist throughout the entire program execution. The static allocation inherent in this section guarantees that once declared, variables retain their state over the complete runtime, thereby offering a stable memory environment in contrast to transient or dynamically allocated storage. Variables are defined using explicit formatting directives, such as the *PIC* clause, which meticulously determines their visual representation and operational constraints. This premeditated approach to memory allocation not only secures the persistence of data items but also lays a foundation for predictable behavior in complex computation sequences.

Hierarchical Structures and Data Semantics

The declarative syntax of the WORKING-STORAGE section benefits from a hierarchical organization achieved through the assignment of level numbers. These level numbers, for instance 01, 05, and others, impose a structured layering that delineates group items from elementary variables. This hierarchical model is instrumental in crafting composite data constructs where related variables are nested within larger groupings. The rigorous ordering facilitates both clarity in data semantics and precision in physical memory mapping. By adhering to this structural paradigm, the section bridges abstract data definitions with their concrete realization in memory, ensuring that every variable's context and interrelationships are unequivocally established.

Declarative Precision and Memory Configuration

The role of the WORKING-STORAGE section extends beyond mere declaration; it asserts a dual responsibility for defining and configuring the program's memory. Variables are declared with deliberate precision using explicit PIC clauses and deliberate initializations which enforce stringent formatting, range constraints, and storage types. This articulate specification ensures that the memory footprint of each variable is immutable and systematically managed. Such a robust declarative framework contributes to the overall reliability of the program, as variables preserve interprocedural state information and facilitate seamless data manipulation. The meticulous design merge of syntactic clarity with physical memory configuration exemplifies a refined approach to persistent variable management in a static memory model.

Cobol Code Snippet

```
IDENTIFICATION DIVISION.
PROGRAM-ID. WORKSTORAGE-DEMO.

ENVIRONMENT DIVISION.
* For this demonstration no file I/O is required.
```

```
INPUT-OUTPUT SECTION.

DATA DIVISION.
WORKING-STORAGE SECTION.
* Hierarchical declaration of persistent variables using group
↪  items.
01 CALCULATION-GROUP.
    05 WS-NUMBER     PIC 9(3)    VALUE 10.
    05 WS-SUM        PIC 9(5)    VALUE 0.
    05 WS-COUNT      PIC 9(3)    VALUE 1.
    05 WS-RESULT     PIC 9(5)    VALUE 0.
    05 WS-FACTORIAL  PIC 9(8)    VALUE 1.

* Constants used in computed formula.
01 EQUATION-CONSTANTS.
    05 WS-MULTIPLIER PIC 9(2)    VALUE 2.
    05 WS-ADDEND     PIC 9(2)    VALUE 5.
    05 WS-DIVISOR    PIC 9(2)    VALUE 3.

* Variable for average calculation with two decimal places.
01 WS-AVERAGE        PIC 9(5)V99 VALUE 0.

PROCEDURE DIVISION.
MAIN-LOGIC.
    * Compute the sum of numbers from 1 to WS-NUMBER.
    PERFORM VARYING WS-COUNT FROM 1 BY 1 UNTIL WS-COUNT > WS-NUMBER
        ADD WS-COUNT TO WS-SUM
    END-PERFORM.
    DISPLAY "Sum of numbers from 1 to " WS-NUMBER " is: " WS-SUM.

    * Compute an important formula:
    * WS-RESULT = (WS-SUM * WS-MULTIPLIER + WS-ADDEND) / WS-DIVISOR.
    COMPUTE WS-RESULT = (WS-SUM * WS-MULTIPLIER + WS-ADDEND) /
        ↪  WS-DIVISOR.
    DISPLAY "Computed formula ((SUM * MULTIPLIER + ADDEND) /
        ↪  DIVISOR) yields: " WS-RESULT.

    * Reinitialize WS-COUNT for factorial computation.
    MOVE 1 TO WS-COUNT.
    * Compute factorial of WS-NUMBER using iterative multiplication.
    PERFORM VARYING WS-COUNT FROM 1 BY 1 UNTIL WS-COUNT > WS-NUMBER
        COMPUTE WS-FACTORIAL = WS-FACTORIAL * WS-COUNT
    END-PERFORM.
    DISPLAY "Factorial of " WS-NUMBER " is: " WS-FACTORIAL.

    * Compute average of the series: AVERAGE = WS-SUM / WS-NUMBER.
    COMPUTE WS-AVERAGE = WS-SUM / WS-NUMBER.
    DISPLAY "Average of numbers from 1 to " WS-NUMBER " is: "
        ↪  WS-AVERAGE.

    STOP RUN.
```

Chapter 8

LOCAL-STORAGE Section Concepts

Definition and Role of Local-Storage

The LOCAL-STORAGE section in COBOL defines a specialized area for temporary variable allocation that is intrinsically tied to the execution context of a program unit. Variables declared within this section are instantiated upon each activation of a procedure and are subsequently relinquished when the activation period concludes. In this configuration, the lifetime of these data items is strictly limited to their respective procedure invocations, ensuring that every call operates on a clean slate with respect to these temporary variables. This mechanism enforces a disciplined separation between transient computational state and the long-lived state maintained in other storage areas, thereby supporting rigorous isolation of data and reducing the risks associated with unintended state persistence.

Memory Allocation and Temporal Control

The allocation strategy for LOCAL-STORAGE variables is fundamentally dynamic, governed by the runtime environment and the precise boundaries of procedural execution. Upon each entry into a procedural block, the system allocates a fresh instance of the LOCAL-STORAGE segment, with each variable reinitialized in accordance with its declaration. This ephemeral allocation is intrinsically bound to the activation record maintained on the runtime stack, which facilitates an automatic reclamation of memory as soon as the routine completes its execution. The temporal control inherent in this design ensures that any intermediate computations, temporary structures, or transient data processing results are confined within the narrowly defined lifecycle of the procedure, thereby minimizing the scope of side effects and promoting a more modular and predictable program behavior.

Comparative Analysis: LOCAL-STORAGE versus WORKING-STORAGE

The design paradigms that distinguish LOCAL-STORAGE from WORKING-STORAGE are rooted in their respective lifetimes and roles within a COBOL program. In contrast to LOCAL-STORAGE, the WORKING-STORAGE section is characterized by static allocation, wherein variables are instantiated once at program initialization and persist throughout the entirety of program execution. This global persistence is conducive to scenarios where long-term state preservation and interprocedural data sharing are requisite. However, the same characteristic also renders WORKING-STORAGE susceptible to issues related to stale data and unintentional cross-call contamination. Conversely, LOCAL-STORAGE is meticulously engineered to encapsulate variables within the narrow temporal confines of a procedural activation. This approach enables a more refined control over data isolation, as every procedure call generates a new instance of the corresponding local data region. The differential behavior is especially significant in complex computational environments where the precision of state management directly influences the robustness and predictability of execution outcomes. The inherent reinitialization of LOCAL-STORAGE variables obviates the complications associated with modifying persistent data, thereby fostering an environment in which transient computations can be performed with enhanced reliability and clarity.

Cobol Code Snippet

```
IDENTIFICATION DIVISION.
PROGRAM-ID. LOCALSTORAGEDEMO.

*----------------------------------------------------
* This program demonstrates the use of the LOCAL-STORAGE
↪   section in
* COBOL by computing the factorial of a given number. The
↪   algorithm
* employs local-storage variables to hold temporary
↪   computation values.
* Note that each invocation of the COMPUTE-FACTORIAL
↪   procedure causes
* a fresh allocation (and initialization) of these variables,
↪   ensuring
* that no previous state persists between calls.
*----------------------------------------------------

ENVIRONMENT DIVISION.
INPUT-OUTPUT SECTION.
* (No external files are utilized in this demonstration)

DATA DIVISION.
WORKING-STORAGE SECTION.
* Global variables are declared here.
01  WS-NUMBER.
    05  WS-NUMBER-VALUE    PIC 9(4) VALUE  7.
01  WS-RESULT.
    05  WS-FACTORIAL    PIC 9(12) VALUE  1.
01  WS-DISPLAY-MSG      PIC X(50) VALUE "The factorial
↪   result is:".

LOCAL-STORAGE SECTION.
*----------------------------------------------------
* Local-storage variables: These are allocated dynamically at
↪   the
* entrance of each procedure call and are deallocated upon
↪   exit.
*----------------------------------------------------
01  LS-COUNTER.
    05  LS-COUNT        PIC 9(4)  VALUE ZERO.
01  LS-PRODUCT.
    05  LS-PROD         PIC 9(12) VALUE 1.

PROCEDURE DIVISION.
MAIN-PARA.
    DISPLAY "Starting Factorial Calculation using
    ↪   LOCAL-STORAGE".
    PERFORM COMPUTE-FACTORIAL
    DISPLAY WS-DISPLAY-MSG, " ", WS-RESULT
    STOP RUN.
```

```
*----------------------------------------------------
* COMPUTE-FACTORIAL: Calculates the factorial of
↪  WS-NUMBER-VALUE
* using a simple iterative algorithm. The local-storage
↪  variables
* LS-COUNT and LS-PROD are used to hold the loop counter and
↪  the
* cumulative product respectively. Note that these variables
↪  are
* reinitialized automatically on every activation of this
↪  procedure.
*----------------------------------------------------
COMPUTE-FACTORIAL.
    MOVE 1 TO LS-COUNT.
    MOVE 1 TO LS-PROD.
    PERFORM UNTIL LS-COUNT > WS-NUMBER-VALUE
        MULTIPLY LS-PROD BY LS-COUNT GIVING LS-PROD
        ADD 1 TO LS-COUNT
    END-PERFORM.
    MOVE LS-PROD TO WS-RESULT.
    EXIT.
```

Chapter 9

LINKAGE Section Concepts

Overview of the LINKAGE Section

The LINKAGE section in COBOL constitutes a dedicated data area that is intrinsically designed to support inter-program data communication and parameter passing. This section defines identifiers that are not allocated by the callee's internal storage mechanisms but are instead resolved at runtime from data supplied by a calling program. The delineation provided by the LINKAGE section establishes a clear boundary between a program's persistent working storage and the temporary parameters received during each invocation. In this arrangement, the identifiers declared in the LINKAGE section serve as formal placeholders which receive externally managed data, thereby enabling a modular and loosely coupled structure for program components.

Mechanisms for Inter-Program Data Communication

The operational framework of inter-program communication in COBOL is heavily reliant on the dynamic resolution of identifiers sourced from the calling environment. Upon the invocation of a subprogram, the runtime environment provides specific memory addresses corresponding to the variables prepared in the calling program's working storage. These addresses are mapped directly to the identifiers declared in the LINKAGE section, thereby ensuring that all data communication adheres to the structured protocols of the execution model. This mapping is performed through a runtime mechanism that associates parameter order and type with the respective identifiers. The design of this mechanism minimizes redundant data copying and leverages address referencing to promote an efficient transfer of state. As a result, the LINKAGE section becomes a conduit for data that is transient by design, allowing for streamlined interactions between distinct program units.

Parameter Passing Techniques

Parameter passing via the LINKAGE section typically follows a call-by-reference paradigm, wherein the calling program provides direct access to its working storage to the invoked subprogram. In this scheme, parameters are not duplicated; rather, the subprogram is granted access to the exact memory location of each supplied datum. Consequently, any modification performed on these parameters within the subprogram can have immediate repercussions on the original data. This approach necessitates a rigorous discipline in type consistency and size specification, ensuring that the externally supplied data structure is faithfully interpreted by the recipient program. The methodology of parameter passing implemented through the LINKAGE section enables a seamless and efficient transmission of data across program boundaries, while simultaneously preserving the integrity of the interfacing contract between caller and callee.

Runtime Dynamics and Memory Organization

The runtime behavior associated with the LINKAGE section is governed by the dynamic allocation of parameter references, which are established during subprogram activation. Rather than allocating separate storage, the runtime system binds external memory locations to the identifiers declared in the LINKAGE section at the onset of execution. This binding is achieved through the manipulation of activation records, wherein pointers to caller-supplied data are transmitted as part of the call protocol. The absence of automatic initialization within the LINKAGE section underscores its role as an interface to externally controlled data. Memory organization under this paradigm emphasizes efficient data access and minimizes overhead through direct pointer referencing. The deliberate design choice to forgo intrinsic allocation within the subprogram reinforces the dependency on the caller for ensuring the accuracy and consistency of passed parameters, thereby integrating the memory management responsibilities across program boundaries.

Cobol Code Snippet

```
IDENTIFICATION DIVISION.
PROGRAM-ID. CALC-EXPRESSION.

DATA DIVISION.
WORKING-STORAGE SECTION.
* Working-storage used for display messages
01 WS-MESSAGE      PIC X(50) VALUE 'Computation Result is:
↪  '.
01 WS-ERROR        PIC X(30) VALUE 'Error: Division by
↪  zero.'.

LINKAGE SECTION.
* The following parameters are passed from the calling
↪  program.
* They are resolved at runtime via call-by-reference.
01 LK-PARAMS.
    05 OPER1       PIC S9(5) COMP.   *> First operand
    05 OPER2       PIC S9(5) COMP.   *> Second operand
    05 OPER3       PIC S9(5) COMP.   *> Third operand
    ↪  factor
    05 MULTIPLIER  PIC S9(3) COMP.   *> Divisor or scaling
    ↪  factor
    05 RESULT      PIC S9(7) COMP.   *> To store computed
    ↪  result

PROCEDURE DIVISION USING LK-PARAMS.
MAIN-PARA.
    * The following algorithm computes the expression:
    *    RESULT = ((OPER1 + OPER2) * OPER3) / MULTIPLIER
    * It demonstrates the use of the LINKAGE Section for
    ↪  parameter passing
    * and utilizes the COMPUTE statement for evaluating an
    ↪  arithmetic formula.

    IF MULTIPLIER = 0
        DISPLAY WS-ERROR
    ELSE
```

```
            COMPUTE RESULT = ((OPER1 + OPER2) * OPER3) /
            ↪  MULTIPLIER.
            DISPLAY WS-MESSAGE RESULT
      END-IF.
      STOP RUN.
```

Chapter 10

PIC Clauses and Data Types

Fundamental Aspects of PIC Clauses

The PIC clause in COBOL represents a declarative specification that dictates the data format and storage layout within a program's data structures. This clause serves as a descriptive blueprint by which a variable's form is rigorously defined in terms of its length, type, and permissible range of values. Structurally, a PIC clause delineates the expected pattern using a combination of symbols and numeric qualifiers. For example, numeric fields are characterized by the digit symbol 9, while character fields are identified with the letter X. This formalism ensures that each data item is assigned a precise physical footprint in memory, thereby contributing to the consistency and predictability of data representations in the program's execution environment.

The intrinsic design of the PIC clause is such that it segregates data types into clearly interpretable categories. Within these categories, modifiers and scaling factors are employed to express additional properties such as sign indication or the presence of an implicit decimal position. By virtue of this explicit specification, the PIC clause not only defines the external appearance of the data but also governs the internal mechanics of data storage and retrieval. The structural rules established by these clauses play an essential role in supporting both arithmetic operations and alphanumeric manipulations by ensuring that every field conforms to an anticipated format.

Defining Numeric Data Types Using PIC Clauses

Numeric data definitions in COBOL leverage the predictive structure provided by PIC clauses to articulate the characteristics of numerical quantities. The basic numeric symbol, denoted by 9, is used to signify a single digit, and multiple occurrences of this symbol establish the overall size of the field. When increased precision is required, successive 9 symbols are grouped, and a repetition qualifier may be employed to indicate an exact number of digits. In some instances, the inclusion of a leading sign, represented by the symbol S, prefaces the numeric declaration to accommodate both positive and negative values. The optional insertion of an implied decimal point, symbolized by V, further refines the specification by demarcating the boundary between integer and fractional components.

Every numeric PIC clause, by virtue of its explicit construction, facilitates the allocation of memory in a manner that is both efficient and predictable. The restriction imposed by the clause precludes ambiguities in numerical precision and supports arithmetic computations by preserving the integrity of each digit's positional value. The methodical structure of these clauses allows for internal representations where scaling factors, such as those indicated by the use of additional editing symbols, ensure that computations adhere to the defined decimal precision. As such, numerical definitions formulated via PIC clauses strike a balance between descriptive clarity and operational robustness, thereby optimizing both runtime efficiency and data consistency.

Defining Alphanumeric Data Types Using PIC Clauses

Alphanumeric data items are defined using PIC clauses that are structurally distinct from their numeric counterparts. The symbol X is employed to represent a single alphanumeric character, and explicit repetition qualifiers enclosed in parentheses specify the total field length. By using this form of definition, each alphanumeric field is fixed in size, offering a consistent layout that is critical for the processing and manipulation of textual data. The inherent simplicity of the X specification belies its utility; it is sufficiently versatile to encompass letters, digits, and an assortment of special characters without invoking the arithmetic constraints applicable to numeric fields.

Moreover, the PIC clause for alphanumeric definitions facilitates predictable memory allocation, ensuring that each field occupies a predetermined number of bytes. This predictability is of paramount importance in scenarios where fixed-length records are processed, as it enables reliable data extraction and storage. The design of these clauses accommodates a broad spectrum of text-based data representations while maintaining strict conformance to a declared size. By explicitly declaring the field length, the PIC clause not only serves as a template for input and output operations but also acts as a safeguard against inadvertent data truncation or overflow during runtime manipulations.

Each aspect of a PIC clause, whether tailored for numeric or alphanumeric data, is devised to provide a rigorous framework for data description. In numeric definitions, every digit and modifier contributes to the precision of arithmetic operations, while in alphanumeric definitions, the fixed-length specification strengthens the structural integrity of textual data. The careful orchestration of these elements under the umbrella of PIC clauses is integral to the disciplined approach that COBOL adopts in data handling and storage.

Cobol Code Snippet

```
IDENTIFICATION DIVISION.
PROGRAM-ID. PICDEMO.

ENVIRONMENT DIVISION.

DATA DIVISION.
WORKING-STORAGE SECTION.
    *------------------------------------------------------------
    * Numeric Variables Defined Using PIC Clauses
    * WS-NUM1: Signed numeric with 4 integer digits and 2 decimals.
    * WS-NUM2: Unsigned numeric with 4 integer digits and 2
    ↳ decimals.
    *------------------------------------------------------------
    01 WS-NUM1        PIC S9(4)V99 VALUE +0123.45.
    01 WS-NUM2        PIC 9(4)V99  VALUE 0067.89.
    01 WS-SUM         PIC S9(5)V99 VALUE ZERO.
```

```cobol
01 WS-DIFF          PIC S9(5)V99 VALUE ZERO.
01 WS-PRODUCT       PIC S9(6)V99 VALUE ZERO.
01 WS-QUOTIENT      PIC S9(4)V99 VALUE ZERO.
01 WS-DIVISOR       PIC 9(4)V99  VALUE 0002.00.


*-------------------------------------------------------------
* Variables for a Sample Algorithm:
* Compute Simple Interest using the formula:
*    Interest = (Principal * Rate * Time) / 100
*-------------------------------------------------------------
01 WS-PRINCIPAL     PIC 9(6)V99 VALUE 5000.00.
01 WS-RATE          PIC 9(2)V99 VALUE 05.25.
01 WS-TIME          PIC 9(2)V99 VALUE 02.00.
01 WS-INTEREST      PIC 9(6)V99 VALUE ZERO.


*-------------------------------------------------------------
* Alphanumeric Variable for Displaying Messages
*-------------------------------------------------------------
01 WS-MSG           PIC X(30)   VALUE "Computation Completed.".

PROCEDURE DIVISION.
    DISPLAY "Starting PIC Code Demonstration".

    *-------------------------------------------------------------
    * Demonstrate Basic Arithmetic Operations
    *-------------------------------------------------------------
    COMPUTE WS-SUM = WS-NUM1 + WS-NUM2.
    DISPLAY "Sum: " WS-SUM.

    COMPUTE WS-DIFF = WS-NUM1 - WS-NUM2.
    DISPLAY "Difference: " WS-DIFF.

    COMPUTE WS-PRODUCT = WS-NUM1 * WS-NUM2.
    DISPLAY "Product: " WS-PRODUCT.

    IF WS-DIVISOR NOT = ZERO
        COMPUTE WS-QUOTIENT = WS-NUM1 / WS-DIVISOR.
        DISPLAY "Quotient: " WS-QUOTIENT.
    ELSE
        DISPLAY "Error: Division by zero.".
    END-IF.

    *-------------------------------------------------------------
    * Execute a More Complex Calculation: Simple Interest
    * Formula: Interest = (Principal * Rate * Time) / 100
    *-------------------------------------------------------------
    COMPUTE WS-INTEREST = (WS-PRINCIPAL * WS-RATE * WS-TIME) / 100.
    DISPLAY "Simple Interest: " WS-INTEREST.

    *-------------------------------------------------------------
    * Display Final Message and Terminate Program
    *-------------------------------------------------------------
    DISPLAY WS-MSG.
```

```
STOP RUN.
```

Chapter 11

Understanding Level Numbers

Concept and Syntax of Level Numbers

Data definitions in COBOL are predicated on the assignment of level numbers that govern the structural arrangement of data items. Level numbers, expressed as numeric tokens such as 01, 05, 10, and so forth, serve to delineate hierarchical relationships in data records. Each level number signifies the degree of nesting within the overall structure; a data item defined at a higher level number is considered subordinate to the data item defined with a lower level number, thereby forming a tree-like architecture within the DATA DIVISION. This syntactic construct imposes rigorous constraints, ensuring that every record and group item adheres to an expected pattern of specification. The numeric nature of the level numbers, unadorned by extraneous symbols, enables a predictable and systematic partitioning of the data environment where each tier in the hierarchy is clearly delineated by its designated level.

Hierarchical Organization of Data Definitions

The utility of level numbers is most evident in their capacity to instill a logical hierarchy within data structures. A definition initiated at level 01 typically represents the highest scope of a record and encapsulates a series of subordinate group items, each marked by a subsequent increase in the level number. In this hierarchical schema, group items function as aggregates of related data fields, and their intrinsic nested arrangement reflects the natural subdivisions of the underlying data. The hierarchical ordering provided by level numbers not only facilitates the organization of individual data items but also establishes the contextual relationships between composite records and their elementary components. The resultant structure allows for a clear demarcation of data boundaries and supports the internal consistency required during both data processing and storage.

Structural Integrity and Syntactic Constraints

The systematic use of level numbers enforces structural integrity throughout the data records in COBOL programs. Hierarchical relationships are maintained by ensuring that a data item defined with a specific level number remains within the confines of its immediate superior item, as denoted by a lower level number. This rule-based approach prevents ambiguities in the association of subordinate fields, thereby reinforcing a coherent data layout. The constraints on level number assignment serve as an essential mechanism for error checking during compilation, as any deviation from the prescribed hierarchical order is flagged by rigorous syntactic validation. The precision afforded by level number designations plays a pivotal role in safeguarding the consistency of data access, manipulation, and storage by ensuring that every element is accurately positioned in relation to its peers and parent groups.

Implications for Data Structuring and Management

The hierarchical structure induced by level numbers has significant implications for data management and program design in COBOL. By clearly articulating the relationships between different data items, level numbers contribute to an organized and modular framework that mirrors complex data constructs found in contemporary computing paradigms. The explicit declaration of hierarchical levels enables sophisticated data groupings that support efficient record traversal and manipulation. Such a framework enhances the maintainability of legacy systems by providing an unambiguous blueprint for data storage, which in turn simplifies tasks such as debugging, system modification, and data transformation. The hierarchical arrangement, governed by meticulously assigned level numbers, thus underpins both the logical integrity and operational efficiency of COBOL data definitions within enterprise-scale applications.

Cobol Code Snippet

```
IDENTIFICATION DIVISION.
PROGRAM-ID. LEVELNUM-EXAMPLE.

ENVIRONMENT DIVISION.
CONFIGURATION SECTION.
SOURCE-COMPUTER. IBM-370.
OBJECT-COMPUTER. IBM-370.

DATA DIVISION.
WORKING-STORAGE SECTION.
01 WS-INDEX              PIC 9(2) VALUE 1.
* Hierarchical data structure demonstrating level numbers
01 EMPLOYEE-RECORD.
   05 EMPLOYEE-ID        PIC 9(4)      VALUE 1001.
   05 EMPLOYEE-INFO.
      10 EMPLOYEE-NAME   PIC A(30)     VALUE "JOHN SMITH".
      10 SALARY-DETAILS.
         15 BASE-SALARY        PIC 9(6)V99 VALUE 50000.00.
         15 BONUS-PERCENTAGE   PIC 9V99    VALUE 0.10.
         15 BONUS-AMOUNT       PIC 9(6)V99 VALUE 0.
         15 TOTAL-SALARY       PIC 9(6)V99 VALUE 0.
* Table of salary adjustments to simulate bonus/reward
↪    criteria
01 ADJUSTMENT-TABLE.
   05 ADJUSTMENT-ENTRY OCCURS 3 TIMES.
      10 ADJUSTMENT-AMOUNT  PIC 9(4)V99 VALUE 0.

PROCEDURE DIVISION.
MAIN-PARA.
    DISPLAY "COBOL Level Number Hierarchy and Calculation
    ↪    Example".
    PERFORM CALCULATE-SALARY.
    PERFORM APPLY-ADJUSTMENTS.
    PERFORM DISPLAY-RESULTS.
    STOP RUN.

CALCULATE-SALARY.
```

```
      * Compute bonus amount using the formula: BONUS =
      ↪   BASE-SALARY * BONUS-PERCENTAGE
       COMPUTE BONUS-AMOUNT = BASE-SALARY * BONUS-PERCENTAGE.
      * Compute total salary: TOTAL = BASE-SALARY +
      ↪   BONUS-AMOUNT
       COMPUTE TOTAL-SALARY = BASE-SALARY + BONUS-AMOUNT.
       EXIT.

   APPLY-ADJUSTMENTS.
      * For demonstration, assign adjustment amounts
       MOVE 150.50 TO ADJUSTMENT-AMOUNT (1).
       MOVE 200.75 TO ADJUSTMENT-AMOUNT (2).
       MOVE 100.25 TO ADJUSTMENT-AMOUNT (3).
       PERFORM VARYING WS-INDEX FROM 1 BY 1 UNTIL WS-INDEX > 3
          COMPUTE BASE-SALARY = BASE-SALARY + ADJUSTMENT-AMOUNT
          ↪   (WS-INDEX)
       END-PERFORM.
      * Recompute total salary after applying adjustments
       COMPUTE TOTAL-SALARY = BASE-SALARY + BONUS-AMOUNT.
       EXIT.

   DISPLAY-RESULTS.
       DISPLAY "Employee ID: " EMPLOYEE-ID.
       DISPLAY "Employee Name: " EMPLOYEE-NAME.
       DISPLAY "Base Salary after Adjustments: " BASE-SALARY.
       DISPLAY "Bonus Percentage: " BONUS-PERCENTAGE.
       DISPLAY "Calculated Bonus: " BONUS-AMOUNT.
       DISPLAY "Total Salary: " TOTAL-SALARY.
       EXIT.
   END PROGRAM LEVELNUM-EXAMPLE.
```

Chapter 12

USAGE Clause in Data Items

Conceptual Overview of the USAGE Clause

The USAGE clause in COBOL serves as a declarative mechanism that specifies the underlying representation and storage characteristics of data items within the DATA DIVISION. This clause delineates the mapping between the high-level data definitions and their attendant machine-level storage formats, thereby influencing both compilation semantics and execution behavior. It designates, for example, whether a data item is to be handled in a human-readable fashion as in the case of $DISPLAY$, or in a more compact and computationally efficient format such as $BINARY$, $COMP$, or $COMP - 3$. The clause functions as a pivotal interface between the logical design of data structures and their physical realization, ensuring that the abstract data models are appropriately aligned with the hardware-oriented aspects of the computing environment.

Representation Modalities: $DISPLAY$, $BINARY$, and Alternative Formats

The spectrum of representation options provided by the USAGE clause encompasses several distinct modalities, each with inherent implications for data storage and computational operations. The $DISPLAY$ format is predominantly associated with text-based representations, ensuring that characters and digits are stored in a human-readable form according to standard encoding schemes. By contrast, the $BINARY$ and $COMP$ options facilitate the storage of numerical data in machine-native formats that are optimized for arithmetic operations and efficient processing. Additionally, the $COMP-3$ format implements a packed decimal representation, employing a compact encoding strategy that reduces the memory footprint while preserving numerical precision. These modalities exhibit nuanced trade-offs; for instance, while $DISPLAY$ prioritizes clarity and ease of verification, $BINARY$, $COMP$, and $COMP-3$ optimize for computational speed and space efficiency.

Memory Representation and Data Encoding Strategies

The internal representation prescribed by the USAGE clause exerts a profound influence on the layout of data in memory and the strategies employed for data encoding. A data item declared with the $DISPLAY$ usage typically utilizes one byte per character or digit, conforming to standard character set encodings, which facilitates straightforward visual inspection and debugging. In contrast, declarations employing $BINARY$ or $COMP$ invoke a mapping to a contiguous block of memory that is structured to support binary arithmetic operations, with multiple bytes allocated as needed to accommodate the range and precision of the numerical value. The $COMP-3$ format, characterized by its packed decimal encoding, minimizes the physical space required by consolidating two decimal digits per byte, with a designated nibble reserved for the sign information. Such encoding strategies are meticulously determined by the interplay between the theoretical model of data representation and the practical exigencies of efficient memory allocation on modern computing systems.

Implications for Computational Fidelity and System Performance

The explicit declaration of data representation through the USAGE clause has direct ramifications for computational fidelity and system performance. By aligning data storage with a designated usage format, the clause mitigates discrepancies between the programmer's abstract data definitions and the machine's interpretation of the stored values. This alignment is particularly critical in arithmetic processing, where the precision and integrity of numerical computations depend on the correct interpretation of the data format. Moreover, the selection of a particular usage modality influences memory allocation efficiency and the speed of data processing. Data items represented in formats such as $BINARY$ or $COMP-3$ may be subject to specialized machine instructions that accelerate arithmetic operations, thus contributing to overall system performance improvements. The USAGE clause, therefore, is instrumental not only in ensuring the logical coherence of data definitions but also in optimizing the correspondence between software abstractions and their hardware implementations.

Cobol Code Snippet

```
IDENTIFICATION DIVISION.
PROGRAM-ID. USAGE-EXAMPLE.

ENVIRONMENT DIVISION.

DATA DIVISION.
WORKING-STORAGE SECTION.
* Variables defined with different USAGE clauses to demonstrate
↪  their representation
01 WS-DISPLAY     PIC 9(5)    USAGE DISPLAY    VALUE 12345.
01 WS-BINARY      PIC 9(5)    USAGE BINARY     VALUE 100.
01 WS-COMP        PIC 9(5)    USAGE COMP       VALUE 10.
01 WS-COMP3       PIC 9(5)    USAGE COMP-3     VALUE 2.
01 WS-RESULT      PIC 9(7)                     VALUE ZERO.
01 WS-MESSAGE     PIC X(50)                    VALUE SPACES.

PROCEDURE DIVISION.
MAIN-PROCEDURE.
    DISPLAY "Starting USAGE Clause Calculation Example - Begin".
    DISPLAY "Initial Values:".
    DISPLAY "  WS-DISPLAY (DISPLAY)  : " WS-DISPLAY.
    DISPLAY "  WS-BINARY  (BINARY)   : " WS-BINARY.
    DISPLAY "  WS-COMP     (COMP)    : " WS-COMP.
    DISPLAY "  WS-COMP3    (COMP-3)  : " WS-COMP3.

    * Performing arithmetic computation using variables with
    ↪  different USAGE clauses.
    * Equation: WS-RESULT = (WS-DISPLAY + WS-BINARY) * WS-COMP /
    ↪  WS-COMP3
```

```
COMPUTE WS-RESULT = ((WS-DISPLAY + WS-BINARY) * WS-COMP) /
↪  WS-COMP3.

DISPLAY "Calculated Result ( (DISPLAY+BINARY)*COMP/COMP-3 ) : "
↪  WS-RESULT.
MOVE "Computation Complete" TO WS-MESSAGE.
DISPLAY WS-MESSAGE.

STOP RUN.
```

Chapter 13

COMP and COMP-3 Formats

Binary Numeric Representation: COMP

The $COMP$ clause specifies a binary representation mechanism for numeric data in which values are stored in a format that mirrors the native binary architecture of the processor. In this configuration, a numerical entity is mapped directly to a contiguous sequence of bytes, allowing arithmetic operations to be executed using the hardware's inherent binary arithmetic capabilities. Typically, the $COMP$ representation employs a two's complement format for sign representation, thereby enabling efficient computation of both positive and negative values. Memory allocation for $COMP$ data is aligned with the processor's word boundaries, which minimizes access latency and maximizes the throughput of arithmetic operations due to reduced data conversion overhead. This method of storing numerals is particularly well suited for operations that demand high performance, as it eliminates intermediary formatting steps and leverages the streamlined execution pathways available in modern computing architectures.

Packed-Decimal Representation: COMP-3

In contrast to the binary approach, the $COMP$-3 format employs a packed-decimal encoding scheme designed to achieve space-efficient storage while preserving decimal precision. Each decimal digit is encoded into a four-bit nibble, thereby allowing two decimal digits to be stored per byte. The final nibble is reserved for the sign, resulting in a compact representation wherein a numeric item defined with n decimal digits occupies $\lceil \frac{n+1}{2} \rceil$ bytes. This precise packing of decimal digits minimizes the physical footprint of numerical data and ensures that the exactness of decimal arithmetic is retained. Despite the increased computational overhead occasionally encountered when converting between the packed-decimal format and binary representations, the $COMP$-3 method affords a distinct advantage in applications that require meticulous adherence to decimal precision, such as financial computations and commercial data processing.

Memory Alignment, Data Efficiency, and Arithmetic Implications

A rigorous examination of the memory alignment and efficiency inherent in the $COMP$ and $COMP$-3 formats reveals distinct trade-offs between computational performance and storage economy. Memory allocation for data defined with the $COMP$ clause is typically governed by the architecture's standard word size, which facilitates optimally aligned data accesses and enables arithmetic operations to be performed with minimal latency. Conversely, the $COMP$-3 format is engineered to reduce the number of bytes required by densely packing decimal digits into half-byte segments, thus achieving a higher degree of storage efficiency. However, this compactness necessitates additional processing steps during arithmetic operations, as the packed decimal data must often be decoded or converted into a binary format prior to computation. Compiler optimizations and hardware-supported conversion routines may alleviate some of these processing delays, but the inherent design of $COMP$-3 prioritizes precise decimal representation over raw execution speed. The divergent strategies embodied by the $COMP$ and $COMP$-3 representations underscore a fundamental balance between the immediacy of binary arithmetic and the stringent requirements for decimal accuracy and space conservation.

Cobol Code Snippet

```
IDENTIFICATION DIVISION.
PROGRAM-ID. COMP-ALGORITHM.
ENVIRONMENT DIVISION.
CONFIGURATION SECTION.
SOURCE-COMPUTER. IBM-370.
OBJECT-COMPUTER. IBM-370.

DATA DIVISION.
WORKING-STORAGE SECTION.
*------------------------------------------------------------
* Definition of numeric fields using COMP and COMP-3 formats
*------------------------------------------------------------
01  WS-NUMBERS.
    05 WS-NUM-BIN       PIC S9(6) COMP.      *> Binary
    ↪  representation (two's complement)
    05 WS-NUM-COMP3     PIC S9(6) COMP-3.      *>
    ↪  Packed-decimal representation (COMP-3)
    05 WS-SUM           PIC S9(6) COMP.      *> Sum stored
    ↪  as binary
    05 WS-PRODUCT       PIC S9(9) COMP-3.      *> Product
    ↪  stored as packed-decimal
    05 WS-RESULT        PIC 9(8).            *> Alphanumeric
    ↪  display field

PROCEDURE DIVISION.
MAIN-PARA.

    ↪  *-----------------------------------------------------------
    * Initialize the numeric variables with sample values

    ↪  *-----------------------------------------------------------
    MOVE 123456 TO WS-NUM-BIN.
    MOVE 654321 TO WS-NUM-COMP3.


    ↪  *-----------------------------------------------------------
    * Display the initial values with their respective
    ↪  formats

    ↪  *-----------------------------------------------------------
    DISPLAY "Initial Binary Value (COMP): " WS-NUM-BIN.
    DISPLAY "Initial Packed Decimal Value (COMP-3): "
    ↪  WS-NUM-COMP3.
```

61

```
↪    *-------------------------------------------------------------
* Compute the sum of the binary and packed-decimal
↪    values.
* Note: COBOL performs arithmetic independent of the
↪    storage
* format so the addition works seamlessly.

↪    *-------------------------------------------------------------
COMPUTE WS-SUM = WS-NUM-BIN + WS-NUM-COMP3.
DISPLAY "Sum (Binary Computation): " WS-SUM.


↪    *-------------------------------------------------------------
* Compute a product by multiplying the packed-decimal
↪    value
* by a constant factor to demonstrate arithmetic
↪    operations.

↪    *-------------------------------------------------------------
COMPUTE WS-PRODUCT = WS-NUM-COMP3 * 3.
DISPLAY "Product (Packed Decimal Computation): "
↪    WS-PRODUCT.


↪    *-------------------------------------------------------------
* Demonstrate a compound computation:
* Equation: RESULT = (Sum + Product) / 2
* This combines both COMP and COMP-3 calculations into an
* intermediate result which is then converted for
↪    display.

↪    *-------------------------------------------------------------
COMPUTE WS-RESULT = ( WS-SUM + WS-PRODUCT ) / 2.
DISPLAY "Final Result ((Sum + Product) / 2): " WS-RESULT.

STOP RUN.
```

Chapter 14

Numeric Editing with PIC Modifiers

Fundamental Principles of PIC Editing

Within COBOL's data description paradigm, the PIC clause functions as a declarative mechanism through which numeric values are formatted for output. The clause incorporates a series of editing symbols that act as both placeholders and directives, thereby establishing patterns for digit display, alignment, and sign indication. In this context, symbols such as 9 and Z assume critical roles. The digit symbol 9 represents a mandatory numeric position, ensuring that each allocated field is populated with a numeral when available. In contrast, the placeholder symbol Z is employed to conditionally suppress leading zeros, substituting them with spaces to enhance output clarity. These symbols, together with other elements such as the decimal point (.) and comma (,), collectively determine the mapping between the inherent numerical data and its formatted presentation, adhering strictly to the predefined spatial and syntactical constraints.

Elaboration of Editing Symbols and Their Functional Roles

The editing symbols embedded in a PIC clause serve multiple functions that harmonize raw numerical representation with human-readable formatting. The 9 symbol dictates the placement of each digit, thereby enforcing a structure wherein every significant or non-significant numeral occupies a fixed position. In juxtaposition, the Z symbol facilitates a nuanced suppression of non-essential zeros, effectively converting them into blank spaces when they precede significant digits. This mechanism is particularly advantageous in mitigating visual clutter and aligning output fields. Additionally, the inclusion of punctuation characters such as the period (.) and comma (,) within the PIC string specifies the segmentation of integer and fractional parts as well as the demarcation of digit groups for enhanced legibility. Moreover, modifiers associated with sign representation, typically interwoven with these editing symbols, comprehensively manage the display of positive and negative indicators. The integration of these symbols engenders a robust system wherein each character within the PIC format contributes to a coherent, precise, and standardized numeric output.

Implications for Output Presentation and Data Integrity

The deliberate application of editing symbols within PIC clauses exerts a significant influence on the consistency and precision of numeric outputs. By enforcing fixed digit positions and incorporating optional suppression through symbols like Z, the resultant formatted field exhibits both visual uniformity and operational accuracy. The interplay between explicit digit characters and conditional placeholders ensures that the transformation from internal numeric representation to external display is executed with meticulous adherence to formatting protocols. This systematic approach not only upholds the structural integrity of the data but also synchronizes the displayed output with established conventions, thereby facilitating clear communication within data-intensive environments. The carefully calibrated use of symbols such as 9, Z, and punctuation characters guarantees that numeric displays maintain a balanced alignment between computational fidelity and aesthetic rigor, a duality that is indispensable in applications where both precision and clarity are paramount.

Cobol Code Snippet

```
IDENTIFICATION DIVISION.
PROGRAM-ID. NUMERIC-EDIT-DEMO.
AUTHOR. Maxwell_Vector.

ENVIRONMENT DIVISION.
CONFIGURATION SECTION.
SOURCE-COMPUTER. IBM-370.
OBJECT-COMPUTER. IBM-370.

DATA DIVISION.
WORKING-STORAGE SECTION.
* Variables for basic arithmetic operations
01  NUM-A              PIC 9(4) VALUE 1234.
01  NUM-B              PIC 9(4) VALUE 5678.
01  ADD-RESULT         PIC 9(5) VALUE ZERO.
01  AVERAGE            PIC 9(5)V99 VALUE ZERO.
01  COMPLEX-RESULT     PIC 9(6)V99 VALUE ZERO.

* Variables for financial calculation demonstration
01  PRINCIPAL          PIC 9(6)V99 VALUE 100000.00.
01  RATE               PIC 9(3)V99 VALUE 5.25.
01  TIME               PIC 9(2) VALUE 2.
01  INTEREST           PIC 9(6)V99 VALUE ZERO.
01  FORMATTED-INTEREST PIC ZZZ,ZZZ,ZZ9.99.

PROCEDURE DIVISION.
MAIN-PARA.
    DISPLAY "COBOL Numeric Editing with PIC Modifiers Demo".

    *-------------------------------------------------
    * Perform arithmetic operations using formulas:
    * (1) Simple Addition: NUM-A + NUM-B
    * (2) Average Calculation: (NUM-A + NUM-B) / 2
    * (3) Complex Formula: ((NUM-A + NUM-B) * 12) / 4
    *-------------------------------------------------

    ADD NUM-A TO NUM-B GIVING ADD-RESULT.
    DISPLAY "Addition Result (NUM-A + NUM-B): " ADD-RESULT.

    COMPUTE AVERAGE = (NUM-A + NUM-B) / 2.
    DISPLAY "Average (NUM-A + NUM-B)/2: " AVERAGE.

    COMPUTE COMPLEX-RESULT = (NUM-A + NUM-B) * 12 / 4.
    DISPLAY "Complex Calculation ((NUM-A+NUM-B)*12/4): "
    ↪  COMPLEX-RESULT.

    *-------------------------------------------------
    * Financial Calculation Example:
    * Compute Interest = (Principal * Rate * Time) / 100
    * and format it using a PIC clause with editing symbols.
```

```
*--------------------------------------------------

COMPUTE INTEREST = (PRINCIPAL * RATE * TIME) / 100.
MOVE INTEREST TO FORMATTED-INTEREST.
DISPLAY "Calculated Interest (Principal * Rate * Time /
↪  100): "
        FORMATTED-INTEREST.

STOP RUN.
```

Chapter 15

Overview of the PROCEDURE DIVISION

Defining the Nature and Functionality of the PROCEDURE DIVISION

The PROCEDURE DIVISION constitutes the dynamic nucleus of a COBOL program, serving as the repository for explicit algorithmic instructions and operational logic. This division delineates the sequence in which computational tasks are executed and embodies the imperative paradigm by specifying the transformative processes applied to data. Its structure is devised to translate static program specifications into a series of deterministic operations that govern state transitions and resource manipulation. Within this paradigm, individual computational steps are carefully orchestrated to ensure that both arithmetic evaluations and decision-making constructs are seamlessly integrated within a coherent operational framework.

Structural Composition and Control Flow within the PROCEDURE DIVISION

The internal architecture of the PROCEDURE DIVISION is characterized by a meticulous segmentation into paragraphs and sections, each encapsulating discrete units of logic. This modular assembly facilitates a hierarchical organization of control flow, where sequences of statements are linked together to effectuate the overall program functionality. Structural elements such as conditional constructs (for example, IF and EVALUATE) and iterative control mechanisms (exemplified by various forms of PERFORM) are deployed to regulate the progression of execution. The deliberate arrangement of these constructs ensures that the transfer of control adheres to a well-defined sequence, thereby promoting clarity and precision in the management of program state and computational order.

Integration of Data Processing and Computational Logic

Positioned as the intermediary between static data definitions and dynamic operational execution, the PROCEDURE DIVISION plays a pivotal role in the manifestation of data processing. By invoking and manipulating variables defined in preceding divisions, it enacts a series of computational routines that transform raw input data into processed outputs. The execution semantics embedded within this division leverage arithmetic and relational operations, as well as logical evaluations, to perform systematic modifications on data elements. This integration not only supports the implementation of sophisticated algorithms but also reinforces data integrity by ensuring that each processing step is conducted within the rigorously defined structural confines of the program.

Cobol Code Snippet

```
IDENTIFICATION DIVISION.
PROGRAM-ID. PROCEDURE-EXAMPLE.
AUTHOR. Maxwell_Vector.

ENVIRONMENT DIVISION.

DATA DIVISION.
WORKING-STORAGE SECTION.
     * Variables for arithmetic computations.
     77   NUM1        PIC 9(4) VALUE 120.
     77   NUM2        PIC 9(4) VALUE 30.
     77   NUM3        PIC 9(4) VALUE 15.
     77   RESULT      PIC 9(7)V99 VALUE 0.
```

```
    77  TEMP          PIC 9(7)V99 VALUE 0.

    * Variables for iterative computation (loop and sum).
    77  I             PIC 9(2) VALUE 1.
    77  LIMIT         PIC 9(2) VALUE 10.
    77  SUM           PIC 9(7)V99 VALUE 0.
    77  AVERAGE       PIC 9(7)V99 VALUE 0.

    * Flag used in conditional evaluation.
    77  FLAG          PIC X    VALUE 'N'.

PROCEDURE DIVISION.
MAIN-LOGIC.
    DISPLAY "Starting complex computations in the PROCEDURE
    ↪  DIVISION.".

    *----------------------------------------------------
    * Compute a complex arithmetic equation:
    * RESULT = ((NUM1 + NUM2) * NUM3) / (NUM1 - NUM2)
    *----------------------------------------------------
    IF NUM1 > NUM2
        COMPUTE RESULT = ((NUM1 + NUM2) * NUM3) / (NUM1 - NUM2)
    ELSE
        DISPLAY "Error: Invalid arithmetic operation; potential
        ↪  division by zero."
    END-IF.
    DISPLAY "Computed RESULT: " RESULT.

    *----------------------------------------------------
    * Calculate the sum of natural numbers from 1 to LIMIT using
    ↪  PERFORM.
    *----------------------------------------------------
    PERFORM VARYING I FROM 1 BY 1 UNTIL I > LIMIT
        COMPUTE SUM = SUM + I
    END-PERFORM.
    DISPLAY "Sum of numbers from 1 to " LIMIT " is: " SUM.

    *----------------------------------------------------
    * Compute the average of three numbers using the COMPUTE
    ↪  statement.
    *----------------------------------------------------
    COMPUTE AVERAGE = (NUM1 + NUM2 + NUM3) / 3.
    DISPLAY "Average of NUM1, NUM2, and NUM3: " AVERAGE.

    *----------------------------------------------------
    * Evaluate the RESULT using multi-branch logic with the EVALUATE
    ↪  statement.
    * Depending on the computed value, a FLAG is set accordingly.
    *----------------------------------------------------
    EVALUATE TRUE
        WHEN RESULT > 1000
            MOVE 'Y' TO FLAG
            DISPLAY "Outcome: High RESULT detected. FLAG set to Y."
```

```
        WHEN RESULT > 500
            MOVE 'Y' TO FLAG
            DISPLAY "Outcome: Moderate RESULT detected. FLAG set to
            ↪  Y."
        WHEN OTHER
            MOVE 'N' TO FLAG
            DISPLAY "Outcome: Low RESULT value. FLAG remains N."
    END-EVALUATE.


    *-------------------------------------------------
    * Final Debug Output: Display all critical variable values.
    *-------------------------------------------------
    DISPLAY "=== Final Computation Summary ===".
    DISPLAY "NUM1: " NUM1.
    DISPLAY "NUM2: " NUM2.
    DISPLAY "NUM3: " NUM3.
    DISPLAY "RESULT: " RESULT.
    DISPLAY "SUM (1 to " LIMIT "): " SUM.
    DISPLAY "AVERAGE: " AVERAGE.
    DISPLAY "FLAG: " FLAG.

    STOP RUN.
```

Chapter 16

Structuring Code: Paragraphs and Statements

Foundations of Procedural Segmentation

Within the PROCEDURE DIVISION, the deliberate demarcation of code into paragraphs establishes a structural paradigm that underlies both the functional decomposition and the logical sequencing of operations. This segmentation reflects a commitment to modular design whereby each paragraph encapsulates a specific subset of computational tasks. In this context, the organization of paragraphs is closely aligned with the formal principles of separation of concerns and abstraction, ensuring that discrete algorithmic operations are coherently isolated. By partitioning the execution flow into logically distinct units, the overall design mitigates complexity and facilitates a rigorous analytical approach to program behavior.

Paragraphs as Discrete Units of Functionality

Paragraphs serve as the primary granules of code segmentation within the PROCEDURE DIVISION. Each paragraph is uniquely identified by a designated label that conveys semantic meaning and delineates the boundaries of a self-contained functional entity. This labeling system not only aids in the navigation of the codebase but also underpins the capacity to apply localized modifications without necessitating extensive alterations to adjacent sections. The encapsulation achieved through paragraph-based structuring mirrors the theoretical constructs of modular programming, where the isolation of operations promotes precision in execution and streamlines the process of debugging and verification. The meticulous arrangement of statements within these paragraphs is instrumental in preserving the integrity of logical sequences and ensuring that the transformation of data proceeds in an orderly and predictable manner.

Sections as Aggregators of Logical Blocks

Sections introduce an additional hierarchical layer by aggregating multiple paragraphs that share related operational contexts. This structural configuration allows for the consolidation of functionally cohesive paragraphs into broader thematic units, thereby enhancing the overall coherence of the program's flow. The organizational utility of sections becomes particularly evident in large-scale systems, where the collation of related processing routines into a unified section serves to reduce cognitive overhead. The sectional grouping further supports advanced code analysis by delineating clear boundaries between different phases of the computational process. This methodology aligns with established practices in software engineering, as it systematically partitions the code into distinctly manageable segments, ensuring that purpose and functionality are transparently communicated through the architecture.

Implications for Readability and Maintainability

The systematic partitioning of the PROCEDURE DIVISION into finely structured paragraphs and aggregated sections exerts a profound influence on both the readability and maintainability of the code. By localizing specific computational operations within dedicated paragraphs, the code attains a high degree of clarity that facilitates both human comprehension and automated analysis. The precise and systematic labeling of these components ensures that alterations and enhancements can be implemented with minimal risk of unintended interference across the program. Furthermore, the hierarchical aggregation provided by sections introduces an additional level of organization, thereby reinforcing the modular architecture and supporting scalability. This architectural approach adheres to rigorous standards of software design, where the deliberate structuring of statements into logically coherent units directly contributes to the robustness and longevity of the system.

Cobol Code Snippet

```
IDENTIFICATION DIVISION.
PROGRAM-ID. QUADRATIC-SOLVER.
AUTHOR. Maxwell_Vector.

ENVIRONMENT DIVISION.
INPUT-OUTPUT SECTION.

DATA DIVISION.
WORKING-STORAGE SECTION.
77  WS-COEFF-A       PIC S9(4)V99 VALUE 0.
77  WS-COEFF-B       PIC S9(4)V99 VALUE 0.
77  WS-COEFF-C       PIC S9(4)V99 VALUE 0.
77  WS-DISCRIMINANT  PIC S9(6)V99 VALUE 0.
77  WS-SQRT-DISC     PIC S9(4)V99 VALUE 0.
77  WS-ROOT1         PIC S9(4)V99 VALUE 0.
77  WS-ROOT2         PIC S9(4)V99 VALUE 0.
77  WS-DISCRIM-ABS   PIC S9(6)V99 VALUE 0.

PROCEDURE DIVISION.
MAIN-PARA.
    PERFORM READ-COEFFS.
    PERFORM COMPUTE-DISCRIMINANT.
    PERFORM CHECK-DISCRIMINANT.
    STOP RUN.

READ-COEFFS.
    DISPLAY "Enter coefficient A (non-zero):".
    ACCEPT WS-COEFF-A.
    IF WS-COEFF-A = 0
        DISPLAY "Coefficient A cannot be zero. Terminating program."
        STOP RUN
    END-IF.
    DISPLAY "Enter coefficient B:".
    ACCEPT WS-COEFF-B.
    DISPLAY "Enter coefficient C:".
    ACCEPT WS-COEFF-C.
    EXIT.
```

```
COMPUTE-DISCRIMINANT.
    COMPUTE WS-DISCRIMINANT = (WS-COEFF-B * WS-COEFF-B)
                             - (4 * WS-COEFF-A * WS-COEFF-C).
    EXIT.

CHECK-DISCRIMINANT.
    IF WS-DISCRIMINANT < 0
        DISPLAY "Discriminant is negative. The equation has complex
        ↪  roots."
        COMPUTE WS-DISCRIM-ABS = FUNCTION ABS (WS-DISCRIMINANT)
        PERFORM COMPUTE-COMPLEX-ROOTS
    ELSE
        PERFORM COMPUTE-REAL-ROOTS
    END-IF.
    EXIT.

COMPUTE-REAL-ROOTS.
    COMPUTE WS-SQRT-DISC = FUNCTION SQRT (WS-DISCRIMINANT).
    COMPUTE WS-ROOT1 = ((-1 * WS-COEFF-B) + WS-SQRT-DISC) / (2 *
    ↪  WS-COEFF-A).
    COMPUTE WS-ROOT2 = ((-1 * WS-COEFF-B) - WS-SQRT-DISC) / (2 *
    ↪  WS-COEFF-A).
    PERFORM DISPLAY-REAL-ROOTS.
    EXIT.

COMPUTE-COMPLEX-ROOTS.
    COMPUTE WS-SQRT-DISC = FUNCTION SQRT (WS-DISCRIM-ABS).
    DISPLAY "Complex Roots:".
    DISPLAY "Real Part: " ((-1 * WS-COEFF-B) / (2 * WS-COEFF-A)).
    DISPLAY "Imaginary Part: " (WS-SQRT-DISC / (2 * WS-COEFF-A)) "
    ↪  i".
    EXIT.

DISPLAY-REAL-ROOTS.
    DISPLAY "Real Roots:".
    DISPLAY "Root 1: " WS-ROOT1.
    DISPLAY "Root 2: " WS-ROOT2.
    EXIT.
```

Chapter 17

MOVE Statement in Detail

Conceptual Framework and Motivation

The MOVE statement occupies a central role in COBOL's data handling paradigm by effecting the transfer of data between distinct memory-resident variables and fields. This operation serves as the fundamental mechanism for establishing correspondence between a source element and a destination element across the various divisions of a program. Within this conceptual framework, the essence of the MOVE statement lies in its capacity to mediate data assignment with an implicit adherence to type and format compatibility. The operation is not a mere physical copy; rather, it embodies a transformation process whereby the intrinsic properties of the source data—such as its length, format, and semantic constraints—are reconciled and imposed upon the target structure. The design of this mechanism reflects a deliberate abstraction that reduces programming complexity through standardized data transportation procedures, ensuring that data is systematically aligned with the architectural requirements of the broader system.

Syntactic Structure and Formal Semantics

At the syntactic level, the MOVE statement is characterized by a declarative structure that clearly delineates the source operand from the destination operand. The formulation adheres to a prescribed syntax that is unambiguous within the context of COBOL's rigid formatting rules. In formal terms, the statement can be considered as an operation mapping a specific data entity S (source) to another entity D (destination), wherein the mapping function is governed by conversion rules, padding behavior, and truncation policies as specified by the underlying data definitions. Such a definition is not merely lexical; it is defined by precise semantic rules that prescribe how character strings, numeric values, and alphanumeric data are to be reconciled. Notably, any disparity between the lengths or types of S and D initiates a series of implicit operations, ensuring adherence to COBOL's stringent data integrity constraints and preserving the logical consistency of the information transferred.

Type Conversion and Data Coercion Mechanisms

A critical aspect of the MOVE statement lies in its ability to perform type conversion and data coercion during data transfer. When the operation involves operands of disparate types or differing picture clauses, an internal conversion process is invoked. For instance, the transformation from an alphanumeric source to a numeric destination requires the MOVE statement to interpret the textual representation and reconstitute it into a numerical value consistent with the target's defined precision. Conversely, when numerical values are transferred into alphanumeric fields, the statement mandates the insertion of appropriate formatting or blank padding to reconcile the length and display requirements. Such conversion mechanisms are essential in ensuring that despite heterogeneous data definitions, the resultant assignment retains semantic homogeneity. The formal semantics governing these operations are defined by a set of conversion rules that govern not only the normalization of data but also error handling in scenarios where data incompatibility is detected.

Operational Dynamics and Data Integrity Considerations

The practical implementation of the MOVE statement is marked by its deterministic approach to data transfer, where the destination field is assigned a value that reflects the full, albeit sometimes reformatted, content of the source. Attention to detail is paramount when considering the operational dynamics, as the statement manages issues such as field truncation and the propagation of extraneous characters, thereby influencing the overall data integrity of the application. Each execution of the MOVE statement is an atomic operation that consolidates reading and transformation phases into a single, logically contiguous process. Moreover, the statement ensures that potential discrepancies arising from differences in field definitions are resolved at runtime through well-defined, algorithmic adjustments. Such adjustments serve to minimize ambiguities associated with data representation, thereby establishing a robust framework for predictable program behavior. The MOVE statement, in this respect, is instrumental in safeguarding both the fidelity of the transferred value and the consistency of the application's data landscape.

Cobol Code Snippet

```
IDENTIFICATION DIVISION.
PROGRAM-ID. MOVEDEMO.
AUTHOR. Maxwell_Vector.
DATE-WRITTEN. 2024-10-10.

ENVIRONMENT DIVISION.
CONFIGURATION SECTION.
    SOURCE-COMPUTER. IBM-370.
    OBJECT-COMPUTER. IBM-370.

DATA DIVISION.
WORKING-STORAGE SECTION.
* Define an alphanumeric variable containing a numeric string.
77  WS-ALPHA   PIC X(10)  VALUE "000123   ".
* Define a numeric variable to receive the converted value.
77  WS-NUMERIC PIC 9(5)   VALUE ZERO.
* Variable to hold the result of arithmetic operation.
77  WS-CALC    PIC 9(5)   VALUE ZERO.
* Alphanumeric variable to demonstrate numeric-to-string conversion
↪   with padding.
```

```
77  WS-NUM-PAD PIC X(10)  VALUE SPACES.
* Variable to illustrate truncation: receiving a longer string into
↪  a fixed-length field.
77  WS-RESULT  PIC X(10)  VALUE SPACES.

PROCEDURE DIVISION.
MAIN-PARA.
    DISPLAY "Initial alphanumeric value: " WS-ALPHA.

    * MOVE from alphanumeric to numeric with implicit type
    ↪  conversion.
    MOVE WS-ALPHA TO WS-NUMERIC.
    DISPLAY "After MOVE to numeric: " WS-NUMERIC.

    * Perform arithmetic operation: add 100 to the numeric value.
    COMPUTE WS-CALC = WS-NUMERIC + 100.
    DISPLAY "After arithmetic (WS-NUMERIC + 100): " WS-CALC.

    * Convert numeric result back to an alphanumeric field.
    MOVE WS-CALC TO WS-NUM-PAD.
    DISPLAY "Numeric value moved to alphanumeric (padded): "
    ↪  WS-NUM-PAD.

    * Demonstrate truncation: moving a longer string to a
    ↪  fixed-length field.
    MOVE "HELLO WORLD" TO WS-RESULT.
    DISPLAY "Result after MOVE with truncation: " WS-RESULT.

    STOP RUN.
```

Chapter 18

Arithmetic Operations: ADD and SUBTRACT

Conceptual Basis of Numerical Operations

The arithmetic operations in COBOL, encapsulated through the ADD and SUBTRACT statements, constitute a fundamental mechanism for the transformation of numerical data between memory-resident entities. These operations are intrinsically bound to a formal model in which each operand is rigorously defined by a PIC clause that specifies attributes such as precision, scale, and sign. The ADD and SUBTRACT statements are not merely syntactic sugar but represent a systematic approach to numerical manipulation, adhering to strict semantic rules that ensure arithmetic consistency. In this framework, each operation functions within an abstract space where the numerical values are treated as elements in a set, typically modeled as
$mathbbZ$ for integers, and the operations are defined in a manner that guarantees deterministic behavior under constrained computational conditions.

Syntactic and Semantic Structure of the ADD Statement

The ADD statement is engineered to perform summation over one or more numerical operands, mapping them to a single destination

variable. Formally, this operation can be represented as a function
f :
$mathbbZ^n$
to
$mathbbZ$, where n denotes the number of summands. Each source
operand is subjected to an implicit conversion process, ensuring
its numerical representation is coherent with the constraints imposed by the target variable's definition. The operation adheres
to the associative property, which mathematically guarantees that
the grouping of operands does not influence the outcome, provided
that issues such as truncation or overflow do not occur. The explicit
delineation of sources and destination fields within the ADD construct reinforces a model where data portability and integrity are
preserved through stringent syntactic and semantic stipulations.

Syntactic and Semantic Structure of the SUBTRACT Statement

The SUBTRACT statement is responsible for effecting the arithmetic difference between numerical quantities. It operates as a
binary function g :
$mathbbZ$
$times$
$mathbbZ$
to
$mathbbZ$, wherein the operation involves deducting one or more
subtrahend values from an initial minuend. The formal semantics
of the subtraction process emphasize adherence to type compatibility and precision management, ensuring that any deviation in
operand sizes triggers an internal conversion mechanism. The fundamental nature of subtraction, characterized by its non-commutative
and non-associative properties, introduces additional layers of complexity that are managed by the language's evaluation model. Careful specification of operand sequencing and explicit mapping into
destination storage mitigates potential discrepancies, thus consolidating numeric accuracy within the functional boundaries set by
the COBOL standard.

Operational Considerations and Numeric Precision

The execution of ADD and SUBTRACT operations in COBOL is subject to a set of operational rules designed to preserve numeric precision and ensure arithmetic integrity. During evaluation, each operand is verified against the field-length constraints and numeric precision as defined by its PIC specification. In scenarios where the computed result exceeds the capacity of the destination field, systematic truncation or rounding is invoked in order to reconcile any mismatch between the computed value and the storage format. Such mechanisms are an essential aspect of COBOL's fixed-point arithmetic system, where the deterministic and atomic nature of arithmetic instructions guarantees that every operation results in a consistent and precisely defined numerical output. The rigorous enforcement of these constraints ensures that arithmetic expressions yield results that remain faithful to the intended mathematical computation even under the limitations of finite digital representation.

Theoretical Underpinnings and Formal Properties

From an algebraic perspective, the operations realized by the ADD and SUBTRACT statements can be interpreted within the context of fundamental arithmetic theory. The ADD operation naturally reflects the properties of commutativity and associativity; for arbitrary elements a, b, and c in $mathbbZ$, the equalities $a+b = b+a$ and $(a+b)+c = a+(b+c)$ hold true, provided that the numerical precision is maintained throughout the computation. Conversely, the SUBTRACT operation, defined by the binary mapping $a - b$, lacks commutativity and associativity, thereby necessitating a precise ordering of operations. These formal properties are deeply integrated into the COBOL execution model, which incorporates detailed conversion functions that guarantee that every arithmetic operation adheres to the rigid formalism required for consistent numeric computation. Such an approach ensures that arithmetic results remain both mathematically valid and compatible with the system's storage definitions.

Cobol Code Snippet

```
IDENTIFICATION DIVISION.
PROGRAM-ID. ARITHMETIC-OP.

ENVIRONMENT DIVISION.
CONFIGURATION SECTION.
INPUT-OUTPUT SECTION.

DATA DIVISION.
WORKING-STORAGE SECTION.
* Define numeric fields with fixed point precision.
01 NUM-A       PIC S9(4)V99 VALUE 1234.56.
01 NUM-B       PIC S9(4)V99 VALUE  789.12.
01 NUM-C       PIC S9(4)V99 VALUE   56.78.

01 RESULT-ADD-1 PIC S9(5)V99 VALUE ZERO.
01 RESULT-ADD-2 PIC S9(5)V99 VALUE ZERO.
01 TEMP-VAR     PIC S9(5)V99 VALUE ZERO.

01 DIFF-1      PIC S9(5)V99 VALUE ZERO.
01 DIFF-2      PIC S9(5)V99 VALUE ZERO.

PROCEDURE DIVISION.
MAIN-PARA.
    DISPLAY "COBOL ARITHMETIC OPERATIONS DEMO".
    DISPLAY "-----------------------------------".

    ↪   *-----------------------------------------------------------
    * Demonstrate Associativity of the ADD Operation.
    * Compute (NUM-A + NUM-B) + NUM-C.

    ↪   *-----------------------------------------------------------
    ADD NUM-A NUM-B GIVING TEMP-VAR.
    ADD TEMP-VAR NUM-C GIVING RESULT-ADD-1.

    * Compute NUM-A + (NUM-B + NUM-C).
    ADD NUM-B NUM-C GIVING TEMP-VAR.
    ADD NUM-A TEMP-VAR GIVING RESULT-ADD-2.

    DISPLAY "Result of (NUM-A + NUM-B) + NUM-C: "
    ↪   RESULT-ADD-1.
    DISPLAY "Result of NUM-A + (NUM-B + NUM-C): "
    ↪   RESULT-ADD-2.


    ↪   *-----------------------------------------------------------
    * Demonstrate Non-Associativity of the SUBTRACT
    ↪   Operation.
    * Compute (NUM-A - NUM-B) - NUM-C.
```

```
↪   *------------------------------------------------------------
MOVE NUM-A TO TEMP-VAR.
SUBTRACT NUM-B FROM TEMP-VAR GIVING DIFF-1.
SUBTRACT NUM-C FROM DIFF-1 GIVING DIFF-1.

* Compute NUM-A - (NUM-B - NUM-C).
SUBTRACT NUM-C FROM NUM-B GIVING TEMP-VAR.
SUBTRACT TEMP-VAR FROM NUM-A GIVING DIFF-2.

DISPLAY "Result of (NUM-A - NUM-B) - NUM-C: " DIFF-1.
DISPLAY "Result of NUM-A - (NUM-B - NUM-C): " DIFF-2.

STOP RUN.
```

Chapter 19

Arithmetic Operations: MULTIPLY and DIVIDE

Conceptual Basis of Multiplicative and Divisive Processes

The operations of multiplication and division in COBOL are governed by a framework that emphasizes a fixed-point numerical model designed to execute complex arithmetic expressions within the constraints specified by picture clauses. The multiplication process is grounded in the notion of repeated addition, yet it is abstracted into a direct operation that maps a pair or set of operands into a single product. In formal terms, a multiplicative function $\mu : \mathbb{Z}^n \to \mathbb{Z}$ is realized such that each operand, defined through its respective PIC clause, is first converted implicitly into a common numerical representation. Conversely, division is treated as a twofold process: a quotient is computed and, where necessary, a remainder is optionally derived. This process can be mathematically conceived as a partial function $\delta : \mathbb{Z} \times (\mathbb{Z} \setminus \{0\}) \to \mathbb{Z}$ that enforces the condition $b \neq 0$ for a division operation $a \div b$. Both operations are integrated into COBOL's arithmetic model, which mandates rigorous adherence to numeric precision, arithmetic integrity, and deterministic evaluation.

Syntactic and Semantic Considerations for the MULTIPLY Statement

The MULTIPLY statement in COBOL is characterized by its ability to handle one or more multiplicands in a single instruction. The syntactic structure ensures that operands are processed in a manner consistent with their defined storage formats. From a semantic perspective, the multiplication operation is implemented as an evaluative function that computes the product by performing a series of implicit type conversions, aligning the storage definitions specified in each operand's PIC clause. The operation is inherently associative; that is, for any operands a, b, and c satisfying the required constraints, the equality

$$(a \times b) \times c = a \times (b \times c)$$

holds under ideal arithmetic conditions, subject to the limitations imposed by fixed-point representations. The design of the COBOL MULTIPLY construct further accommodates the conversion of intermediate results to prevent overflow, ensuring that the final computed product conforms to the predetermined field length and precision.

Syntactic and Semantic Considerations for the DIVIDE Statement

The DIVIDE statement is intrinsically more complex owing to its dual-output nature, where the primary result is the quotient and an optional secondary result represents the remainder. The operation is structurally divided into distinct phases involving the determination of the numerical quotient and the calculation of any residual value. In formal notation, the quotient is given by a function $\delta_Q : \mathbb{Z} \times (\mathbb{Z} \setminus \{0\}) \to \mathbb{Z}$ where $\delta_Q(a, b)$ approximates the result of $a \div b$. The optional remainder is defined via an auxiliary function $\delta_R : \mathbb{Z} \times (\mathbb{Z} \setminus \{0\}) \to \mathbb{Z}$ such that the relationship

$$a = b \times \delta_Q(a, b) + \delta_R(a, b)$$

is maintained, provided that the divisor is nonzero. The COBOL evaluation model employs stringent type compatibility checks and automatic conversion mechanisms to align operand precision and scale prior to execution. This ensures that the division operation, while mathematically non-associative and non-commutative, systematically produces results that are consistent with the semantic expectations derived from the associated PIC descriptors.

Operational Considerations and Numeric Precision in Complex Arithmetic Operations

Multiplicative and divisive operations in COBOL are executed within a computational environment where numeric precision is paramount. The arithmetic engine verifies that each operand satisfies the field-length and scale constraints imposed by the corresponding PIC clause. In multiplication, the potential for intermediate results to exceed the precision of the destination variable necessitates the implementation of rounding or truncation mechanisms. The system-level conversion functions dynamically adjust operand representations to preclude overflow and maintain arithmetic integrity. Similarly, the division operation must contend with issues of finite representation; rounding policies are rigorously enforced to reconcile the inherent imprecision associated with the division of integers when interpreted in a fixed-point context. In both cases, the evaluation model is designed to ensure that every arithmetic instruction completes in an atomic fashion, thereby guaranteeing that the computed results remain within the bounds of deterministic behavior defined by the COBOL standard.

Formal and Theoretical Underpinnings of Multiplicative and Divisive Operations

The mathematical foundation underpinning the MULTIPLY and DIVIDE statements is deeply rooted in established algebraic structures. Within the realm of fixed-point arithmetic, multiplication is viewed as an operation in a commutative monoid with an identity element 1, satisfying the properties:

$$a \times b = b \times a \quad \text{and} \quad a \times (b \times c) = (a \times b) \times c,$$

provided that the effects of rounding and truncation are negligibly managed. Division, by contrast, is defined as a partial function on a set with nonzero divisors and exhibits a decomposition that yields both a quotient and a remainder. The formal treatment of division adheres to the algorithmic formulation

$$a = b \times q + r, \quad 0 \leq r < |b|,$$

where q represents the computed quotient and r the residual, subject to rounding conventions intrinsic to the computational model. This dual-faceted approach reflects the nuanced balance between theoretical arithmetic ideals and the practical constraints of digital representation. The implementation of these operations within COBOL ensures that arithmetic processes are encapsulated within a robust framework, offering precise control over computational behavior while harmonizing with the overall design of the language's fixed-point arithmetic paradigm.

Cobol Code Snippet

```
IDENTIFICATION DIVISION.
PROGRAM-ID. ARITHMETIC-DEMO.
*-----------------------------------------------------
*   This program demonstrates COBOL arithmetic operations:
*   - Multiplication of two fixed-point numbers.
*   - Division producing both a quotient and a remainder.
*   - Verification of the fundamental relationship:
*       NUM1 = NUM2 * QUOTIENT + REMAINDER
*   It also illustrates the internal handling of precision and
↪   the
*   conversion steps necessary in a fixed-point arithmetic
↪   system.
*-----------------------------------------------------


ENVIRONMENT DIVISION.

DATA DIVISION.
WORKING-STORAGE SECTION.
* Define two sample numbers adhering to fixed-point
↪   constraints.
77 NUM1              PIC 9(6)V99 VALUE 12345.67.
77 NUM2              PIC 9(6)V99 VALUE 123.45.

* Variables to store the outcome of arithmetic operations.
77 PRODUCT           PIC 9(12)V99.     * Result of
↪   multiplication.
77 QUOTIENT          PIC 9(6)V99.      * Result of division
↪   (quotient).
77 REMAINDER         PIC 9(6)V99.      * Result of division
↪   (remainder).
```

```
77 CHECK-VALUE        PIC 9(12)V99.     * For verifying NUM1 =
↪    NUM2*QUOTIENT+REMAINDER.

PROCEDURE DIVISION.
    DISPLAY "COBOL Arithmetic Operations Demo".

    *---------------------------------------------------
    * Multiplicative Operation:
    * Compute the product of NUM1 and NUM2.
    * Equation: PRODUCT = NUM1 * NUM2
    * Internal conversion handles alignment per PIC clauses.
    *---------------------------------------------------
    MULTIPLY NUM1 BY NUM2 GIVING PRODUCT.
    DISPLAY "PRODUCT (NUM1 * NUM2): " PRODUCT.

    *---------------------------------------------------
    * Divisive Operation:
    * Perform division of NUM1 by NUM2.
    * This statement computes both the quotient and the
    ↪    remainder.
    * Equation: NUM1 = NUM2 * QUOTIENT + REMAINDER
    * Type-checking and rounding mechanisms ensure precision.
    *---------------------------------------------------
    DIVIDE NUM1 BY NUM2 GIVING QUOTIENT REMAINDER REMAINDER.
    DISPLAY "QUOTIENT (NUM1 / NUM2): " QUOTIENT.
    DISPLAY "REMAINDER: " REMAINDER.

    *---------------------------------------------------
    * Verification Step:
    * Re-calculate NUM2 * QUOTIENT and add REMAINDER to
    ↪    verify:
    *    CHECK-VALUE = NUM2 * QUOTIENT + REMAINDER   NUM1
    * This confirms that the arithmetic integrity is
    ↪    maintained.
    *---------------------------------------------------
    MULTIPLY NUM2 BY QUOTIENT GIVING CHECK-VALUE.
    ADD REMAINDER TO CHECK-VALUE GIVING CHECK-VALUE.
    DISPLAY "Verification (NUM2 * QUOTIENT + REMAINDER): "
    ↪    CHECK-VALUE.

    STOP RUN.
```

Chapter 20

COMPUTE Statement Fundamentals

Syntactic Structure and Expression Composition

The COMPUTE statement represents a comprehensive syntactic construct that permits the evaluation of complex arithmetic expressions within a single declarative statement. In this context, individual operands, each defined by their respective picture clauses, are combined with arithmetic operators to form a single evaluable expression. The expression can be abstractly represented as a tree structure where each internal node corresponds to an operator (such as $+$, $-$, $\times$, or $\div$) and each leaf node represents a fixed-point numeric operand. The ordering of operations is unambiguously defined by the language's operator precedence rules, ensuring that, for example, multiplication and division are performed prior to addition and subtraction unless explicit parentheses are employed to alter the natural hierarchy. This structure not only supports nested arithmetic but also enforces consistency between the symbolic representation of the expression and the eventual numeric result.

Semantic Considerations: Evaluation, Type Coercion, and Error Handling

At the semantic level, the COMPUTE statement functions as an evaluative mechanism that maps an arithmetic expression to a singular, deterministic numerical result. Prior to execution, every operand undergoes implicit type coercion to achieve compatibility with an internal common representation. This conversion ensures that translation between various PIC definitions is seamlessly managed within the computation process. Formally, if an expression E is composed of operands a, b, c, and so on, there exists an underlying function $\kappa : \mathcal{E} \to \mathbb{R}$ that resolves the expression E to its computed value, subject to the finite storage and precision constraints imposed by fixed-point arithmetic. In the event that an operand cannot be converted without loss of fidelity, the evaluation mechanism incorporates error-handling protocols designed to preclude undefined computational states, thereby maintaining the integrity of the overall arithmetic process.

Arithmetic Precision and Rounding Mechanisms

A critical feature of the COMPUTE statement is its integrated approach to managing numeric precision. Each arithmetic operation within the statement is subject to the limitations imposed by a fixed-point numerical model, where intermediate results may possess a precision exceeding that of the final target field. To mitigate potential overflow or loss of significance, the arithmetic engine employs rounding functions that adhere to predetermined algorithms. For instance, consider an expression of the form

$$x = a + b \times c,$$

where the product $b \times c$ might produce additional fractional digits. The evaluation process incorporates a rounding mechanism denoted by a function $r(\cdot)$, such that the final value of x is given by

$$x = r\Big(a + \big(b \times c\big)\Big).$$

This guarantees that the result conforms to the fixed precision specified by its picture clause, thereby ensuring that the computed outcome remains within the definitional limits of the storage variable.

Operational Efficiency and Expressive Power

The COMPUTE statement consolidates the evaluation of recursively nested arithmetic operations into a solitary instruction, enhancing operational efficiency by reducing the overhead associated with multiple discrete arithmetic statements. This conciseness allows for the construction of sophisticated expressions without the introduction of intermediate variables or auxiliary calculations. Internally, the compiler translates the complex expression into an optimized parse tree where constant sub-expressions may be precomputed and redundant evaluations eliminated. The result is an expression evaluation strategy that not only simplifies source code but also promotes a reduction in runtime computational complexity. Consequently, the COMPUTE statement embodies a synthesis of expressive power and operational rigor, facilitating the precise and efficient resolution of complex arithmetic operations within the constraints of COBOL's fixed-point arithmetic paradigm.

Cobol Code Snippet

```
IDENTIFICATION DIVISION.
PROGRAM-ID. COMPUTE-EXAMPLE.

ENVIRONMENT DIVISION.
* This example does not use external file I/O.

DATA DIVISION.
WORKING-STORAGE SECTION.
* Define fixed-point numeric variables with PIC clauses.
77  A          PIC S9(4)V99 VALUE 123.45.
77  B          PIC S9(4)V99 VALUE  67.89.
77  C          PIC S9(4)V99 VALUE   0.12.
77  PRODUCT    PIC S9(5)V99 VALUE ZERO.
77  RESULT     PIC S9(5)V99 VALUE ZERO.
77  COMPLEX-RES PIC S9(6)V99 VALUE ZERO.
77  WS-MESSAGE PIC X(50).

PROCEDURE DIVISION.
MAIN-PARA.
    DISPLAY "Starting COMPUTE Statement Example...".

    *-------------------------------------------------------------
    * Compute the product of B and C with rounding.
    * This demonstrates operand type coercion, operator precedence,
    * and the application of the ROUNDED clause.
    *-------------------------------------------------------------
```

```
COMPUTE PRODUCT = B * C ROUNDED
    ON SIZE ERROR
        DISPLAY "Error: Multiplication overflow."
        STOP RUN
END-COMPUTE.
DISPLAY "Computed PRODUCT (B * C): " PRODUCT.


*------------------------------------------------------------
* Compute a combined expression: RESULT = A + (B * C)
* The operation reflects the tree-structured evaluation where
* multiplication is performed prior to addition.
*------------------------------------------------------------
COMPUTE RESULT = A + (B * C) ROUNDED
    ON SIZE ERROR
        DISPLAY "Error: Addition overflow."
        STOP RUN
END-COMPUTE.
DISPLAY "Final RESULT (A + B * C): " RESULT.


*------------------------------------------------------------
* Compute a more complex nested arithmetic expression to
* illustrate the operational efficiency and expressive power.
* Expression: COMPLEX-RES = (A + (B * C)) - (B / C) + (A - C)
*------------------------------------------------------------
COMPUTE COMPLEX-RES = (A + (B * C)) - (B / C) + (A - C) ROUNDED
    ON SIZE ERROR
        DISPLAY "Error: Complex computation overflow."
        STOP RUN
END-COMPUTE.
DISPLAY "Nested Expression Result: " COMPLEX-RES.


STOP RUN.
```

Chapter 21

Conditional Processing with IF

Syntactic Structure of the IF Statement

The IF statement constitutes a primary control construct that delineates the execution flow based on the evaluation of a logical predicate. The abstract syntax of the statement is defined by a header that contains the keyword IF immediately followed by a conditional expression. This conditional expression is composed of one or more relational operators, such as $=$, $<$, $>$, $\leq$, and $\geq$, which compare operands conforming to the prescribed data formats. The inherent structure allows for an optional alternate branch, typically introduced by an ELSE clause, which delineates a divergent execution pathway when the predicate evaluates to false. This bifurcation simplifies the logical structure of decision-making by partitioning the execution into mutually exclusive segments, thereby enhancing both the readability and the formal rigor of the program.

Semantic Considerations in Conditional Evaluation

The semantics of the IF statement are rooted in the deterministic evaluation of logical predicates and the controlled redirection of program flow. Each operand is assessed within the context of implicit type coercion, ensuring that values originating from different numeric or alphanumeric representations are internally normalized for coherent comparison. The evaluation mechanism adheres to a strict order of operations as defined by standard relational logic, mapping complex expressions onto a Boolean domain. Formally, if a predicate P is expressed as a function $P : \mathcal{D} \rightarrow \{\text{true}, \text{false}\}$, then the outcome of the IF statement is predicated on whether P produces a truth value of true. In scenarios in which the condition is not fulfilled, the execution control is transferred to the alternative branch if one is specified; otherwise, the sequential flow of the program continues without interruption. This deterministic behavior is essential for preserving the logical integrity of the control structure in environments where fixed-point arithmetic and implicit rounding may otherwise introduce subtle deviations.

Common Usage Scenarios and Execution Paradigms

The IF statement is employed extensively in contexts where conditional execution is necessary for regulating operational semantics and optimizing code pathways. One common scenario involves the validation of variable states, wherein conditions are used to verify that data values fall within acceptable ranges or conform to expected formats. Such validations are typically constructed by juxtaposing the current state against predetermined thresholds, with the IF construct isolating the regular processing logic from error handling or exceptional processing routines. In addition to data validation, the IF statement supports the implementation of branching logic in control flows, enabling recursive or nested conditional constructs. These complex arrangements allow for the hierarchical resolution of decision criteria, where sub-conditions are evaluated only if an antecedent condition is satisfied. This encapsulation of multifaceted decision logic into a single control envelope not only streamlines program design but also provides an opportunity for optimization by eliminating redundant checks. The execution paradigm inherent in this conditional structure ensures that the program exhibits both clarity in its logic and efficiency in its run-time performance.

Cobol Code Snippet

```
IDENTIFICATION DIVISION.
PROGRAM-ID. IFDEMO.

ENVIRONMENT DIVISION.
* Optional: System and configuration details may be added
↪  here.

DATA DIVISION.
WORKING-STORAGE SECTION.
* Variable declarations for arithmetic and conditional
↪  evaluation
01  NUM1       PIC 9(4) VALUE 0100.
01  NUM2       PIC 9(4) VALUE 0060.
01  SUM        PIC 9(4) VALUE ZERO.
01  AVG        PIC 9(3)V9(2) VALUE ZERO.
01  THRESHOLD  PIC 9(3) VALUE 075.
01  DIFFERENCE PIC 9(4) VALUE ZERO.
01  RESULT     PIC X(30) VALUE SPACES.

PROCEDURE DIVISION.
MAIN-LOGIC.
    DISPLAY "Starting IF demo program".

    * Compute arithmetic expressions as part of the algorithm
    COMPUTE SUM = NUM1 + NUM2.
    COMPUTE DIFFERENCE = NUM1 - NUM2.
    COMPUTE AVG = SUM / 2.

    DISPLAY "NUM1: " NUM1 "  NUM2: " NUM2.
    DISPLAY "SUM : " SUM.
    DISPLAY "AVERAGE: " AVG.
    DISPLAY "DIFFERENCE: " DIFFERENCE.

    * Use IF statement to evaluate if the computed average
    ↪  exceeds the threshold.
    IF AVG > THRESHOLD THEN
        MOVE "Average exceeds threshold." TO RESULT
    ELSE
        MOVE "Average does not exceed threshold." TO RESULT
    END-IF.
    DISPLAY "Result: " RESULT.

    * Nested IF construct to further analyze the difference
    ↪  value.
    IF DIFFERENCE = 40 THEN
        DISPLAY "Exact difference is 40."
    ELSE
        IF DIFFERENCE > 40 THEN
            DISPLAY "Difference is greater than 40."
        ELSE
```

```
            DISPLAY "Difference is less than 40."
        END-IF
END-IF.

STOP RUN.
```
_____

Chapter 22

Multi-branch Logic with EVALUATE

Syntactic Structure and Expressiveness

The EVALUATE statement is architected to encapsulate multiple decision pathways within a single construct, thereby obviating the need for deeply nested conditional statements. Its syntactic design commences with a header that demarcates the initiation of the evaluation, followed by a series of case clauses that articulate the specific conditions and corresponding actions. Each clause is constructed in a manner that permits the association of one or more candidate expressions with a distinct computational branch, ensuring that the grammar supports a flexible yet rigorous formulation. In formal terms, if an expression is represented by E, the subsequent clauses in the statement delineate mappings from E to an action subset, effectively partitioning the state space into mutually exclusive segments. This structure facilitates a clear and concise representation of multi-branch logic, promoting both syntactic clarity and structural integrity in complex programmatic contexts.

Semantic Underpinnings and Formal Considerations

The semantic framework of the EVALUATE statement rests on a deterministic mapping of evaluated expressions to specific execution paths. Viewed through the lens of formal logic, the statement may be conceptualized as a function $f\colon \mathcal{S} \to \mathcal{A}$, where $\mathcal{S}$ denotes the set of possible states derived from evaluating expression E, and $\mathcal{A}$ denotes the set of actions corresponding to the evaluated conditions. Under this paradigm, the EVALUATE construct inspects the current state and subsequently selects the first clause for which the condition holds true, executing the associated action. This sequential and non-ambiguous evaluation process adheres to strict Boolean logic and order of operations, thus ensuring that each possible branch is both well-defined and exclusive. Furthermore, the treatment of composite and nested conditions within the statement follows rigorous formal rules, thereby precluding the ambiguities that typically plague less structured conditional constructs. The semantic clarity afforded by this mechanism is instrumental in maintaining the logical integrity of complex control flows.

Comparative Analysis with Nested IF Constructs

Relative to traditional nested IF constructs, the EVALUATE statement offers a pronounced improvement in both readability and maintenance. Nested IF constructs, while functionally capable, often lead to cascading levels of indentation that obscure the underlying logical structure. In contrast, the EVALUATE statement consolidates multiple condition checks into a single, coherent block, providing a more streamlined and legible alternative. This consolidation not only simplifies the visual parsing of conditional logic but also facilitates formal reasoning about the control flow, as the logical branches are delineated in a uniform and hierarchical fashion. The inherent design mitigates the potential for inadvertent fall-through and logically inconsistent executions, which are risks that are more pronounced in deeply nested constructs. As a result, the EVALUATE statement serves as both an efficient and robust method for implementing multi-way conditional logic, ensuring that each conditional pathway is explicitly defined and systematically managed.

Cobol Code Snippet

```
IDENTIFICATION DIVISION.
PROGRAM-ID. MULTIEVALUATEDEMO.

ENVIRONMENT DIVISION.

DATA DIVISION.
WORKING-STORAGE SECTION.
    * Define numeric variables and messages.
    77 NUM1        PIC S9(4) COMP-5 VALUE 15.
    77 NUM2        PIC S9(4) COMP-5 VALUE 5.
    77 RESULT      PIC S9(6) COMP-5 VALUE 0.
    77 OPTION      PIC 9        VALUE 0.
    77 MESSAGE     PIC X(40)    VALUE SPACES.

PROCEDURE DIVISION.
MAIN-LOGIC.
    * Display operation options.
    DISPLAY "Select Operation: 1=ADD, 2=SUBTRACT, 3=MULTIPLY,
    ↪  4=DIVIDE".
    ACCEPT OPTION.

    * Evaluate the user's selection as a mapping function (f: S ->
    ↪  A)
    * where the state (OPTION) determines the action performed.
    EVALUATE OPTION
        WHEN 1
            COMPUTE RESULT = NUM1 + NUM2
            MOVE "Addition Operation Executed" TO MESSAGE
        WHEN 2
            COMPUTE RESULT = NUM1 - NUM2
            MOVE "Subtraction Operation Executed" TO MESSAGE
        WHEN 3
            COMPUTE RESULT = NUM1 * NUM2
            MOVE "Multiplication Operation Executed" TO MESSAGE
        WHEN 4
            IF NUM2 NOT = 0
                COMPUTE RESULT = NUM1 / NUM2
                MOVE "Division Operation Executed" TO MESSAGE
            ELSE
                MOVE "Error: Division by Zero" TO MESSAGE
            END-IF
        WHEN OTHER
            MOVE "Invalid Option Selected" TO MESSAGE
    END-EVALUATE.

    * Additional evaluation to demonstrate multi-branch logic on the
    ↪  computed result.
    * This second mapping further classifies RESULT based on its
    ↪  sign.
    EVALUATE TRUE
```

99

```
        WHEN RESULT < 0
            MOVE "Computed result is negative." TO MESSAGE
        WHEN RESULT = 0
            MOVE "Computed result is zero." TO MESSAGE
        WHEN RESULT > 0
            MOVE "Computed result is positive." TO MESSAGE
END-EVALUATE.

* Display the final computed result and associated evaluation
↪ message.
DISPLAY "Final Computed Result: " RESULT.
DISPLAY "Evaluation: " MESSAGE.

STOP RUN.
```

Chapter 23

Looping with PERFORM

Foundational Concepts in Iterative Control Flow

Iterative execution serves as a cornerstone in the design of computational processes, and the PERFORM statement emerges as a prominent mechanism to encapsulate repetitive operations within a singular construct. The construct can be formally interpreted as an application of a state transformation function $f: S \to S$, where each iteration effects a transition from one state to a subsequent state within a finite set S. This perspective underscores the determinism and inherent structure of the looping mechanism, as the operation of f is iteratively applied until a prescribed termination condition is satisfied. The abstraction provided by the PERFORM statement embodies a high-level approach to loop control, effectively isolating the iterative block from lower-level control variables and manual state management.

Syntactic Structure and Execution Semantics

The syntactic formulation of the PERFORM statement is characterized by a disciplined arrangement that clearly demarcates the boundaries of the iterative block from its control directives. The statement is constructed to include explicit specification of the repetition parameters, which may be fixed or contingent upon a condition evaluated at runtime. Formal analysis reveals that each iteration represents an execution of a well-defined sequence of operations, followed by a re-evaluation of the iteration's continuation criterion. This behavior is analogous to the repeated application of an iterative function, wherein the operation f is systematically applied to an initial state in order to generate a sequence of successive states. The clear syntactic separation between the loop control mechanism and the operational block permits a rigorous mapping from the written code to its corresponding execution semantics, ensuring that the process remains both predictable and amenable to formal verification.

Comparative Analysis with Conventional Iterative Constructs

When contrasted with iterative constructs found in other programming languages, the PERFORM statement distinguishes itself through its emphasis on declarative iteration. Traditional loop constructs, which often require explicit handling of loop indices or counters, compel the programmer to manage complex state modifications manually. In contrast, the PERFORM statement abstracts such details by encapsulating the repetitive behavior into a single, coherent block of operations. This abstraction not only simplifies the expression of iterative processes but also renders the underlying computation amenable to analysis via formal methods. The dual capability of supporting both fixed-count iteration and conditionally governed repetition further enhances its utility, as it can be seamlessly adapted to a wide range of computational patterns. The juxtaposition of the PERFORM statement against its counterparts illustrates its robustness and flexibility in handling repetitive tasks within the rigid framework of procedural programming.

Cobol Code Snippet

```
IDENTIFICATION DIVISION.
PROGRAM-ID. LOOPDEMO.
AUTHOR. Maxwell_Vector.

ENVIRONMENT DIVISION.
```

```
* The configuration and system-specific settings may be added
↳ here.

DATA DIVISION.
WORKING-STORAGE SECTION.
* Define a number for which we will compute factorial and
↳ summation.
77  WS-NUMBER        PIC 9(04)    VALUE 6.

* Variables for computing factorial.
77  WS-FACTORIAL     PIC 9(18)    VALUE 1.
77  WS-COUNTER       PIC 9(04)    VALUE 1.

* Variable for computing summation.
77  WS-SUM           PIC 9(18)    VALUE 0.

PROCEDURE DIVISION.
MAIN-PROCESS.

    *----------------------------------------------------
    * Display introductory messages.
    *----------------------------------------------------
    DISPLAY '----------------------------------------'.
    DISPLAY '   DEMONSTRATING LOOPING WITH PERFORM'.
    DISPLAY '----------------------------------------'.

    *----------------------------------------------------
    * Factorial Calculation:
    * The iterative state transformation is modeled by
    ↳ applying
    * the function f: S -> S defined as:
    *       f(STATE) = STATE * CURRENT-COUNTER
    * where STATE is initially 1 and CURRENT-COUNTER iterates
    ↳ from 1 to WS-NUMBER.
    *----------------------------------------------------
    DISPLAY 'Calculating Factorial of ' WS-NUMBER ' using
    ↳ iterative transformation:';
    PERFORM VARYING WS-COUNTER FROM 1 BY 1 UNTIL WS-COUNTER >
    ↳ WS-NUMBER
        COMPUTE WS-FACTORIAL = WS-FACTORIAL * WS-COUNTER
        DISPLAY 'Iteration ' WS-COUNTER ': Factorial = '
        ↳ WS-FACTORIAL
    END-PERFORM.
    DISPLAY 'Final Factorial of ' WS-NUMBER ' is '
    ↳ WS-FACTORIAL.

    *----------------------------------------------------
    * Summation Calculation:
    * This loop demonstrates a conditionally governed
    ↳ repetition.
    * We sum the integers from 1 to WS-NUMBER as an alternate
    ↳ example of
    * iterative processing using the PERFORM UNTIL construct.
```

```
*----------------------------------------------------
DISPLAY '----------------------------------------'.
DISPLAY 'Calculating Sum from 1 to ' WS-NUMBER.
MOVE 1 TO WS-COUNTER.
PERFORM UNTIL WS-COUNTER > WS-NUMBER
    ADD WS-COUNTER TO WS-SUM
    DISPLAY 'Iteration ' WS-COUNTER ': Sum = ' WS-SUM
    ADD 1 TO WS-COUNTER
END-PERFORM.
DISPLAY 'Final Sum = ' WS-SUM.


*----------------------------------------------------
* End of Program.
*----------------------------------------------------
STOP RUN.
```

Chapter 24

Inline vs. Out-of-line PERFORM

Inline PERFORM: Syntactic Characteristics and Immediate Execution

The inline embodiment of the PERFORM construct integrates the iterative block directly within the immediate procedural context. This approach defines a sequence of operations that is executed in situ, without reference to an external label or separate code section. Conceptually, the iterative mechanism may be represented as the successive application of a transformation function $f: S \to S$, where each invocation of f modifies the state S in a deterministic fashion. The syntactic structure of the inline PERFORM guarantees that the series of instructions is contiguous to the invoking statement, thereby enforcing a strict ordering of operations that maintains a tight coupling with its surrounding context. Such proximity facilitates straightforward evaluation of the loop's invariant properties, as well as simplified management of local variable scopes and control flow parameters.

Out-of-line PERFORM: Modular Encapsulation and Deferred Execution

In contrast to the inline implementation, the out-of-line PERFORM construct segregates the iterative block from its point of invocation by assigning it a distinct identifier in the form of a paragraph or section. This modular encapsulation allows the iterative sequence to be defined externally and then referenced through a PERFORM statement, effectively decoupling the control directive from the operational content. The out-of-line approach supports a design paradigm wherein the iterative process is treated as an autonomous unit, thereby enabling independent verification, reusability, and isolated analysis of the loop's operational semantics. The mechanism adheres to the notion of deferred execution: the control flow transfers to a labeled block where the series of operations is executed, and upon completion, the program resumes its primary sequence of instructions. This structural separation enhances the clarity of code segmentation and supports comprehensive formal analysis of the loop's behavior.

Comparative Analysis: Semantic Implications and Structural Considerations

A meticulous juxtaposition of the inline and out-of-line PERFORM constructs reveals inherent differences in both syntactic presentation and semantic interpretation. In the inline formulation, the iterative block is embedded within the direct flow of control, which minimizes abstraction and facilitates immediate state transitions as embodied by the function f applied repeatedly to an initial state S. This integration offers advantages in terms of reduced overhead and enhanced visibility of local computational context. Conversely, the out-of-line formulation introduces an additional layer of abstraction by isolating the iterative code into a separately defined block. This decoupling promotes a modular architecture that aids in isolating loop invariants and optimizing code reuse. From a semantic standpoint, both methods ultimately effectuate an iterative state transformation; however, the inline method emphasizes uninterrupted sequential execution, while the out-of-line method affords a delineated structure that is amenable to independent static analysis and potential reuse across disparate segments of the procedural logic.

Cobol Code Snippet

```
IDENTIFICATION DIVISION.
PROGRAM-ID. PERFORM-DEMO.

ENVIRONMENT DIVISION.
CONFIGURATION SECTION.
SOURCE-COMPUTER. IBM-370.
OBJECT-COMPUTER. IBM-370.

DATA DIVISION.
WORKING-STORAGE SECTION.
* STATE represents the program state S.
01  STATE           PIC 9(4)      VALUE 1.
01  I               PIC 9(4)      VALUE 1.
01  MAX-ITERATIONS  PIC 9(4)      VALUE 5.
01  BLANK-LINE      PIC X(1)      VALUE " ".

PROCEDURE DIVISION.
MAIN-PROCEDURE.
    DISPLAY "***** Inline PERFORM Transformation *****".
    DISPLAY "Initial STATE: " STATE.

    * Inline PERFORM:
    * Directly executing an iterative block that applies the
    ↪   function f: S -> S,
    * here defined as f(S)=S * 2.
    PERFORM VARYING I FROM 1 BY 1 UNTIL I > MAX-ITERATIONS
        DISPLAY "Iteration " I " - STATE before
        ↪   transformation: " STATE.
        COMPUTE STATE = STATE * 2
        DISPLAY "Iteration " I " - STATE after
        ↪   transformation: " STATE.
    END-PERFORM.

    DISPLAY "Final STATE after Inline PERFORM: " STATE.
    DISPLAY BLANK-LINE.

    * Reset state and counter for out-of-line demonstration.
    MOVE 100 TO STATE.
    MOVE 1 TO I.
    DISPLAY "***** Out-of-line PERFORM Transformation *****".
    DISPLAY "Initial STATE: " STATE.

    * Out-of-line PERFORM:
    * The iterative transformation f(S)=S - 10 is
    ↪   encapsulated in the
    * TRANSFORM-STATE paragraph, thereby decoupling the logic
    ↪   from the main flow.
    PERFORM TRANSFORM-STATE THRU TRANSFORM-STATE-EXIT.

    DISPLAY "Final STATE after Out-of-line PERFORM: " STATE.
```

```
        STOP RUN.

TRANSFORM-STATE.
    DISPLAY ">> Entering TRANSFORM-STATE Paragraph, starting
    ↪  STATE: " STATE.
    PERFORM VARYING I FROM 1 BY 1 UNTIL I > MAX-ITERATIONS
        DISPLAY "Iteration " I " - STATE before
        ↪  transformation: " STATE.
        COMPUTE STATE = STATE - 10
        DISPLAY "Iteration " I " - STATE after
        ↪  transformation: " STATE.
    END-PERFORM.
    EXIT.

TRANSFORM-STATE-EXIT.
    EXIT.
```

Chapter 25

Basic String Handling in COBOL

Representation of String Data in COBOL

Textual data in COBOL is characterized by its static declaration and fixed-length representation, as typically defined in the DATA DIVISION. The underlying mechanism employs alphanumeric specifications using a PICTURE clause such as $PIC\ X(n)$, where the parameter n denotes the number of character positions allocated. Such declarations establish the physical storage format and impact both the input and output treatment of the string data. The inherent fixed-length nature of these fields necessitates an awareness of trailing spaces and the padding that may occur when textual values occupy fewer positions than allocated. Furthermore, the static allocation of string variables permits the anticipation of storage requirements and facilitates deterministic memory layouts, which are essential for both performance optimization and precise data formatting.

1 Alphanumeric Data Declaration

In COBOL, the declaration of alphanumeric string variables is achieved through explicit specification within the PICTURE clause. The use of the format $PIC\ X(n)$ results in a literal assignment of n character spaces, ensuring that every string conforms to the pre-established data width. The alphanumeric type thereby distinguishes itself from purely numeric types, given that it is intended to capture a sequence of characters rather than a numerical quantity. This designation promotes rigorous control over the way textual data is stored and manipulated, underpinning operations that involve fixed-width formatting and predetermined memory allocation.

2 Fixed Length Versus Logical String Length

The disparity between the allocated fixed length and the effective, or logical, string length introduces considerations intrinsic to COBOL string handling. While variables are instantiated with a specific number of character positions, the meaningful content may be shorter, with trailing spaces serving as implicit delimiters. This distinction influences manipulation techniques, particularly during operations that involve comparison, concatenation, or substring extraction. The management of blank characters and the enforcement of strict field boundaries exemplify the deterministic behavior imposed by COBOL's data definitions, and facilitate precise control over textual data processing.

Intrinsic Mechanisms for String Manipulation

COBOL encompasses a repertoire of built-in mechanisms that support the manipulation of string data within the constraints of its static data definitions. The language provides intrinsic operations that embody classic string processing paradigms, including the concatenation of discrete literals into a singular, contiguous sequence, as well as the extraction and partitioning of segments from a larger string. These operations adhere to the fixed-width nature of the underlying fields, thereby ensuring predictable behavior when textual data is restructured or recombined.

1 Concatenation and Substring Extraction

The concatenation process in COBOL involves the assembly of multiple alphanumeric literals into a singular composite string, a procedure that must account for the possibility of interstitial blank characters and the invariance of field lengths. Substring extraction is similarly governed by the predetermined positions within a string; an extraction operation is sensitive to the starting index and the length of the segment to be isolated. In both cases, the operations are mathematically analogous to function compositions defined on ordered sets, wherein the transformation function $f : S \rightarrow S$ operates on the original string S to yield a new string that occupies a subspace of the original domain. Such operations are executed with strict adherence to the boundaries imposed by the PICTURE clause, ensuring that the resultant string remains well-defined within the fixed-length format.

2 Inspection and Modification Operations

Manipulation of textual data in COBOL also encompasses mechanisms designed to examine and modify the contents of a string without altering its overall structure. Inspection operations allow for the systematic traversal of a string, enabling the quantification and identification of specific character patterns or substrings. Modifications, when applied, are constrained by the field's fixed-length specification, thereby necessitating careful consideration of position and length. The symbolic representation of these operations may be formalized through mappings that associate each position within the string with its corresponding character element. In the context of alterations, the transformation function $g : S \rightarrow S$ may be applied selectively to designated segments, yielding a new string that reflects the intended amendment while preserving the overall format.

Implications for Data Structure Design

The rigid structure imposed by COBOL's static memory allocation for textual data engenders a set of design constraints that are critical to the construction of reliable data processing routines. The interaction between the defined field length and operations performed on string data demands meticulous planning, as the misalignment between physical storage and logical content can precipitate errors during the manipulation of textual information. Consequently, the design of data structures in COBOL frequently incorporates extensive considerations of field boundaries, padding behavior, and the consistency of alphanumeric formatting. This deterministic approach not only ensures uniformity in data handling but also facilitates subsequent formal analysis of program behavior through clearly defined operational semantics. The explicit mapping of each character position within a string to its corresponding memory location underscores the precision inherent in COBOL's treatment of textual data and informs the broader architectural strategy for robust data manipulation.

Cobol Code Snippet

```
IDENTIFICATION DIVISION.
PROGRAM-ID. STRING-EXAMPLE.

DATA DIVISION.
WORKING-STORAGE SECTION.
01 WS-FIRST-STR      PIC X(20) VALUE 'HELLO, COBOL        '.
01 WS-SECOND-STR     PIC X(20) VALUE 'STRING HANDLING     '.
01 WS-COMPOSITE-STR  PIC X(40).
01 WS-SUBSTR         PIC X(10).
01 WS-TEMP-STR       PIC X(40).
01 WS-COUNT          PIC 9(02) VALUE 0.
01 WS-INDEX          PIC 9(02) VALUE 1.
01 WS-LENGTH         PIC 9(02) VALUE 0.

PROCEDURE DIVISION.
    *----------------------------------------------------
    * Concatenation:
    * Combine two fixed-length alphanumeric strings into one
    ↪   composite string.
    *----------------------------------------------------
    STRING WS-FIRST-STR DELIMITED BY SIZE
           WS-SECOND-STR DELIMITED BY SIZE
           INTO WS-COMPOSITE-STR.
    DISPLAY 'Composite String: ' WS-COMPOSITE-STR.


    *----------------------------------------------------
    * Substring Extraction:
    * Extract a substring from position 6 with a length of 10
    ↪   characters.
    * This implements the f: S -> S transformation for
    ↪   substring extraction.
    *----------------------------------------------------
    MOVE WS-COMPOSITE-STR(6:10) TO WS-SUBSTR.
    DISPLAY 'Extracted Substring (positions 6 to 15): '
    ↪   WS-SUBSTR.


    *----------------------------------------------------
    * Inspection:
    * Count the occurrence of the character 'O' in the
    ↪   composite string.
    * This demonstrates an inspection operation to analyze
    ↪   string content.
```

112

```
*------------------------------------------------------
MOVE 0 TO WS-COUNT.
INSPECT WS-COMPOSITE-STR TALLYING WS-COUNT FOR ALL '0'.
DISPLAY 'Number of 0''s in Composite String: ' WS-COUNT.

*------------------------------------------------------
* Modification:
* Replace all blank spaces with hyphens to modify the
↪   string display.
* This represents a g: S -> S transformation for
↪   selective alteration.
*------------------------------------------------------
MOVE WS-COMPOSITE-STR TO WS-TEMP-STR.
INSPECT WS-TEMP-STR REPLACING ALL ' ' BY '-'.
DISPLAY 'Modified String with Hyphens: ' WS-TEMP-STR.

*------------------------------------------------------
* Algorithm: Logical Length Calculation
* Determine the effective (logical) length of the
↪   composite string by
* counting the number of non-space characters.
*------------------------------------------------------
MOVE 0 TO WS-LENGTH.
PERFORM VARYING WS-INDEX FROM 1 BY 1 UNTIL WS-INDEX > 40
    IF WS-COMPOSITE-STR(WS-INDEX:1) NOT = ' '
        ADD 1 TO WS-LENGTH
    END-IF
END-PERFORM.
DISPLAY 'Logical Length (non-space characters): '
↪   WS-LENGTH.

STOP RUN.
```

Chapter 26

Concatenating Strings with STRING

Conceptual Foundations

The operation of concatenating strings within COBOL is achieved through the STRING statement, an imperative construct that encapsulates the fundamental principles of static data manipulation. At its core, the statement models a transformation of a finite sequence of fixed-length alphanumeric strings into a single aggregate string. This process may be formalized by a function $f : S^n \to S$, where each $s_i \in S$ represents an individual source string and the resulting concatenation $f(s_1, s_2, \ldots, s_n)$ is a composite that preserves the ordering and boundary constraints inherent to the source data. The design of the STRING statement reflects rigorous adherence to predetermined memory layouts, ensuring that the amalgamation of discrete strings does not compromise the fixed-width structure defined in the DATA DIVISION of a COBOL program. The consolidation of multiple tokens into one contiguous field exemplifies the deterministic operational paradigm that COBOL enforces for data integrity and predictable formatting.

Syntactic Structure and Delimiting Mechanisms

The syntax of the STRING statement is defined by a well-structured pattern, which begins with the introductory keyword and is succeeded by a series of source strings. Each source element is immediately followed by a delimiter clause—typically expressed as DELIMITED BY—that determines the precise endpoint of that string's effective content. This clause is critical, as it prevents the inadvertent inclusion of extraneous trailing spaces that may extend beyond the intended logical content. The terminal portion of the syntax is marked by the INTO clause, which designates the target variable that will contain the resultant concatenated string. The explicit requirement for delimiter specification serves not only to enforce structural constraints but also to optimize memory usage by ensuring that only the substantively meaningful portions of each source string are concatenated. In this manner, the STRING statement integrates both syntactic strictness and semantic clarity, enabling programmers to construct composite strings with precision and reliability.

Operational Semantics and Practical Application Considerations

The operational semantics of the STRING statement are governed by the deterministic behavior of fixed-length data structures. Upon execution, each source string is evaluated in sequence, with its effective portion determined by the corresponding delimiter clause. The process assimilates these substrings into the target memory area while strictly adhering to the boundaries defined by the fixed size of the destination field. In practical applications, the concatenation mechanism is indispensable for tasks that require the assembly of compound data elements, such as the formation of formatted record fields or the orchestration of complex data transmission procedures. The sequential nature of the operation ensures that the order of source strings is preserved and that any allocated but unused field space is either left intact or managed in accordance with predetermined truncation policies. This deterministic approach is essential for subsequent data validation and analysis within the broader context of automated processing routines. The interplay between syntactic rigour and semantic precision embodied by the STRING statement exemplifies COBOL's overarching strategy for managing structured textual data within a statically defined memory architecture.

Cobol Code Snippet

```
IDENTIFICATION DIVISION.
PROGRAM-ID. STRINGCONCAT.
AUTHOR. Maxwell_Vector.

ENVIRONMENT DIVISION.
CONFIGURATION SECTION.
SOURCE-COMPUTER. IBM-370.
OBJECT-COMPUTER. IBM-370.

DATA DIVISION.
WORKING-STORAGE SECTION.
*----------------------------------------------------
* This section defines four fixed-length alphanumeric
↪   strings.
* The underlying idea is the functional transformation:
*    f(s1, s2, s3, s4) = concatenated-string
* where each input string is concatenated preserving its
↪   order.
* The delimiter clause ensures that only the effective
↪   portion
* (up to the specified delimiter) is concatenated.
*----------------------------------------------------
01  WS-STRING-1    PIC X(15) VALUE "Hello, ".
01  WS-STRING-2    PIC X(15) VALUE "World".
01  WS-STRING-3    PIC X(15) VALUE "! Today is ".
01  WS-STRING-4    PIC X(15) VALUE "COBOL.".

* Destination field must be wide enough to hold the composite
↪   string.
01  WS-DEST-STRING PIC X(60) VALUE SPACES.

PROCEDURE DIVISION.
MAIN-PROGRAM.
    DISPLAY "Concatenation of Strings using STRING
    ↪   Statement".
    DISPLAY "Input Strings:".
    DISPLAY "  1: " WS-STRING-1.
    DISPLAY "  2: " WS-STRING-2.
    DISPLAY "  3: " WS-STRING-3.
    DISPLAY "  4: " WS-STRING-4.


    *----------------------------------------------------
```

```
* The following STRING statement performs the
↪ concatenation:
* It takes each source string, determines the effective
↪ portion
* using the specified delimiter (SPACE), and appends them
↪ sequentially.
* This operation implements the function f: S^n -> S.
*--------------------------------------------------
STRING WS-STRING-1 DELIMITED BY SPACE
       WS-STRING-2 DELIMITED BY SPACE
       WS-STRING-3 DELIMITED BY SPACE
       WS-STRING-4 DELIMITED BY SPACE
       INTO WS-DEST-STRING
END-STRING.

DISPLAY "Concatenated Result:" WS-DEST-STRING.
STOP RUN.
```

Chapter 27

Splitting Strings with UNSTRING

Conceptual Foundations

The function executed by the UNSTRING statement is central to the systematic decomposition of a contiguous character sequence into discrete substrings. The operation may be mathematically represented as a transformation

$$g : S \times D \to S_1 \times S_2 \times \cdots \times S_n,$$

where S denotes the original composite string, D represents the set of delimiter tokens, and each S_i corresponds to a resultant substring generated during the parsing process. This transformation is performed in a deterministic manner, ensuring that the sequential order of the substrings is strictly preserved, thereby maintaining fidelity with the original data structure. The UNSTRING operation is expressly designed to facilitate the extraction of meaningful subcomponents from a unified data stream by utilizing well-defined delimiter criteria, a process that upholds the integrity of fixed-length data constructs and aligns with the rigorous design principles in static data architectures.

Syntactic Characteristics

The syntactic structure of the UNSTRING statement adheres to the formal grammar of the COBOL language, exhibiting a clear and methodical pattern. The construction is initiated with the keyword UNSTRING followed by the specification of the source string. This is immediately succeeded by one or more delimiter clauses, conventionally expressed as

DELIMITED BY $\langle delimiter \rangle$,

which precisely define the termination point of each component extracted from the source. The statement concludes with an INTO clause, designating the target fields that will sequentially receive the extracted substrings. This syntactic configuration enforces strict adherence to the boundaries of the input sequence, ensuring that only the characters preceding a delimiter—and those lying between successive delimiters—are captured. Such a structure minimizes ambiguity and guarantees that the parsing operation remains consistent with the fixed-width constraints and predetermined layouts characteristic of COBOL's DATA DIVISION.

Operational Semantics

The execution of the UNSTRING statement is underpinned by a sequential scanning process that operates in a left-to-right manner over the source string. At each step, the algorithm evaluates the current segment of the string, accumulating characters until a token matching one of the specified delimiters is encountered. At that juncture, the accumulated substring is committed to its designated target field, and the scanning process recommences immediately after the delimiter. This systematic approach may be characterized by a finite state machine model, wherein state transitions are triggered by the detection of delimiter characters. Of particular note is the handling of any residual segment that does not conclude with a delimiter; such segments are either assigned to an additional, predefined target or are processed in accordance with established truncation policies. The clear, deterministic nature of this operation is crucial for the accurate parsing of static textual data, thereby ensuring that the segmentation process is both precise and invariant under the constraints imposed by the memory architecture.

Cobol Code Snippet

```
IDENTIFICATION DIVISION.
PROGRAM-ID. UNSTRING-DEMO.

ENVIRONMENT DIVISION.
CONFIGURATION SECTION.
    SOURCE-COMPUTER. IBM-370.
    OBJECT-COMPUTER. IBM-370.

DATA DIVISION.
WORKING-STORAGE SECTION.
*-- Define the original composite string.
01  WS-SOURCE-STRING     PIC X(50)
        VALUE 'COBOL-UNSTRING-DEMO-EXAMPLE-PARSING'.

*-- Define the delimiter token used for splitting.
01  WS-DELIMITER         PIC X VALUE '-'.

*-- Pointer to track the current scanning position.
01  WS-POINTER           PIC S9(4) COMP VALUE ZERO.

*-- Target fields to hold each substring extracted.
01  WS-TOKEN-1           PIC X(15) VALUE SPACES.
01  WS-TOKEN-2           PIC X(15) VALUE SPACES.
01  WS-TOKEN-3           PIC X(15) VALUE SPACES.
01  WS-TOKEN-4           PIC X(15) VALUE SPACES.
01  WS-TOKEN-5           PIC X(15) VALUE SPACES.
01  WS-TOKEN-6           PIC X(15) VALUE SPACES.

PROCEDURE DIVISION.
MAIN-LOGIC.
    * Display the original composite string.
    DISPLAY 'Original String: ' WS-SOURCE-STRING.

    * The UNSTRING statement below embodies the algorithm:
    * It transforms the original string into its component
    ↪   substrings.
    * The operation scans WS-SOURCE-STRING from
    ↪   left-to-right,
    * accumulating characters until the delimiter token
    ↪   (WS-DELIMITER)
    * is encountered. Each resulting segment is stored in the
    ↪   corresponding
    * target field (WS-TOKEN-n). The WITH POINTER clause
    ↪   captures the final
    * reading position, facilitating any further processing
    ↪   if required.
    UNSTRING WS-SOURCE-STRING
        DELIMITED BY WS-DELIMITER
        INTO WS-TOKEN-1
            WS-TOKEN-2
```

```cobol
            WS-TOKEN-3
            WS-TOKEN-4
            WS-TOKEN-5
            WS-TOKEN-6
    WITH POINTER WS-POINTER.

* Display each extracted token.
DISPLAY 'Token 1: ' WS-TOKEN-1.
DISPLAY 'Token 2: ' WS-TOKEN-2.
DISPLAY 'Token 3: ' WS-TOKEN-3.
DISPLAY 'Token 4: ' WS-TOKEN-4.
DISPLAY 'Token 5: ' WS-TOKEN-5.
DISPLAY 'Token 6: ' WS-TOKEN-6.

* Terminate program execution.
STOP RUN.
```

Chapter 28

Using INSPECT for String Analysis

Conceptual Foundations

The INSPECT statement occupies a central role in the analysis and transformation of character strings within the COBOL language. This construct enables the examination of a fixed-length string by systematically scanning its contents and identifying specific sub-patterns based on predetermined criteria. In its essence, the INSPECT operation affords a dual modality: it permits both the counting of occurrences of a particular character or substring and the replacement of such characters with alternative values. The underlying concept is rooted in the notion of pattern matching, whereby the string is conceived as an ordered sequence of symbols $S = s_1 s_2 \cdots s_n$. Through the application of the INSPECT statement, the operation delineates a function $f : S \to S'$ such that the original sequence is maintained in structure, yet selective sections are either quantitatively assessed or altered. This methodical approach ensures that any modifications or tallying actions are executed in a deterministic manner, preserving the inherent order of the string while enabling precise analytical operations.

Syntactic Characteristics

The formal syntax of the INSPECT statement is rigorously defined, reflecting the precise nature of COBOL's language standards. The statement is initiated by the keyword INSPECT, immediately followed by the specification of the source string expression. Subsequent clauses define the operational context; for instance, a TALLYING phrase may be used to continuously accumulate a count in a designated numeric field, or a REPLACING clause may specify the substitution of identified characters. Each clause adheres to a structured pattern, for example, the syntax for counting is often expressed as

INSPECT ⟨string⟩ TALLYING ⟨counter⟩ FOR ⟨character-set⟩,

which is then extended appropriately to accommodate additional characters or substrings. Similarly, for replacement operations, the syntax dictates a clear correspondence between the source and the target substrings. The language's formal grammar requires that these operations respect the boundaries of the original string, ensuring that any replacement does not violate the fixed-length constraints intrinsic to COBOL's DATA DIVISION. The resultant syntactic structure is both unambiguous and amenable to static analysis, providing a transparent framework for string manipulation.

Operational Semantics

The execution model of the INSPECT statement is characterized by a sequential left-to-right traversal of the source string. During this sweep, each character is evaluated against a set of predetermined conditions as specified by the INSPECT clauses. When operating in a counting mode, the statement increments an associated accumulator each time a character matching the given criteria is encountered. This accumulation process can be described by the function

$$k = \sum_{i=1}^{n} \delta(s_i, c),$$

where $\delta(s_i, c) = 1$ if s_i corresponds to the targeted character c, and $\delta(s_i, c) = 0$ otherwise. In the replacement mode, the operation simultaneously scans the string while effecting character substitution in a non-overlapping manner. Upon encountering a segment that satisfies the match condition, the original symbol is overwritten by the specified replacement character or sequence. The deterministic nature of the state transitions during this operation ensures that once a sequence is modified, it is not subjected to further changes during the same pass. The complete transformation of the string can be encapsulated by the mapping

$$g : S \rightarrow S',$$

where the output string S' reflects the precise modifications imposed by the INSPECT operation. Through these well-defined processes, the INSPECT statement provides a robust mechanism for both analytical and transformative string processing within the COBOL programming paradigm.

Cobol Code Snippet

```
IDENTIFICATION DIVISION.
PROGRAM-ID. INSPECT-DEMO.
AUTHOR. Maxwell_Vector.

ENVIRONMENT DIVISION.
CONFIGURATION SECTION.
SOURCE-COMPUTER. IBM-370.
OBJECT-COMPUTER. IBM-370.

DATA DIVISION.
WORKING-STORAGE SECTION.
    * Define a fixed-length string to demonstrate INSPECT
    ↪ operations.
01 WS-ORIGINAL-STRING  PIC X(19) VALUE "ABACADAEBAADFAECAAC".
01 WS-CNT            PIC 9(03)    VALUE 0.
01 WS-MODIFIED-STRING PIC X(19) VALUE SPACES.

PROCEDURE DIVISION.
MAIN-PARA.
    * Copy the original string to a modifiable working storage
    ↪ variable.
    MOVE WS-ORIGINAL-STRING TO WS-MODIFIED-STRING.

    * Count the occurrences of the character 'A' in the original
    ↪ string.
    * This implements the algorithm: k = [(s_i, "A")],
    * where (s_i, "A") = 1 if the character s_i equals "A",
    ↪ otherwise 0.
    INSPECT WS-ORIGINAL-STRING TALLYING WS-CNT FOR ALL "A".

    * Replace all occurrences of the character 'B' with 'Y'
    * in the string, demonstrating a non-overlapping, deterministic
    ↪ transformation.
    INSPECT WS-MODIFIED-STRING REPLACING ALL "B" BY "Y".
```

```
* Display the results including the original string, count of
↪  A's, and modified string.
DISPLAY "Original String: " WS-ORIGINAL-STRING.
DISPLAY "Count of A's   : " WS-CNT.
DISPLAY "Modified String: " WS-MODIFIED-STRING.

STOP RUN.
```

Chapter 29

User Input with ACCEPT

Conceptual Foundations

Within the COBOL programming paradigm, the ACCEPT statement occupies a central role as the formal mechanism for integrating external data into a program's internal state. This operation is designed to capture input from a variety of sources, including interactive user devices and other external interfaces, and to assign such data to pre-declared variables with predetermined structural formats. The process is governed by the constraint that the receiving variable is defined according to a PIC clause, thereby ensuring that the incoming data conforms to fixed-length or specific data-type requirements. This deterministic process guarantees that any data received from the external environment is seamlessly assimilated into the program without violating the rigid structural constraints imposed by the language standard.

Syntactic Construction and Characteristics

The syntactic formulation of the ACCEPT statement is both concise and unambiguous, adhering strictly to the formal grammar rules of COBOL. The construction commences with the keyword ACCEPT, immediately followed by the identifier of the target variable. In abstract terms, if the external input is denoted by I and the target variable by V, the operation enacts the mapping

$$V \leftarrow I,$$

where the content of the input source is directly transferred to the storage location corresponding to V. This direct assignment is subject to the inherent structural constraints of V, ensuring that only data conforming to the associated PIC definition is accepted. The simplicity of the syntax belies the underlying complexity of input validation and format preservation, both of which are embedded within the strict parsing and semantic analysis enforced by the compiler.

Semantic Execution and Operational Behavior

During program execution, the ACCEPT statement initiates a well-defined sequence of operations that govern the acquisition of external data. Initially, an input buffer, denoted by B, is allocated to temporarily hold the incoming data. The runtime environment then performs a state transformation represented by the function

$$\Phi : B \to V,$$

where the function Φ encapsulates the processing steps that validate the input against the data type and formatting requirements of V. The content of B is examined in its entirety, ensuring that the data adheres to the conventions stipulated by the PIC clause. This execution model is characterized by a single-pass evaluation mechanism, wherein the input is processed sequentially without recursive reexamination. Such a linear, deterministic evaluation strategy ensures that once data is transferred from B to V, it is integrated into the program's operational context in its original, intended format. The robustness of this mechanism is critical to maintaining both data integrity and the overall stability of the execution environment when interfacing with a variety of external input sources.

Cobol Code Snippet

```
IDENTIFICATION DIVISION.
PROGRAM-ID. ACCEPT-DEMO.

ENVIRONMENT DIVISION.
CONFIGURATION SECTION.
SOURCE-COMPUTER. IBM-370.
OBJECT-COMPUTER. IBM-370.

DATA DIVISION.
WORKING-STORAGE SECTION.
* Define variables to hold user input and computed results.
01 WS-INPUT-NUMBER    PIC 9(05)    VALUE ZEROS.
01 WS-INPUT-TEXT      PIC X(20)    VALUE SPACES.
01 WS-CALC-VALUE      PIC 9(06)    VALUE ZEROS.
01 WS-RESULT          PIC X(50)    VALUE SPACES.

PROCEDURE DIVISION.
MAIN-PROGRAM.
    DISPLAY 'Enter a 5-digit number:'.
    * The ACCEPT statement below performs the operation:
    *   V <- I
    * where WS-INPUT-NUMBER represents V and the incoming data
    ↪ is I.
    ACCEPT WS-INPUT-NUMBER.

    DISPLAY 'Enter a text string (max 20 characters):'.
    ACCEPT WS-INPUT-TEXT.


    ↪  *------------------------------------------------------------
    * The following COMPUTE statement illustrates a simple
    * arithmetic operation representing the essential
    ↪  transformation
    * of the accepted numeric input. Here we add 100 to the
    ↪  input,
    * mimicking a processing function : B → V (B as input
    ↪  buffer).


    ↪  *------------------------------------------------------------
    COMPUTE WS-CALC-VALUE = WS-INPUT-NUMBER + 100.


    ↪  *------------------------------------------------------------
    * Using the STRING statement, we concatenate literals and
    ↪  variable
    * contents to form a comprehensive output that shows both
    ↪  the raw
    * input and the computed result.

    ↪  *------------------------------------------------------------
```

```
       STRING 'Input Number: ' DELIMITED BY SIZE
              WS-INPUT-NUMBER  DELIMITED BY SIZE
              '  |  Computed Value (Input + 100): ' DELIMITED BY
              ↪  SIZE
              WS-CALC-VALUE    DELIMITED BY SIZE
              INTO WS-RESULT.
       DISPLAY WS-RESULT.

       DISPLAY 'Text Entered: ' WS-INPUT-TEXT.

       STOP RUN.
```
_____

Chapter 30

Output with DISPLAY

Conceptual Foundations

The DISPLAY statement functions as the primary conduit for transferring textual data and variable values from the program's internal state to an external output interface, such as a console or screen. It encapsulates the transformation of structured in-memory representations into a sequential stream of characters that are immediately perceivable by an external observer. The intrinsic purpose of the statement is to render both literal strings and computed variable contents in a human-readable form while preserving the precise formatting dictated by fixed-format rules. The operation can be regarded as a direct mapping, one that transposes the internal state S of designated data items into an ordered output stream, thereby ensuring that the semantic integrity of variable values is maintained during display.

Syntactic Considerations

The formal syntax of the DISPLAY statement adheres to the strict grammatical constructs of the COBOL language. The statement is characterized by its unembellished structure, initiating with the keyword *DISPLAY* followed by a sequence of operands. Each operand may represent either a literal string or an identifier corresponding to a data item defined in the program. These operands are subject to the constraints imposed by their respective PIC clauses, which specify the permissible format and length of the data. The syntax is intentionally terse, yet it is sufficient to disambiguate between data elements and textual constants. This syntactic clarity facilitates a straightforward compilation process that translates the written statement into a set of operations capable of rendering the specified output without misinterpretation or data loss.

Semantic Execution and Data Mapping

At the semantic level, the operation of the DISPLAY statement is governed by a deterministic evaluation that ensures a seamless transition from internal representations to their corresponding external displays. Upon invocation, the runtime system initiates a transformation function, denoted Ψ, which systematically maps each operand O—whether it is a literal or a variable—to its string representation. Specifically, if a variable V holding a numeric or alphanumeric value is encountered, the function Ψ computes a corresponding textual output $\Psi(V)$, preserving fixed-length formatting and inherent data precision. This process entails the integration of multiple operands into a single contiguous output stream that is dispatched to the designated output device. The semantic model underlying the DISPLAY statement guarantees that the transformation is executed in a single, linear pass, thereby precluding the possibility of recursive or iterative reprocessing. Such a mechanism is crucial for ensuring that the portrayal of both static and dynamically computed data remains consistent and unambiguous on the output medium.

Cobol Code Snippet

```
IDENTIFICATION DIVISION.
PROGRAM-ID. DISPLAYDEMO.
AUTHOR. Maxwell_Vector.

ENVIRONMENT DIVISION.
* No file I/O is performed in this demo program

DATA DIVISION.
WORKING-STORAGE SECTION.
* Variables representing internal state and operands for
↪   transformation
01 WS-STATE.
    05 WS-NUM          PIC 9(5)       VALUE 12345.
```

```
       05 WS-ALPHA        PIC X(20)    VALUE "COBOL DEMO OUTPUT".
01 WS-A                PIC 9(5)     VALUE 01000.
01 WS-B                PIC 9(5)     VALUE 00235.
01 WS-SUM              PIC 9(5)     VALUE ZERO.
01 WS-PROD             PIC 9(9)     VALUE ZERO.
01 WS-QUOTIENT         PIC 9(5)V99  VALUE ZERO.
01 WS-NUM-STR          PIC X(6)     VALUE SPACES.
01 WS-DISPLAY-LINE     PIC X(80)    VALUE SPACES.

PROCEDURE DIVISION.
MAIN-PROCESS.
    *-------------------------------------------------------------
    * Demonstrating arithmetic operations transformation
    * The transformation function  maps numeric values to their
    * string representations for external display.
    *-------------------------------------------------------------
    COMPUTE WS-SUM = WS-A + WS-B.
    DISPLAY "Computed Sum (WS-A + WS-B): " WS-SUM.

    COMPUTE WS-PROD = WS-A * WS-B.
    DISPLAY "Computed Product (WS-A * WS-B): " WS-PROD.

    IF WS-B NOT = 0
        COMPUTE WS-QUOTIENT = WS-A / WS-B
    ELSE
        MOVE ZERO TO WS-QUOTIENT
    END-IF.
    DISPLAY "Computed Quotient (WS-A / WS-B): " WS-QUOTIENT.

    *-------------------------------------------------------------
    * Updating internal state and displaying updated numeric value
    *-------------------------------------------------------------
    ADD 1 TO WS-NUM.
    DISPLAY "Updated WS-NUM (internal state incremented): " WS-NUM.

    *-------------------------------------------------------------
    * Displaying alphanumeric data directly
    *-------------------------------------------------------------
    DISPLAY "Alphanumeric Data: " WS-ALPHA.

    *-------------------------------------------------------------
    * Transformation Function  Demonstration:
    * Mapping the numeric internal state into its string equivalent
    * and concatenating with literal text to form a comprehensive
    * output message.
    *-------------------------------------------------------------
    MOVE WS-NUM TO WS-NUM-STR.
    STRING "Mapping WS-NUM: "
           WS-NUM-STR
           " yields output "
           WS-ALPHA
           DELIMITED BY SIZE
           INTO WS-DISPLAY-LINE
```

132

```
END-STRING.
DISPLAY "Transformation Function  output: " WS-DISPLAY-LINE.

STOP RUN.
```
_____

Chapter 31

File-Control Paragraph Details

Conceptual Framework of File-Control Paragraphs

The file-control paragraph within the ENVIRONMENT Division constitutes a declarative mechanism that rigorously specifies the attributes and associations of external file resources. This construct delineates the logical file identifiers from their respective physical representations by establishing an unambiguous mapping between the two. The structural role of the file-control paragraph involves the articulation of file properties—such as organization type, access mode, and disposition rules—in a manner that directly influences the operational behavior of file input/output (I/O) routines. In formal terms, the association can be interpreted as a mapping function $\Theta : I \to P$, where I represents the set of logical identifiers and P signifies the set of physical file specifications. Such a conceptual framework ensures that file assignment during runtime adheres strictly to the predefined configuration, thereby safeguarding data integrity and consistency in file operations.

Syntactic Structure and Declarative Grammar

The syntactic architecture of the file-control paragraph is governed by a context-sensitive grammar that underpins the COBOL language. The clause is composed of a series of tokens and keywords arranged in a fixed format, each of which contributes to a hierarchical representation of file attributes. The declarative nature of this construct mandates that every file identifier is accompanied by a series of subordinate clauses that specify parameters such as file organization—whether sequential, indexed, or relative—as well as access modes and record-locking strategies. This ordered syntactic structure guarantees that the compiler generates a parse tree with clear delineations between the logical intent and the physical file descriptor configurations. Through this formalism, the file-control paragraph operates as an interpretable specification that bridges the semantic gap between source code directives and the system-level file management routines.

File Assignment and Access Mechanisms

Within the domain of file assignment, the file-control paragraph functions as the nexus between abstract file definitions and their corresponding physical entities. Here, logical file identifiers are systematically associated with specific device paths or system-level file names, a process that can be abstracted by a function $\Phi : I \to D$, where D encapsulates device-specific descriptors. This mapping is critical to ensuring that I/O operations, whether they involve sequential reads or keyed access in an indexed organization, are executed against the intended file resources. The mechanism imposes strict constraints on file accessibility by predefining parameters such as read/write permissions and buffering strategies, thereby eliminating ambiguity during the file-opening process. The precision of this assignment mechanism is instrumental in maintaining consistency across diverse system environments and supports a deterministic translation from logical constructs to operational file descriptors.

Operational Semantics and Runtime Integration

At the runtime level, the operational semantics derived from the file-control paragraph are pivotal in orchestrating file access and ensuring system-level compliance with the predefined file schema. The directives contained within the paragraph are translated into internal representations that the runtime system employs to initialize file channels. This translation may be conceptualized as a function Ψ, where $\Psi(F)$ yields a fully instantiated file descriptor that conforms to the system's I/O abstraction. The runtime integration is characterized by the direct invocation of these descriptors during file-opening routines, thereby enabling structured access to external data resources. Furthermore, the operational semantics encapsulate error-handling provisions by mandating early detection of discrepancies between the declared file attributes and the actual state of the file system. In this manner, the file-control paragraph serves as a critical interface between static program declarations and dynamic file-handling mechanisms, ensuring that the transformation from declarative file assignments to concrete operational entities is executed with precision and reliability.

Cobol Code Snippet

```
IDENTIFICATION DIVISION.
PROGRAM-ID. FILECONTROLDEMO.
AUTHOR. Maxwell_Vector.
DATE-WRITTEN. 2024.

ENVIRONMENT DIVISION.
INPUT-OUTPUT SECTION.
FILE-CONTROL.
    SELECT LOGICAL-FILE ASSIGN TO 'DATAFILE.DAT'
        ORGANIZATION IS SEQUENTIAL
        ACCESS MODE IS SEQUENTIAL
        FILE STATUS IS WS-FILSTAT.

DATA DIVISION.
FILE SECTION.
FD  LOGICAL-FILE.
01  LOGICAL-RECORD.
    05  RECORD-DATA     PIC X(80).

WORKING-STORAGE SECTION.
```

```
01  WS-FILSTAT          PIC XX      VALUE SPACES.
01  END-FLAG            PIC X       VALUE 'N'.
    88  END-OF-FILE     VALUE 'Y'.
    88  NOT-END-OF-FILE VALUE 'N'.
01  WS-LOGICAL-ID       PIC X(10)   VALUE 'FILELOGIC'.
01  WS-PHYSICAL-ID      PIC X(20)   VALUE 'DATAFILE.DAT'.
01  WS-DEVICE-DESC      PIC X(20)   VALUE 'DISK STORAGE'.
01  WS-INST-FILEDESC    PIC X(20).

PROCEDURE DIVISION.
MAIN-PROGRAM.
    PERFORM INITIALIZE-MAPPINGS
    PERFORM OPEN-FILES
    PERFORM PROCESS-FILE UNTIL END-FLAG = 'Y'
    PERFORM CLOSE-FILES
    STOP RUN.

INITIALIZE-MAPPINGS.

    ↪   *-------------------------------------------------------------
    * Simulate Mapping Function Theta:  Logical ID ->
    ↪   Physical ID.
    * Here, WS-PHYSICAL-ID is assigned to the instantiated
    ↪   file descriptor.

    ↪   *-------------------------------------------------------------
    MOVE WS-PHYSICAL-ID TO WS-INST-FILEDESC.
    DISPLAY "Mapping Theta: " WS-LOGICAL-ID " -> "
    ↪   WS-INST-FILEDESC.


    ↪   *-------------------------------------------------------------
    * Simulate Mapping Function Phi: Logical ID -> Device
    ↪   Descriptor.
    * This links the logical file identifier to its system
    ↪   storage type.

    ↪   *-------------------------------------------------------------
    DISPLAY "Mapping Phi: " WS-LOGICAL-ID " -> "
    ↪   WS-DEVICE-DESC.


    ↪   *-------------------------------------------------------------
    * Simulate Mapping Function Psi: Instantiation of File
    ↪   Descriptor.
    * This step embodies runtime transformation from
    ↪   declaration to
    * an operational file descriptor used for I/O processing.

    ↪   *-------------------------------------------------------------
    DISPLAY "Mapping Psi: Initialized file descriptor "
    ↪   WS-INST-FILEDESC.
    .
```

```
OPEN-FILES.
    OPEN INPUT LOGICAL-FILE.
    IF WS-FILSTAT NOT = "00"
        DISPLAY "Error opening file, status: " WS-FILSTAT
        STOP RUN
    END-IF.
    DISPLAY "File opened successfully.".
    .

PROCESS-FILE.
    READ LOGICAL-FILE
        AT END
            MOVE 'Y' TO END-FLAG
        NOT AT END
            DISPLAY "Record Read: " RECORD-DATA
            PERFORM PROCESS-RECORD
    END-READ.
    .

PROCESS-RECORD.

    ↪  *------------------------------------------------------------
    * Placeholder for record processing algorithm.
    * This section can include computations, validations, and
    * any transformations applied to each record read.

    ↪  *------------------------------------------------------------
    DISPLAY "Processing Record: " RECORD-DATA.
    .

CLOSE-FILES.
    CLOSE LOGICAL-FILE.
    DISPLAY "File closed successfully.".
    .
```

Chapter 32

Defining File Records in the File Section

Structural Foundations of File Record Definitions

The File Section within the DATA DIVISION is dedicated to the precise specification of the physical record layout as stored in external files. This section establishes a declarative framework that determines both the granular composition and the overall structure of each file record. The design encapsulates every byte of information by assigning explicit field definitions that mirror the on-disk representation. In this context, the record length, alignment, and field order are defined in a manner that ensures consistency between the program's internal abstractions and the external file system. The framework is underpinned by fixed-format and context-sensitive grammatical rules that guide the formal declaration of data structures, resulting in a deterministic mapping between the logical description and its stored manifestation.

Declarative Syntax and Hierarchical Organization

The syntax employed within the File Section adheres to a strict hierarchical organization, where each data item is associated with a level number that establishes parent-child relationships between fields. Such a hierarchy forms a tree structure $T = (V, E)$, in which each node $v \in V$ represents a field or group of fields, and each edge $(u, v) \in E$ conveys the nesting and relative positioning of these fields. The descriptive elements provided by the PICTURE clause and the associated USAGE specification contribute to the formal semantics of the file record. Field definitions indicate not only the size and type of each attribute but also contextual constraints, such as the permissible range of values and the expected formatting. The interplay between these syntactic components ensures that the resulting record layout encapsulates the intended physical ordering and data representation.

Mapping Physical Structures to Software Abstractions

A central aspect of defining file records is the abstraction of physical file data into well-structured software representations. The File Section serves as an interface where each defined record is directly mapped to an external data structure. In this mapping process, the declarative specifications yield a correspondence function $M : F \to S$, where F denotes the set of physical file records and S represents the structured in-memory data entities. This function is instrumental in bridging the gap between the static configuration provided by the source code and the dynamic runtime environment. The explicit description of the physical record's layout, including field boundaries and positions, contributes to a robust mechanism for data retrieval, error detection, and validation, ensuring that the intrinsic attributes of a file are faithfully preserved during program execution.

Design Considerations in Record Definition

The design of file records within the File Section necessitates careful attention to several engineering concerns. The explicit declaration of fields must account for potential alignment issues, padding requirements, and the need for compatibility with external file specifications. Design decisions encompass the determination of record size L, where the sum of the individual field lengths does not exceed system limitations and adheres to the file system's constraints.

Furthermore, the flexibility to employ redefinitions allows a single physical storage area to be interpreted in multiple ways, thereby optimizing storage usage without sacrificing clarity. The formal description within the File Section imparts precise control over field ordering, while the use of hierarchical level numbers provides a coherent structure that can be statically verified for consistency. Through rigorous adherence to these design principles, the record definitions ensure the integrity and reliability of file I/O operations across diverse computing environments.

Cobol Code Snippet

```
        IDENTIFICATION DIVISION.
        PROGRAM-ID. FILE-RECORD-DEFINITION.

        ENVIRONMENT DIVISION.
        INPUT-OUTPUT SECTION.
        FILE-CONTROL.
            SELECT CUSTOMER-FILE ASSIGN TO "CUSTOMER.DAT"
                ORGANIZATION IS SEQUENTIAL
                FILE STATUS IS WS-FILE-STATUS.

        DATA DIVISION.
        FILE SECTION.
        *----------------------------------------------------
        * The following FD defines the physical record layout for the
        * customer file. The hierarchical structure (levels) encodes
        ↪   the
        * tree T = (V, E), where V denotes individual fields and E
        ↪   the
        * nesting relations. This ensures a clear mapping from file
        ↪   data
        * (F) to the in-memory structure (S), i.e., M : F -> S.
        *----------------------------------------------------
        FD  CUSTOMER-FILE.
        01  CUSTOMER-RECORD.
            05  CUST-ID        PIC X(10).
            05  CUST-NAME      PIC X(20).
            05  CUST-ADDRESS   PIC X(30).
            05  CUST-AMOUNT    PIC 9(6)V99.
        * Optionally, one can redefine the record for alternative
        ↪   views:
        * 01  CUSTOMER-RECORD.
        *     05  ORIGINAL-FORM.
        *         10  CUST-ID        PIC X(10).
        *         10  CUST-NAME      PIC X(20).
        *         10  CUST-ADDRESS   PIC X(30).
        *         10  CUST-AMOUNT    PIC 9(6)V99.
```

```
*      05  ALT-REPRESENTATION REDEFINES ORIGINAL-FORM.
*          10  COMBINED-RECORD   PIC X(70).

WORKING-STORAGE SECTION.
*------------------------------------------------------
* Variables to support file status, computation of the total
* record length (L) and intermediate arithmetic operations.
* Equation: L = Len(CUST-ID) + Len(CUST-NAME) +
*               Len(CUST-ADDRESS) + Len(CUST-AMOUNT)
* Here, lengths correspond to the predefined values in the
↪  FD.
*------------------------------------------------------
01  WS-FILE-STATUS     PIC XX     VALUE SPACES.
01  WS-RECORD-LENGTH.
    05  WS-LEN-CUST-ID      PIC 9(03)  VALUE 10.
    05  WS-LEN-CUST-NAME    PIC 9(03)  VALUE 20.
    05  WS-LEN-CUST-ADDR    PIC 9(03)  VALUE 30.
    05  WS-LEN-CUST-AMNT    PIC 9(03)  VALUE 8.  *> 6 digits
↪  + 2 implied decimals
01  WS-TOTAL-LENGTH    PIC 9(04)  VALUE ZERO.
01  WS-COMPUTE-RESULT  PIC 9(06)V99 VALUE ZERO.

PROCEDURE DIVISION.
MAIN-PROCEDURE.

↪  *------------------------------------------------------------
* Calculate the total record length based on individual
↪  field sizes.
* This demonstrates the formal equation L =
↪  WS-LEN-CUST-ID +
*                                      WS-LEN-CUST-NAME
↪  +
*                                      WS-LEN-CUST-ADDR
↪  +
*
↪  WS-LEN-CUST-AMNT.

↪  *------------------------------------------------------------
COMPUTE WS-TOTAL-LENGTH = WS-LEN-CUST-ID +
                          WS-LEN-CUST-NAME +
                          WS-LEN-CUST-ADDR +
                          WS-LEN-CUST-AMNT.
DISPLAY "Calculated Record Length (L): " WS-TOTAL-LENGTH.


↪  *------------------------------------------------------------
* Open the file and demonstrate the mapping from physical
↪  file
* records to structured in-memory variables.

↪  *------------------------------------------------------------
OPEN INPUT CUSTOMER-FILE.
```

```
PERFORM UNTIL WS-FILE-STATUS = "10"
    READ CUSTOMER-FILE
        AT END
            MOVE "10" TO WS-FILE-STATUS
        NOT AT END
            * Mapping example: interpret the CUST-AMOUNT
            ↪  field.
            MOVE FUNCTION NUMVAL(CUST-AMOUNT) TO
            ↪  WS-COMPUTE-RESULT
            DISPLAY "Customer ID: " CUST-ID
            DISPLAY "Name       : " CUST-NAME
            DISPLAY "Address    : " CUST-ADDRESS
            DISPLAY "Amount     : " WS-COMPUTE-RESULT
    END-READ
END-PERFORM.

CLOSE CUSTOMER-FILE.
STOP RUN.
```

Chapter 33

Sequential File Organization

Fundamental Concepts and Data Layout

Sequential file organization is characterized by the contiguous arrangement of records that form a strictly ordered sequence. In this paradigm, a file is regarded as an ordered set $R = \{r_1, r_2, \ldots, r_n\}$, where each r_i represents a data record conforming to a predetermined structure. The physical layout of the file is such that records are stored one after the other, maintaining a linear progression that reflects both storage constraints and access patterns. This methodical configuration permits a deterministic mapping between the logical composition of data and its physical manifestation, thus ensuring that the sequential order is preserved from the point of data creation through subsequent retrieval operations.

Record Access Mechanisms

The mechanism for accessing records in a sequentially organized file adheres to a linear traversal model. Beginning at the first record, each subsequent record is accessed in the order it appears within the file. The absence of non-sequential indexing implies that the retrieval process is inherently iterative, with the operational complexity scaling as $O(n)$ relative to the number of records. Each read operation advances the file pointer to the next record until a terminal condition, commonly defined by an end-of-file indicator, is encountered. This method of record access ensures consistency in processing since the position and order of each record remain fixed, thereby simplifying algorithmic implementations for data scanning and extraction.

Operational Semantics of Sequential Processing

Within the sequential file framework, the processing of records is governed by a continuous, linear progression. The sequential access model integrates closely with state-transition paradigms wherein the file pointer's movement from one record to the next is formalized through a series of well-defined states. At each state transition, the record currently in focus is subjected to processing routines that interpret its structured fields as defined by the file's layout specifications. The temporal progression inherent in this model permits the application of stream processing techniques, wherein the data flows in a single direction without the need for random access. As a consequence, the operational semantics define a clear, unidirectional pathway through which the entirety of the file is processed in a methodical and predictable manner.

Design Considerations in Sequential File Systems

The design of sequential file systems entails rigorous attention to record composition, storage alignment, and the establishment of effective buffering strategies. A central design criterion involves the precise determination of record boundaries and field lengths, ensuring that the cumulative record size conforms to both logical and physical constraints. This detailed specification is essential when considering padding methods and alignment requirements dictated by hardware architectures. In addition, the inherent simplicity of the sequential model facilitates the deployment of prefetching and caching mechanisms that improve input/output performance by exploiting the predictable order of record access. The resultant architecture reflects a harmonious balance between theoretical rigor and pragmatic efficiency, as it affords both the precision of a formally defined data structure and the operational expediency demanded by high-throughput processing environments.

Cobol Code Snippet

```
IDENTIFICATION DIVISION.
PROGRAM-ID. SEQUENTIALFILEDEMO.

*-------------------------------------------------------------
* This program demonstrates sequential file organization.
* The file is logically viewed as a set R = {r1, r2, ..., rn},
* where each record is processed in a linear O(n) traversal.
* The program reads each record, aggregates a numeric field,
* and computes the average (i.e., Average = Sum / Count).
*-------------------------------------------------------------

ENVIRONMENT DIVISION.
INPUT-OUTPUT SECTION.
FILE-CONTROL.
    SELECT INFILE ASSIGN TO "DATAFILE.DAT"
        ORGANIZATION IS SEQUENTIAL
        ACCESS MODE IS SEQUENTIAL
        FILE STATUS IS WS-FILE-STATUS.

DATA DIVISION.
FILE SECTION.
FD  INFILE.
01  DATA-RECORD.
    05  REC-ID      PIC 9(4).
    05  REC-VALUE   PIC 9(5).

WORKING-STORAGE SECTION.
01  WS-FILE-STATUS  PIC XX.
01  WS-END-OF-FILE  PIC X VALUE "N".
    88  END-OF-FILE     VALUE "Y".
01  WS-REC-COUNT    PIC 9(5) VALUE ZERO.
01  WS-SUM          PIC 9(9) VALUE ZERO.
01  WS-AVERAGE      PIC 9(9)V99 VALUE ZERO.

PROCEDURE DIVISION.
MAIN-LOGIC.
    OPEN INPUT INFILE
    PERFORM UNTIL WS-END-OF-FILE = "Y"
        READ INFILE
            AT END
                MOVE "Y" TO WS-END-OF-FILE
            NOT AT END
                ADD 1 TO WS-REC-COUNT
                ADD REC-VALUE TO WS-SUM
        END-READ
    END-PERFORM
    CLOSE INFILE

    IF WS-REC-COUNT > 0
        COMPUTE WS-AVERAGE = WS-SUM / WS-REC-COUNT
```

```
END-IF

DISPLAY "Total Records Processed: " WS-REC-COUNT
DISPLAY "Sum of Record Values: " WS-SUM
DISPLAY "Average of Record Values: " WS-AVERAGE

STOP RUN.
```

Chapter 34

Indexed File Organization

Theoretical Foundations of Key-Based Indexing

Indexed file organization employs an auxiliary mapping structure that associates each record with a unique key, thereby facilitating rapid access to a record's physical location. This mapping can be formalized as a function

$$f : K \to L,$$

where K represents the set of key values derived from record attributes and L signifies the set of corresponding physical record addresses. The function f is constructed to preserve a strict ordering among keys, a property that is essential for ensuring both uniqueness and an efficient lookup mechanism. This formal framework underpins the transformation of a traditional sequential file into one that supports expedited search operations through key-based addressing.

Structural Characteristics and Order Preservation

The intrinsic structure of an index in file organization is designed to maintain an ordered sequence of keys paired with pointers to their associated records. Typically, this index is implemented using hierarchical data structures—such as balanced trees—that inherently enforce a total order on the key set. When keys are arranged in increasing order, binary search techniques can be employed, reducing the average search complexity from $O(n)$ in a sequential scan to $O(\log n)$. The ordering invariant not only supports direct record access but also enhances the efficiency of range queries by enabling contiguous traversal through the ordered key values. This design ensures that every key maintains a definitive position within the sequence, thereby streamlining the retrieval process even under conditions of high data volume.

Search Complexity and Retrieval Efficiency

The adoption of a key-based indexing strategy yields significant improvements in the efficiency of search operations. By leveraging a multi-level, hierarchical index structure, the retrieval of a specific record is transformed from a linear search into a logarithmically bounded operation. In this context, the worst-case time complexity for a lookup operation is reduced to

$$O(\log n),$$

where n is the total number of entries in the index. This enhanced performance becomes particularly evident in data-intensive applications that require rapid, non-sequential access to records. Furthermore, the ordered nature of the index permits the seamless execution of range queries, where the set of keys between any two given values can be traversed in order with minimal additional overhead. This dual capability of random and range-based retrieval illustrates the profound impact of key-based indexing on overall system performance.

Operational Considerations in Index Maintenance

The dynamic maintenance of an index in an evolving file system introduces a range of operational considerations. Insertions, updates, and deletions of records necessitate corresponding adjustments in the index to preserve its structural properties and ordering invariants. Algorithms for index maintenance must be robust in handling these modifications while ensuring that the index remains balanced and that the integrity of key-to-record mappings is not compromised. Techniques such as deferred updates and batched reorganization are commonly employed to mitigate the maintenance overhead and to optimize throughput. Additionally, rigorous consistency checks are integral to safeguarding the index against transient errors that may arise during concurrent operations. The careful management of these operational aspects is critical to sustaining the high access speeds and reliability that are the principal advantages of indexed file organization.

Cobol Code Snippet

```
* Program: Indexed Search Example demonstrating key-based
↪  indexing and
* the mapping function f: K -> L. This example simulates an
↪  indexed file
* where keys are maintained in a sorted index table and a
↪  binary search is
* used to locate a record. The binary search reduces lookup
↪  time to O(log n).

IDENTIFICATION DIVISION.
PROGRAM-ID. INDEXED-SEARCH.

ENVIRONMENT DIVISION.
INPUT-OUTPUT SECTION.
FILE-CONTROL.
    SELECT IDXFILE ASSIGN TO "INDEXED.DAT"
        ORGANIZATION IS INDEXED
        ACCESS MODE IS RANDOM
        RECORD KEY IS REC-KEY.

DATA DIVISION.
FILE SECTION.
FD  IDXFILE.
01  IDX-RECORD.
    05 REC-KEY      PIC 9(4).
    05 REC-DATA     PIC X(50).

WORKING-STORAGE SECTION.
* Variables for binary search over the index table.
01 WS-SEARCH-KEY    PIC 9(4).
01 WS-INDEX-LOWER   PIC 9(4) VALUE 1.
01 WS-INDEX-UPPER   PIC 9(4) VALUE 10.
01 WS-MID           PIC 9(4).
01 WS-FIND-FLAG     PIC X VALUE "N".
```

```
* Simulated index table representing the mapping function f:
↪   K -> L,
* where each entry consists of a key (K) and its
↪   corresponding physical
* record address (L). The table is maintained in strictly
↪   increasing order.
01 INDEX-TABLE.
    05 IT-ENTRY OCCURS 10 TIMES INDEXED BY ITX.
        10 IT-KEY      PIC 9(4).
        10 IT-ADDR     PIC 9(4).

PROCEDURE DIVISION.
MAIN-LOGIC.
    PERFORM INITIALIZE-INDEX.
    DISPLAY "Enter Key to Search:".
    ACCEPT WS-SEARCH-KEY.
    PERFORM BINARY-SEARCH.
    IF WS-FIND-FLAG = "Y"
        DISPLAY "Key found in Index Table. Retrieving
        ↪   record..."
        PERFORM READ-RECORD
    ELSE
        DISPLAY "Key " WS-SEARCH-KEY " not found in Index
        ↪   Table."
    STOP RUN.

INITIALIZE-INDEX.
    * Populate the index table with dummy sorted keys and
    ↪   simulated file addresses.
    MOVE 1000 TO IT-KEY (1)     *> f(1000) maps to physical
    ↪   address 1.
    MOVE 1    TO IT-ADDR (1)
    MOVE 1010 TO IT-KEY (2)     *> f(1010) maps to physical
    ↪   address 2.
    MOVE 2    TO IT-ADDR (2)
    MOVE 1020 TO IT-KEY (3)
    MOVE 3    TO IT-ADDR (3)
    MOVE 1030 TO IT-KEY (4)
    MOVE 4    TO IT-ADDR (4)
    MOVE 1040 TO IT-KEY (5)
    MOVE 5    TO IT-ADDR (5)
    MOVE 1050 TO IT-KEY (6)
    MOVE 6    TO IT-ADDR (6)
    MOVE 1060 TO IT-KEY (7)
    MOVE 7    TO IT-ADDR (7)
    MOVE 1070 TO IT-KEY (8)
    MOVE 8    TO IT-ADDR (8)
    MOVE 1080 TO IT-KEY (9)
    MOVE 9    TO IT-ADDR (9)
    MOVE 1090 TO IT-KEY (10)
    MOVE 10   TO IT-ADDR (10)
    EXIT.
```

```
BINARY-SEARCH.
    * Implements binary search on the sorted index table.
    MOVE "N" TO WS-FIND-FLAG.
    MOVE 1   TO WS-INDEX-LOWER.
    MOVE 10  TO WS-INDEX-UPPER.
    PERFORM UNTIL WS-INDEX-LOWER > WS-INDEX-UPPER
        COMPUTE WS-MID = (WS-INDEX-LOWER + WS-INDEX-UPPER) /
        ↪  2
        IF IT-KEY (WS-MID) = WS-SEARCH-KEY
            MOVE "Y" TO WS-FIND-FLAG
            EXIT PERFORM
        ELSE
            IF IT-KEY (WS-MID) > WS-SEARCH-KEY
                COMPUTE WS-INDEX-UPPER = WS-MID - 1
            ELSE
                COMPUTE WS-INDEX-LOWER = WS-MID + 1
            END-IF
        END-IF
    END-PERFORM.
    EXIT.


READ-RECORD.
    READ IDXFILE
        RECORD KEY WS-SEARCH-KEY
        INVALID KEY
            DISPLAY "Error: Record not found in physical
            ↪  file."
        END-READ.
    DISPLAY "Record Retrieved: Key = " REC-KEY " Data = "
    ↪  REC-DATA.
    EXIT.
```

Chapter 35

Relative File Organization

Conceptual Framework of Relative File Organization

Relative file organization constitutes a methodology in which each record is assigned a fixed numerical identifier, commonly referred to as the relative record number (RRN). This identifier directly corresponds to a predetermined physical position within the file infrastructure. In this arrangement, files are segmented into uniform slots or records, where the invariance of record size permits the application of straightforward arithmetic to compute the exact location of any given record. The design promotes a robust mapping between the logical sequential order and the underlying physical layout, thereby eliminating the need for iterative search routines when accessing records.

Mathematical Foundations of Relative Addressing

The efficiency of relative file organization is anchored in precise mathematical formulations that establish a direct correlation between record numbering and physical addresses. Let B denote the base address of the file, and let L represent the fixed length of each record. For a record with relative record number r, the corresponding physical address A is determined by the expression

$$A = B + (r - 1) \times L.$$

This linear mapping guarantees constant-time, or $O(1)$, access to records regardless of the total number of entries in the file. More generally, this mapping can be expressed as a function $g : \mathbb{N} \to \mathbb{A}$, where $\mathbb{N}$ is the set of natural numbers representing potential record positions, and $\mathbb{A}$ is the set of physical addresses allocated to the file. The simplicity and determinism of this function underpin the performance advantages inherent in the relative file organization scheme.

Access Patterns and Performance Characteristics

The deterministic nature of relative file organization yields predictable access patterns that are independent of the overall file size. When a record's relative number is known, its physical location is computed directly using the established arithmetic, thereby facilitating immediate access without traversing intervening records. This direct addressing mechanism minimizes latency and contributes to a performance profile that remains stable even as the file scales in size. The uniform partitioning of the storage medium further ensures that the retrieval cost remains constant, reinforcing the suitability of this method for applications that demand rapid, random-access operations.

Physical Layout and System-Level Implications

The physical layout in a relative file organization system is a direct function of the fixed record size and the contiguous allocation of storage space. Such a configuration minimizes the overhead associated with file management, as the spatial relationship between records is inherently maintained by the storage design. In practice, the contiguous arrangement aids in reducing fragmentation and enhances the overall efficiency of input/output operations.

Conversely, deviations from uniform record lengths or the occurrence of deletions may introduce complexities that require auxiliary mechanisms to preserve the integrity of the addressing scheme. At the system level, these considerations necessitate a careful balance between the rigidity of fixed-size allocation and the flexibility needed to manage dynamic record modifications within the storage medium.

Cobol Code Snippet

```
IDENTIFICATION DIVISION.
PROGRAM-ID. RELATIVE-FILE-ADDRESS.

ENVIRONMENT DIVISION.
CONFIGURATION SECTION.
        SOURCE-COMPUTER. IBM-370.
        OBJECT-COMPUTER. IBM-370.

DATA DIVISION.
WORKING-STORAGE SECTION.
01 BASE-ADDR       PIC 9(6) VALUE 100000.
01 REC-LENGTH      PIC 9(4) VALUE 0080.
01 REL-REC-NUM     PIC 9(5) VALUE ZERO.
01 PHYS-ADDR       PIC 9(8) VALUE ZERO.
01 WS-MSG          PIC X(50).

PROCEDURE DIVISION.
MAIN-LOGIC.
    *> Prompt the user for the relative record number.
    DISPLAY "Enter Relative Record Number:".
    ACCEPT REL-REC-NUM.

    *> Compute the physical address using the formula:
    *>    PHYS-ADDR = BASE-ADDR + (REL-REC-NUM - 1) * REC-LENGTH
    COMPUTE PHYS-ADDR = BASE-ADDR + (REL-REC-NUM - 1) * REC-LENGTH.

    *> Display the calculated physical address.
    MOVE "Calculated Physical Address: " TO WS-MSG.
    DISPLAY WS-MSG PHYS-ADDR.

    STOP RUN.
```

Chapter 36

Designing Record Layouts

Conceptual Foundations for Record Layout Design

The design of record layouts in file storage systems necessitates the articulation of a coherent strategy that integrates both abstract data modeling and practical constraints imposed by physical storage media. Records are conceptualized as structured aggregates of data fields, where each field is allocated a predefined length and position. In many instances, the overall record size, denoted by

$$R = \sum_{i=1}^{n} L_i,$$

serves as a primary metric in evaluating space utilization, with L_i representing the length of the ith field. A rigorous approach requires that the process of layout design accommodate the semantic relationships among data elements while optimizing for retrieval speed and memory efficiency. The theoretical framework underpinning record layout is rooted in the principles of structured design and is deeply intertwined with the operational characteristics of file management systems, ensuring that logical organization is inextricably linked to physical storage considerations.

Data Segmentation and Field Prioritization

A principal consideration in the construction of an effective record layout is the segmentation of the record into logical clusters that mirror the frequency and patterns of access observed in file operations. Individual fields within a record are not merely arranged sequentially; rather, their positioning is influenced by factors such as access latency, data interdependency, and the likelihood of simultaneous retrieval. If $f(i)$ denotes the access frequency of the ith field, an optimal design may seek to minimize the weighted access cost represented by

$$\sum_{i=1}^{n} f(i) \cdot L_i,$$

subject to the constraints imposed by fixed block sizes and hardware limitations. Such a formulation ensures that fields with higher access frequencies are situated in contiguous memory segments, thereby reducing the need for multiple I/O operations. Strategic grouping of fields based on their semantic and operational affinities enables the system to capitalize on cache locality and prefetching mechanisms, fostering a design that is both efficient and inherently logical.

Alignment, Padding, and Efficient Use of Storage

The precise alignment of data elements within a record is critical to achieving optimal performance on contemporary storage hardware. Given the importance of alignment constraints, it is essential that each field occupies a memory address that conforms to the hardware's alignment requirements. For instance, if every field must be aligned on an address boundary that is a multiple of A, then the condition

$$\text{address}(F_i) \mod A = 0$$

must hold for each field F_i. To satisfy such constraints, padding may be introduced between fields, an approach that, while potentially increasing the overall record size, reduces the cost of misaligned data access and minimizes processor stalls. The trade-off between space efficiency and retrieval performance is therefore a key consideration, with design strategies often favoring the deliberate insertion of minimal padding to preserve alignment while respecting the overall space constraints imposed by the storage medium.

Integration with File System Storage Architecture

The integration of record design with the underlying file system architecture represents a critical junction at which logical data structures meet physical storage realities. File systems typically impose a block-based organization, with a fixed block size B dictating the granularity of I/O operations. Accordingly, the record layout must be devised in such a way that the size R of each record is conducive to efficient block utilization. For example, the maximum number of records that can be stored within a single block is determined by the integer division

$$\lfloor B/R \rfloor,$$

a relationship that underscores the importance of aligning record boundaries with physical block dimensions. This correspondence minimizes the fragmentation of data and reduces the frequency of block reallocation during file operations. Furthermore, the mapping between logical record structures and disk layout is influenced by the efficiency of indexing and retrieval techniques; a thoughtfully engineered record layout enhances both sequential and random access performance by harmonizing with the file system's intrinsic organizational patterns.

Cobol Code Snippet

```
IDENTIFICATION DIVISION.
PROGRAM-ID. RECORDLAYOUT.

ENVIRONMENT DIVISION.
CONFIGURATION SECTION.

DATA DIVISION.
WORKING-STORAGE SECTION.
* Number of fields in the record layout
01 NUM-FIELDS        PIC 99 VALUE 5.

* Table to hold each field's length and its access frequency
```

```
01 FIELD-TABLE.
   05 FIELD-ENTRY OCCURS 5 TIMES.
      10 FIELD-LENGTH   PIC 9999.
      10 ACCESS-FREQ    PIC 9999.

* Variables for computed values
01 TOTAL-RECORD-SIZE   PIC 99999 VALUE 0.
01 WEIGHTED-COST       PIC 999999 VALUE 0.

* Alignment related variables
01 ALIGN-BOUNDARY      PIC 9999 VALUE 4.
01 FIELD-ADDRESS       PIC 99999 VALUE 0.

* File system block size and maximum records per block
01 BLOCK-SIZE          PIC 99999 VALUE 1024.
01 MAX-RECORDS         PIC 9999 VALUE 0.

* Loop counter
01 I                   PIC 99 VALUE 1.

PROCEDURE DIVISION.
MAIN-LOGIC.
    DISPLAY "Initializing Field Table Values".
    MOVE 100 TO FIELD-ENTRY(1).FIELD-LENGTH.
    MOVE 5   TO FIELD-ENTRY(1).ACCESS-FREQ.
    MOVE 200 TO FIELD-ENTRY(2).FIELD-LENGTH.
    MOVE 3   TO FIELD-ENTRY(2).ACCESS-FREQ.
    MOVE 150 TO FIELD-ENTRY(3).FIELD-LENGTH.
    MOVE 8   TO FIELD-ENTRY(3).ACCESS-FREQ.
    MOVE 120 TO FIELD-ENTRY(4).FIELD-LENGTH.
    MOVE 2   TO FIELD-ENTRY(4).ACCESS-FREQ.
    MOVE 180 TO FIELD-ENTRY(5).FIELD-LENGTH.
    MOVE 6   TO FIELD-ENTRY(5).ACCESS-FREQ.

    DISPLAY "Calculating Total Record Size (R) and Weighted Access
    ↪ Cost".
    PERFORM VARYING I FROM 1 BY 1 UNTIL I > NUM-FIELDS
        ADD FIELD-ENTRY(I).FIELD-LENGTH TO TOTAL-RECORD-SIZE
        COMPUTE WEIGHTED-COST = WEIGHTED-COST +
            (FIELD-ENTRY(I).FIELD-LENGTH *
            ↪ FIELD-ENTRY(I).ACCESS-FREQ)
    END-PERFORM.

    DISPLAY "Total Record Size (R): " TOTAL-RECORD-SIZE.
    DISPLAY "Weighted Access Cost: " WEIGHTED-COST.

    DISPLAY "Checking Field Alignment (Alignment Boundary = "
    ↪ ALIGN-BOUNDARY ")".
    MOVE 0 TO FIELD-ADDRESS.
    PERFORM VARYING I FROM 1 BY 1 UNTIL I > NUM-FIELDS
        ADD FIELD-ENTRY(I).FIELD-LENGTH TO FIELD-ADDRESS
        IF FUNCTION MOD(FIELD-ADDRESS, ALIGN-BOUNDARY) = 0
```

159

```
            DISPLAY "Field " I " is properly aligned at address: "
            ↳  FIELD-ADDRESS
        ELSE
            DISPLAY "Field " I " requires padding for alignment;
            ↳  current address: " FIELD-ADDRESS
        END-IF
END-PERFORM.

DISPLAY "Calculating Maximum Records per Block using
↳  floor(B/R)".
IF TOTAL-RECORD-SIZE > 0
    COMPUTE MAX-RECORDS = FUNCTION INTEGER(BLOCK-SIZE /
    ↳  TOTAL-RECORD-SIZE)
ELSE
    MOVE 0 TO MAX-RECORDS
END-IF.
DISPLAY "Maximum Records per Block: " MAX-RECORDS.

STOP RUN.
```

Chapter 37

FD (File Description) Entries Explained

Foundations of FD Entries

File Description (FD) entries constitute the formal mechanism by which COBOL specifies the structure and organization of external files. An FD entry is declared within the FILE SECTION of the DATA DIVISION and establishes a comprehensive definition of record layouts, thereby delineating the correspondence between the in-memory representation and the physical file structure. The FD entry articulates the characteristics of file records, prescribing attributes such as record length, hierarchical field groupings, and the sequential arrangement of elementary items. In effect, the FD entry provides an invariant schema that governs both input and output operations, ensuring data integrity and consistency across all file manipulations.

Declarative Syntax and Structural Composition

The declaration of an FD entry adheres to a formal syntax which encapsulates the structural composition of a file. A typical FD entry commences with the FD keyword, followed by a unique file identifier, and is succeeded by a sequence of record descriptors that employ level-number notation to denote hierarchical relationships.

Each record descriptor specifies the characteristics of a group or elementary item, including its picture clause for data type and size determination. The resulting structure is both layered and modular, permitting the explicit characterization of complex record formats. This declarative approach facilitates rigorous error checking and enables the automatic enforcement of record boundaries and field alignments by the COBOL runtime environment.

Mapping Logical File Structures to Physical Storage

FD entries serve as the critical interface between logical data models and physical file storage systems. By defining the layout of records, FD entries establish the foundational parameters that determine file accessibility, block alignment, and record retrieval efficiency. For instance, if a file is partitioned into records whose total length is denoted by

$$R = \sum_{i=1}^{n} L_i,$$

where L_i is the length of the ith field, then the FD entry essentially encapsulates this summation by specifying fixed field lengths and predefined positions. Such a quantitative description enables file management systems to optimize storage by aligning records with hardware block sizes and by leveraging file buffering strategies. Additionally, the FD entry aids in the formulation of record indexing schemes that optimize both sequential and random access patterns.

Semantic Nuances and Extended Structural Features

Beyond mere syntactical representation, FD entries embody a range of semantic nuances that enhance the robustness of file definitions. Detailed annotations within an FD entry often distinguish between different record types—such as headers, details, and trailers—thereby facilitating segmented file processing. This layered semantic description permits independent handling of diverse record categories within a single file, thereby accommodating complex data interchange scenarios. In scenarios involving overlapping data

162

or multiple interpretations of a memory area, FD entries can be augmented through constructs that resolve ambiguities by means of redefinitions and conditional structures. Such features are essential in contexts requiring high levels of data integrity and consistency, particularly when disparate file access modes are employed.

Implications for File Organization and Data Integrity

The precise description afforded by FD entries has profound implications for both file organization and data integrity. Through a detailed architectural blueprint of each record, FD entries provide the necessary parameters for aligning logical fields with physical storage requirements. This alignment minimizes data fragmentation and enhances the efficiency of I/O operations. The formal structure defined by FD entries also underpins rigorous consistency checks that are instrumental in detecting discrepancies between the expected and actual file formats. By ensuring that every record conforms to predetermined specifications, FD entries act as the first line of defense against data corruption and misinterpretation. The explicitness of the record layout description thereby contributes to a robust file management ecosystem, where every access and update operation can be confidently correlated with its corresponding physical manifestation.

Cobol Code Snippet

```
IDENTIFICATION DIVISION.
PROGRAM-ID. FDALGO.

ENVIRONMENT DIVISION.
INPUT-OUTPUT SECTION.
FILE-CONTROL.
    SELECT MYFILE ASSIGN TO "MYDATA.DAT"
        ORGANIZATION IS SEQUENTIAL.

DATA DIVISION.
FILE SECTION.
FD  MYFILE.
01  RECORD-STRUCTURE.
    05  FIELD1          PIC X(10).
    05  FIELD2          PIC X(15).
    05  FIELD3          PIC X(5).
```

163

```
WORKING-STORAGE SECTION.
* Constants representing the lengths of each field as
↪ specified in the FD entry.
77  WS-FIELD1-LEN       PIC 9(4) VALUE 10.
77  WS-FIELD2-LEN       PIC 9(4) VALUE 15.
77  WS-FIELD3-LEN       PIC 9(4) VALUE 5.
77  WS-TOTAL-LENGTH     PIC 9(4) VALUE 0.

* Table to hold the length of each field (n = 3 fields).
01  FIELD-LENGTHS.
    05  LENGTH-TABLE OCCURS 3 TIMES INDEXED BY IDX.
        10  FIELD-LEN   PIC 9(4).

PROCEDURE DIVISION.
MAIN-PROCEDURE.
    * Initialize the table with each field length as defined
    ↪  by the FD entry.
    MOVE WS-FIELD1-LEN TO FIELD-LEN(1).
    MOVE WS-FIELD2-LEN TO FIELD-LEN(2).
    MOVE WS-FIELD3-LEN TO FIELD-LEN(3).

    * Compute the total record length using the formula:
    *        R = L1 + L2 + L3
    MOVE 0 TO WS-TOTAL-LENGTH.
    PERFORM VARYING IDX FROM 1 BY 1 UNTIL IDX > 3
        ADD FIELD-LEN(IDX) TO WS-TOTAL-LENGTH
    END-PERFORM.

    DISPLAY "Computed Total Record Length: " WS-TOTAL-LENGTH.

    STOP RUN.
```

Chapter 38

Utilizing the REDEFINE Clause

Conceptual Framework of Overlapping Data Definitions

The REDEFINE clause establishes a mechanism by which a contiguous memory region may be interpreted in multiple ways. This facility permits a single block of memory to embody alternative data structures without the necessity of additional storage. In this framework, an initially defined data item is subsequently reinterpreted as an alternate group item. The overlapping definitions correspond to a shared physical space, thereby ensuring that any change under one definition is immediately observable under the alternative interpretation. This conceptual approach is fundamental in systems where space optimization and diversified data handling strategies are paramount.

Structural Semantics of the REDEFINE Clause

Within a structured data environment, the REDEFINE clause allows an alternative declaration to occupy the identical memory footprint as a previously established item. If the original memory block is denoted by M with a defined size L, then an overlapping definition may be viewed as a function $\phi : M \to T$, where T represents the alternative type structure. The semantics enforce that the boundaries of the redefined items are congruent to those of the original declaration. Such a constraint ensures mathematical consistency and structural integrity, guaranteeing that each field within both interpretations aligns perfectly with the corresponding segments of memory. The result is a robust mechanism that underpins the integration of multiple data schemas within a single physical region.

Memory Layout and Logical Data Interpretation

The REDEFINE clause harmonizes the physical layout of memory with varied logical interpretations of data. Multiple overlapping definitions impose alternative schemas on the same sequence of bytes, each offering distinct access and manipulation rules. This aspect of reinterpretation is crucial when a system requires different perspectives of the same data, such as in contexts where one interpretation may be used for efficient storage and another for streamlined processing. The invariant nature of the memory block, preserved by the rigid boundaries imposed by the clause, ensures that the total allocated space remains unchanged. Consequently, the logical rearrangement of data does not result in additional memory overhead, and the dual interpretations maintain complete coherence within the static memory allocation.

Implications for Data Integrity and System Flexibility

The ability to reinterpret a memory region through overlapping definitions carries significant implications for both data integrity and system design flexibility. By utilizing the REDEFINE clause, a system can seamlessly adapt to evolving data representation requirements without altering physical storage parameters. The mechanism enforces that every alternative structure is bounded by the same memory limits, which minimizes the risk of data anomalies and fragmentation. This design principle supports a model in which the abstract separation of concerns is maintained, allowing

166

for diversified processing methodologies while preserving the underlying data consistency. Consequently, overlapping data definitions serve as a foundation for resource optimization and improved modularity in the overall system architecture.

Cobol Code Snippet

```
IDENTIFICATION DIVISION.
PROGRAM-ID. REDEFINE-EXAMPLE.

ENVIRONMENT DIVISION.

DATA DIVISION.
WORKING-STORAGE SECTION.
*-------------------------------------------------------------
* Define a memory block (M) with a fixed length (L) holding
* a 6-digit numeric value. This represents the original data.
*-------------------------------------------------------------
01  WS-BLOCK.
    05  WS-FULL-NUMBER          PIC 9(6) VALUE 123456.


*-------------------------------------------------------------
* Redefine the same memory space as an alternative structure.
* This overlapping definition acts as the function : M → T,
* splitting the 6-digit number into two parts:
*    - WS-PART1: First 3 digits.
*    - WS-PART2: Last 3 digits.
*-------------------------------------------------------------
01  WS-OVERLAP   REDEFINES WS-BLOCK.
    05  WS-PART1               PIC 9(3).
    05  WS-PART2               PIC 9(3).


*-------------------------------------------------------------
* Variables for algorithmic computations:
*    WS-PRODUCT is the multiplication of WS-PART1 and
↪    WS-PART2.
*    WS-SUM is the sum of the original full number
↪    (WS-FULL-NUMBER)
*    and the computed product. This demonstrates combining
*    different interpretations of the same memory block.
*-------------------------------------------------------------
01  WS-PRODUCT                 PIC 9(8) VALUE ZERO.
01  WS-SUM                     PIC 9(8) VALUE ZERO.

PROCEDURE DIVISION.
MAIN-LOGIC.
    DISPLAY "COBOL REDEFINE EXAMPLE" UPON CONSOLE.
    DISPLAY "---------------------------------" UPON
↪       CONSOLE.
```

```
* Display the original numeric view.
DISPLAY "Original Full Number: " WS-FULL-NUMBER UPON
↪   CONSOLE.

* Display the reinterpreted parts from the overlapping
↪   definition.
DISPLAY "Redefined Parts: Part1 = " WS-PART1 " and Part2
↪   = " WS-PART2 UPON CONSOLE.

* Compute the product of the two redefined parts.
COMPUTE WS-PRODUCT = WS-PART1 * WS-PART2.
DISPLAY "Product of Parts (Part1 * Part2): " WS-PRODUCT
↪   UPON CONSOLE.

* Compute the final result integrating both views:
* Final Sum = Full Number + Product.
COMPUTE WS-SUM = WS-FULL-NUMBER + WS-PRODUCT.
DISPLAY "Final Sum (Full Number + Product): " WS-SUM UPON
↪   CONSOLE.

STOP RUN.
```

Chapter 39

Implementing OCCURS for Tables

Syntactic and Semantic Properties of the OCCURS Clause

The OCCURS clause in COBOL provides a declarative means to define a table structure, analogous to an array in many modern programming languages. This clause permits a data item to be replicated a fixed number of times, thereby furnishing a homogeneous collection of elements that share an identical format and size. Formally, if an element is defined with a size S and the OCCURS clause specifies N repetitions, the aggregate memory allocation is given by $N \times S$. Such a formulation establishes a one-to-one correspondence between the declared occurrences and the contiguous memory segments assigned to each element. The semantics of the OCCURS clause ensure that each repetition adheres strictly to the initial definition, precluding any variation in structure across the elements and thereby enforcing uniformity in the table's semantic interpretation.

Memory Allocation and Structural Organization

The memory layout in a COBOL program is determined rigidly by the definitions provided in the DATA DIVISION. In the case of an OCCURS table, the compiler calculates the overall memory footprint by sequentially allocating space for each instance of the repeated element. This process results in a contiguous block of memory, wherein the offset for the ith occurrence is computed as $(i - 1) \times S$, where S represents the size of a single element. The deterministic allocation strategy facilitates efficient access and manipulation, as the physical location of any table element may be directly inferred from its index. Such a static memory organization guarantees that the table's structure remains invariant at runtime, thereby enhancing predictability in both access time and memory usage. Furthermore, the strict layout inherent in the OCCURS clause obviates the need for dynamic memory management techniques, by providing compile-time assurances regarding memory boundaries.

Indexing Mechanisms and Element Access

Element access in OCCURS-defined tables relies on a well-defined indexing mechanism that correlates each occurrence with a unique offset within the contiguous memory allocation. When referring to the jth element of the table, the effective address is computed through the arithmetic expression $Base\_Address + (j - 1) \times S$, a formulation that is readily optimized by the compiler. In many implementations, the use of auxiliary index variables supports more complex operations, such as iterative element processing or conditional data manipulation. This approach allows for both sequential traversal and randomized access within the bounds of the allocated table. The principle underlying this mechanism is the abstraction of table elements as entities within a one-dimensional array, where the uniformity of element size serves as a foundation for efficient offset computation and direct addressing.

Nested OCCURS Clauses and Multi-Dimensional Structures

The OCCURS clause also extends to the construction of multidimensional table structures through the mechanism of nesting. By embedding an OCCURS clause within another OCCURS clause, a hierarchical or multi-level table is created, wherein each outer element encapsulates an inner table structure. The effective size calculation for such nested constructs becomes the product of the extents of each level of occurrences. For example, if an outer table is defined with N occurrences and each occurrence contains an inner table with M occurrences, then the overall number of elements is $N \times M$, and the memory offset for an element specified by indices (i, j) is given by

$$Base\_Address + [(i - 1) \times M + (j - 1)] \times S,$$

where S is the size of the innermost element. This nested structure imposes a multi-dimensional logical view upon a unidimensional physical memory allocation. The discipline required to manage such nested OCCURS clauses ensures that each hierarchical level is consistently defined and that overall data integrity is maintained. Such an arrangement is particularly advantageous in scenarios where data exhibits inherent multidimensional correlations, allowing for an elegant representation of complex datasets within the constraints of a static memory model.

Cobol Code Snippet

```
IDENTIFICATION DIVISION.
PROGRAM-ID. OCCURS-EXAMPLE.

ENVIRONMENT DIVISION.
INPUT-OUTPUT SECTION.
FILE-CONTROL.

DATA DIVISION.
WORKING-STORAGE SECTION.
* Define a single-dimensional table using OCCURS.
01  SINGLE-TABLE.
    05  SINGLE-ELEMENT  PIC 9(4) OCCURS 10 TIMES.

* Define a multi-dimensional table using nested OCCURS.
01  NESTED-TABLE.
    05  ROW  OCCURS 5 TIMES.
        10  COLUMN  PIC 9(4) OCCURS 4 TIMES.

* Auxiliary variables for offset calculations and
↪ demonstration.
01  WS-INDEX1       PIC 9(2) VALUE ZERO.
01  WS-INDEX2       PIC 9(2) VALUE ZERO.
01  WS-OFFSET       PIC 9(5) VALUE ZERO.
01  WS-CALC-OFFSET  PIC 9(5) VALUE ZERO.
01  WS-BASE-ADDR    USAGE BINARY PIC S9(4) COMP VALUE ZERO.
```

```
01  WS-ELEMENT-SIZE   USAGE BINARY PIC S9(4) COMP VALUE 4.
01  WS-DISPLAY-VALUE  PIC 9(4).

PROCEDURE DIVISION.
MAIN-LOGIC.
    DISPLAY '--- Single OCCURS Table: Offset Calculation
    ↪   ---'.
    * Calculate offset for the 5th element in SINGLE-TABLE.
    * Using formula: OFFSET = (INDEX - 1) * ELEMENT_SIZE.
    MOVE 5 TO WS-INDEX1.
    COMPUTE WS-CALC-OFFSET = (WS-INDEX1 - 1) *
    ↪   WS-ELEMENT-SIZE.
    DISPLAY 'Offset for 5th element in SINGLE-TABLE: '
    ↪   WS-CALC-OFFSET.

    DISPLAY ' '.
    DISPLAY '--- Nested OCCURS Table: Offset Calculation
    ↪   ---'.
    * Calculate offset for an element in NESTED-TABLE at Row
    ↪   3, Column 2.
    * Formula for nested structure:
    * Effective linear index = (Row - 1) * Number_of_Columns
    ↪   + (Column - 1).
    * Offset = Effective Index * ELEMENT_SIZE.
    MOVE 3 TO WS-INDEX1.
    MOVE 2 TO WS-INDEX2.
    COMPUTE WS-OFFSET = (((WS-INDEX1 - 1) * 4) + (WS-INDEX2 -
    ↪   1)) * WS-ELEMENT-SIZE.
    DISPLAY 'Offset for NESTED-TABLE element at Row 3, Column
    ↪   2: ' WS-OFFSET.

    DISPLAY ' '.
    DISPLAY '--- Demonstration of Effective Memory Address
    ↪   Calculation ---'.
    * Assume a hypothetical base address.
    MOVE 1000 TO WS-BASE-ADDR.
    * For SINGLE-TABLE element 5:
    COMPUTE WS-CALC-OFFSET = WS-BASE-ADDR + (5 - 1) *
    ↪   WS-ELEMENT-SIZE.
    DISPLAY 'Effective address for SINGLE-TABLE element 5: '
    ↪   WS-CALC-OFFSET.

    * For NESTED-TABLE element at Row 3, Column 2:
    COMPUTE WS-OFFSET = WS-BASE-ADDR + (((3 - 1) * 4) + (2 -
    ↪   1)) * WS-ELEMENT-SIZE.
    DISPLAY 'Effective address for NESTED-TABLE element (Row
    ↪   3, Column 2): ' WS-OFFSET.

    STOP RUN.
```

Chapter 40

Indexing and Searching Tables

Architectural Considerations for Indexing OCCURS Tables

Tables defined through the OCCURS clause are allocated as contiguous blocks of memory, a structure that inherently supports deterministic addressing. Given a base memory address B and an element size S, the physical location of the ith element is computed by the formula

$$B + (i - 1) \times S.$$

This regularity enables the construction of an index as an auxiliary data structure that maps key values to their corresponding offsets within the contiguous block. The design of such an index is grounded in the precise memory model enforced by the OCCURS clause, thereby allowing a clear separation between the logical keys and the physical organization of data. The deterministic placement of elements not only simplifies the arithmetic of offset calculation but also provides a robust platform upon which more sophisticated indexing schemes may be built.

Index Structure Design and Optimization

The essence of index structure design lies in establishing a rapid mapping from key values to memory offsets. In the context of OC-CURS tables, an index is typically realized as an ordered collection that maintains associations between the unique identifiers of table elements and their computed addresses. When the index is structured in sorted order, binary search algorithms become applicable, yielding a lookup complexity of $O(\log n)$ for an index containing n elements. Alternatively, hash-based indexing schemes allow for an average-case complexity approaching $O(1)$, provided that a sound hash function and an appropriate collision resolution mechanism are in place.

The selection of an index structure is further influenced by the invariance of the underlying table's memory layout. Since the table elements occupy contiguous and fixed-sized segments, the index can afford to store only the relative offsets or even the precomputed addresses associated with each key. The optimization of the index is thus achieved by minimizing redundant computations, streamlining the mapping process, and ensuring that the maintenance cost of the index remains proportional to the complexity of the data retrieval operation itself.

Search Methodologies in Indexed OCCURS Tables

Search operations on tables defined by the OCCURS clause are inherently enhanced by the presence of a complementary index. The search process initiates with a query to the index data structure in order to retrieve the candidate offset for the desired key. Once identified, the memory address is directly computed by applying the offset to the base address, as given by

$$\text{Address} = B + \text{Offset}.$$

This two-stage process—first resolving the key-to-offset mapping and then directly accessing the element—significantly reduces the overall search latency compared to a full sequential scan of the table.

For cases where multiple key fields define a compound identifier, multi-dimensional indexing techniques may be adopted. In such instances, the index is designed to capture the interdependencies among the key fields, thereby preserving the semantic associations inherent in the data. By partitioning the index structure accordingly, targeted search operations can traverse the multi-level hierarchy to isolate the precise segment of memory that contains the desired information.

Complexity Analysis of Index-Driven Search Operations

The performance of index-driven search operations is characterized by a combination of the computational overhead associated with index traversal and the constant time nature of direct memory access. For an index constructed as a balanced binary search tree, the worst-case lookup time is bounded by $O(\log n)$, where n denotes the number of entries in the index. Once the index has furnished the appropriate offset, the subsequent memory retrieval is achieved in constant time, $O(1)$, owing to the contiguous allocation of table elements.

In scenarios where the index is implemented through a hash table, the expected search time may approach $O(1)$, assuming that the hash function uniformly distributes the keys and that the load factor remains within acceptable limits. The overall efficiency of these search operations is intrinsically linked to the quality of the index design and its alignment with the static memory model enforced by OCCURS tables. The constant-time properties of memory access, when coupled with an optimized index structure, result in a highly efficient mechanism for data search and retrieval within the confines of COBOL's declarative table definitions.

Cobol Code Snippet

```
IDENTIFICATION DIVISION.
PROGRAM-ID. INDEXSEARCH.
ENVIRONMENT DIVISION.
DATA DIVISION.
WORKING-STORAGE SECTION.
    * Base address for table simulation (e.g., memory start address)
    01  B              PIC 9(5)    VALUE 10000.
    * Size of each table element (in bytes)
    01  S              PIC 9(2)    VALUE 50.
    * Number of records in the table
```

175

```cobol
01  NUM-REC        PIC 9(3)   VALUE 5.
* Search key (example: key to find in the table)
01  SEARCH-KEY     PIC 9(4)   VALUE 203.
* Loop index variable
01  I              PIC 9(2)   VALUE 1.
* Table entries defined by OCCURS clause
01  TABLE-ENTRIES.
    05  ENTRY       OCCURS 5 TIMES.
        10 ENTRY-KEY    PIC 9(4).
        10 ENTRY-VALUE  PIC X(20).
* Index table mapping key to offset (computed using formula:
↪   OFFSET = (index - 1) * S)
01  INDEX-TABLE.
    05  INDEX-REC  OCCURS 5 TIMES.
        10 INDEX-KEY   PIC 9(4).
        10 OFFSET      PIC 9(5).
* Variable to hold found record index (0 if not found)
01  FOUND-INDEX    PIC 9(2)   VALUE 0.
* Computed physical address of the found element
* (Address = B + (FOUND-INDEX - 1) * S)
01  COMPUTED-ADDR  PIC 9(7).

PROCEDURE DIVISION.
MAIN-LOGIC.
    PERFORM INITIALIZE-TABLE.
    PERFORM BUILD-INDEX.
    PERFORM SEARCH-TABLE.
    IF FOUND-INDEX > 0
        PERFORM DISPLAY-RESULT
    ELSE
        DISPLAY "Key not found in table."
    END-IF.
    STOP RUN.


INITIALIZE-TABLE.
    * Initialize the table with sample key-value pairs
    MOVE 101 TO ENTRY-KEY (1)
    MOVE "Alice" TO ENTRY-VALUE (1)

    MOVE 203 TO ENTRY-KEY (2)
    MOVE "Bob"   TO ENTRY-VALUE (2)

    MOVE 305 TO ENTRY-KEY (3)
    MOVE "Carol" TO ENTRY-VALUE (3)

    MOVE 407 TO ENTRY-KEY (4)
    MOVE "Dave"  TO ENTRY-VALUE (4)

    MOVE 509 TO ENTRY-KEY (5)
    MOVE "Eve"   TO ENTRY-VALUE (5).
    EXIT.


BUILD-INDEX.
```

176

```
* Build the index table based on the table entries.
* The formula used here is: OFFSET = (I - 1) * S, where I is the
↪  record index.
PERFORM VARYING I FROM 1 BY 1 UNTIL I > NUM-REC
    MOVE ENTRY-KEY (I) TO INDEX-KEY (I)
    COMPUTE OFFSET (I) = (I - 1) * S
END-PERFORM.
EXIT.


SEARCH-TABLE.
    * Linear search through the table to find the matching search
    ↪  key.
    PERFORM VARYING I FROM 1 BY 1 UNTIL I > NUM-REC OR FOUND-INDEX >
    ↪  0
        IF ENTRY-KEY (I) = SEARCH-KEY
            MOVE I TO FOUND-INDEX
        END-IF
    END-PERFORM.
    EXIT.


DISPLAY-RESULT.
    * Compute the physical address using the formula:
    * Address = B + (FOUND-INDEX - 1) * S.
    COMPUTE COMPUTED-ADDR = B + ((FOUND-INDEX - 1) * S)
    DISPLAY "Search Key: " SEARCH-KEY " found at table index: "
    ↪  FOUND-INDEX.
    DISPLAY "Computed Address: " COMPUTED-ADDR.
    DISPLAY "Entry Value: " ENTRY-VALUE (FOUND-INDEX).
    EXIT.
```

Chapter 41

Using the SEARCH Statement

Conceptual Framework of Linear Search in OCCURS Tables

The SEARCH statement implements a linear search mechanism over arrays defined by the OCCURS clause. The table is allocated as a contiguous block of memory, a design choice that guarantees deterministic ordering of elements. In its operation, the SEARCH statement evaluates each element in sequence by comparing a designated field—typically a key—with a specified search value. The simplicity of this procedure belies its critical role in traversing data structures where the relation between logical ordering and physical layout is clearly defined.

1   Operational Semantics of the SEARCH Statement

The fundamental operation of the SEARCH statement involves iterating through each entry of the OCCURS table until a matching key is located. At each iteration, the key field stored in an element is compared against the target value. Given the sequential nature of the OCCURS table, this procedure is analogous to classical linear search algorithms. Termination of the search may occur prior to scanning all elements if a match is encountered, demonstrating an early-exit condition that optimizes the search operation in cases of successful comparisons.

2   Memory Layout and Deterministic Access

The table defined by the OCCURS clause guarantees that each element is placed sequentially in memory. With a base address denoted by B and a fixed record size S, the ith element is located at the computed address

$$B + (i - 1) \times S.$$

This deterministic allocation enhances the efficiency with which the SEARCH statement accesses individual records. The predictable memory architecture reduces the overhead associated with index calculations and allows the search to proceed with constant time delays for each individual comparison. The intimate relationship between the logical ordering of keys and their physical storage optimizes the process of verifying equality conditions across the table.

3   Algorithmic Considerations and Complexity Analysis

The linear nature of the SEARCH operation implies that in the worst-case scenario—where the target key is absent or located at the end of the table—the number of comparisons is equal to the number of elements n. Consequently, the time complexity is expressed as $O(n)$. Even when an early termination occurs on finding a match, the average-case complexity remains proportional to the table size. The method emphasizes minimalistic comparison logic, leveraging the inherent contiguity of memory allocations to perform straightforward key evaluations without the overhead of auxiliary data structures.

Foundational Logic Underpinning the SEARCH Mechanism

The SEARCH statement encapsulates an elegant yet powerful algorithmic strategy: a simple iteration over a statically defined memory block to resolve search queries based on key equivalence. Each element in the OCCURS table is treated as an independent record with explicit key values, and the search mechanism systematically verifies the equivalence of these keys against a provided search criterion. This straightforward approach ensures that the search process is both transparent and predictable, characteristics that are highly valued in systems where data integrity and performance are paramount.

1 Iterative Evaluation and Early Termination Strategy

In practical operation, the SEARCH statement employs an iterative evaluation strategy, wherein each record's key is processed in sequence until a decision point is reached. The underlying logic requires that each comparison yields a binary outcome: either the key matches the search criterion, or it does not. On finding a match, the iteration ceases immediately, and the corresponding record's index is returned to facilitate subsequent direct memory access. This early termination strategy reduces the computational burden in scenarios where the target record is positioned early in the sequence, aligning with efficient algorithmic principles.

2 Integration of Logical Conditions within Structured Data

Underlying the linear search process is the integration of logical conditions within a structured data environment. The SEARCH statement effectively encapsulates the predicate logic necessary for conditional evaluation, ensuring that comparisons remain within the bounds of the structured data model. The statically defined memory layout not only supports a straightforward translation of logical conditions into physical comparisons but also contributes to a robust error-checking mechanism inherent in the data traversal process. Through systematic evaluation, the SEARCH statement preserves both data consistency and computational efficiency.

3 Implications for Data Retrieval Performance

The direct correlation between physical memory layout and logical data ordering culminates in a system where the SEARCH statement can reliably retrieve data with minimal overhead. By relying exclusively on sequential comparisons, the method leverages the simplicity of the OCCURS table structure to afford predictable performance characteristics. The operation's efficiency is intrinsically linked to the size of the table and the distribution of search keys; however, the deterministic access pattern ensures that, in practice, performance remains within acceptable bounds for tables of moderate size. This alignment of memory structure and algorithmic simplicity remains a foundational principle in the design of linear search operations within COBOL programs.

Cobol Code Snippet

```
IDENTIFICATION DIVISION.
PROGRAM-ID. SEARCHDEMO.
ENVIRONMENT DIVISION.
DATA DIVISION.
WORKING-STORAGE SECTION.
*---------------------------------------------------------
* Define an OCCURS table with 5 entries.
* Each entry has a key and associated data.
* The table is indexed by IDX.
*---------------------------------------------------------
01 WS-ENTRY      OCCURS 5 TIMES INDEXED BY IDX.
    05 ITEM-KEY   PIC 99.
    05 ITEM-DATA PIC X(10).


*---------------------------------------------------------
* Variable for the search key.
*---------------------------------------------------------
01 WS-SEARCH-KEY   PIC 99 VALUE 23.
01 WS-MATCHED-INDEX PIC 99 VALUE 0.
01 WS-FOUND        PIC X VALUE 'N'.


*---------------------------------------------------------
* Variables to demonstrate the computed memory address.
* Using the formula: Address = BASE-ADDR + (Index - 1) *
↪   REC-SIZE.
*---------------------------------------------------------
01 BASE-ADDR      PIC S9(04) COMP VALUE 1000.
01 REC-SIZE       PIC S9(04) COMP VALUE 20.
01 CALC-ADDR      PIC S9(04) COMP.

PROCEDURE DIVISION.
MAIN-PARA.

    *---------------------------------------------------
    * Initialize table entries.
    * For each occurrence, assign a unique key and data
    ↪   value.
    *---------------------------------------------------
    MOVE 11 TO ITEM-KEY (1).
```

```cobol
MOVE "Alpha" TO ITEM-DATA (1).

MOVE 23 TO ITEM-KEY (2).
MOVE "Bravo" TO ITEM-DATA (2).

MOVE 35 TO ITEM-KEY (3).
MOVE "Charlie" TO ITEM-DATA (3).

MOVE 47 TO ITEM-KEY (4).
MOVE "Delta" TO ITEM-DATA (4).

MOVE 59 TO ITEM-KEY (5).
MOVE "Echo" TO ITEM-DATA (5).

*----------------------------------------------------
* Perform a linear search using the SEARCH statement.
* The SEARCH statement iterates over the OCCURS table
↪   WS-ENTRY.
* It compares ITEM-KEY (using index IDX) to
↪   WS-SEARCH-KEY.
* On finding a match, the search terminates early.
*----------------------------------------------------
SEARCH WS-ENTRY
    AT END
        DISPLAY "No match found."
    WHEN ITEM-KEY (IDX) = WS-SEARCH-KEY
        MOVE IDX TO WS-MATCHED-INDEX
        MOVE 'Y' TO WS-FOUND
        DISPLAY "Match found at index: " WS-MATCHED-INDEX
END-SEARCH.

*----------------------------------------------------
* Demonstrate computation of a record's memory address.
* Using the formula: Address = BASE-ADDR + ((Index - 1) *
↪   REC-SIZE)
* This reflects the deterministic allocation in memory.
*----------------------------------------------------
IF WS-FOUND = 'Y'
    COMPUTE CALC-ADDR = BASE-ADDR + ((WS-MATCHED-INDEX -
    ↪   1) * REC-SIZE)
    DISPLAY "Computed memory address: " CALC-ADDR
END-IF.

STOP RUN.
```

Chapter 42

Enhanced Searching with SEARCH ALL

Conceptual Foundations of the Binary Search Paradigm

The SEARCH ALL statement represents a significant enhancement over traditional linear search techniques by employing a binary search mechanism on indexed tables. This approach is feasible when the data structure is pre-sorted with respect to the key values, thereby ensuring that each inspection of the midpoint partitions the search space effectively. In a table containing n elements, the binary search mechanism requires, in the worst case, no more than $\lceil \log_2(n) \rceil$ comparisons. This property establishes a time complexity of $O(\log n)$, which is a substantial improvement over the linear time complexity associated with sequential search approaches.

The efficacy of the SEARCH ALL statement is inherently tied to the table's indexed nature, where a well-defined ordering is maintained. The deterministic arrangement of keys within the table guarantees that each binary decision—whether the target key lies in the higher or lower subset—accurately eliminates half of the remaining records. Consequently, the operation not only minimizes the number of comparisons needed but also leverages the advantages conferred by predictable memory organization.

Algorithmic Efficiency and Complexity Characteristics

Within the operational framework of COBOL, the use of the binary search algorithm encapsulated by SEARCH ALL is predicated on the assumption of an ordered data structure. The binary search technique systematically reduces the search interval by computing the midpoint of the current segment and comparing the associated key to the target value. Given that a table of n records supports this halving process, the maximum number of iterations is bounded by $\lceil \log_2(n) \rceil$.

This logarithmic behavior contrasts markedly with the linear progression of traditional search methods. Even when accounting for the minor computational overhead involved in calculating midpoint indices, the aggregate performance gains remain significant for large data sets. The intrinsic efficiency of the binary search paradigm underpins robust performance characteristics and ensures that the search operation scales favorably as the size of the indexed table increases.

Data Structure Integration and Memory Access Patterns

The integration of the SEARCH ALL statement with indexed tables mirrors the convergence of algorithm design with system-level data organization. In COBOL, tables defined with the OCCURS clause are allocated in contiguous memory blocks, providing a deterministic mapping between logical indices and physical memory addresses. For instance, given a base address B and a fixed record size S, the memory location of the ith element is determinable by the expression $B + (i - 1) \times S$.

This explicit calculation facilitates rapid memory access during each iteration of the binary search. At each step, the algorithm directly retrieves the key stored at the computed midpoint, a process that minimizes latency attributed to indirect addressing or cache inefficiencies. The structured nature of the data, combined with the assured sequential memory layout, allows the SEARCH ALL mechanism to exploit modern architectural features such as branch prediction and cache line optimization.

The synthesis of algorithmic precision with disciplined data structure design underscores the enhanced performance of the SEARCH ALL statement. By harnessing the benefits of binary search within the framework of contiguous memory allocation and indexed records, the operation achieves a high degree of computational efficiency while maintaining rigorous adherence to structured programming principles.

Cobol Code Snippet

```
IDENTIFICATION DIVISION.
PROGRAM-ID. BINARY-SEARCH-ALL.
AUTHOR. Maxwell_Vector.
*----------------------------------------------------
* This program demonstrates a binary search using the SEARCH
↪  ALL
* statement on an indexed table. The table is pre-sorted by
↪  the key.
* It highlights key equations:
*   - Worst-case comparisons: CEILING(LOG2(NUM-RECORDS))
*   - Memory location calculation: Base_Address + (i -
↪  1)*Record_Size
*----------------------------------------------------


ENVIRONMENT DIVISION.

DATA DIVISION.
WORKING-STORAGE SECTION.
77  NUM-RECORDS     PIC 9(2)     VALUE 10.
77  TARGET-KEY      PIC 9(4)     VALUE 2345.
77  FOUND-POS       PIC 9(2)     VALUE ZERO.

* Define an indexed table containing sorted records.
01  WS-ENTRY.
    05  WS-RECORD OCCURS 10 TIMES
            INDEXED BY WSINDEX.
        10  WS-KEY   PIC 9(4) COMP.
        10  WS-DATA  PIC X(20).

PROCEDURE DIVISION.
MAIN-PARAGRAPH.

    ↪  *------------------------------------------------------------
    * Initialize the table with sorted key values and related
    ↪  data.
    * Each record is stored in contiguous memory. The memory
    * address for the i-th record can be computed as:
    *   Base_Address + (i - 1) * Record_Size.

    ↪  *------------------------------------------------------------
```

```
MOVE 1001 TO WS-KEY (1).
MOVE "Entry One        " TO WS-DATA (1).

MOVE 1234 TO WS-KEY (2).
MOVE "Entry Two        " TO WS-DATA (2).

MOVE 2345 TO WS-KEY (3).
MOVE "Entry Three      " TO WS-DATA (3).

MOVE 3456 TO WS-KEY (4).
MOVE "Entry Four       " TO WS-DATA (4).

MOVE 4567 TO WS-KEY (5).
MOVE "Entry Five       " TO WS-DATA (5).

MOVE 5678 TO WS-KEY (6).
MOVE "Entry Six        " TO WS-DATA (6).

MOVE 6789 TO WS-KEY (7).
MOVE "Entry Seven      " TO WS-DATA (7).

MOVE 7890 TO WS-KEY (8).
MOVE "Entry Eight      " TO WS-DATA (8).

MOVE 8901 TO WS-KEY (9).
MOVE "Entry Nine       " TO WS-DATA (9).

MOVE 9012 TO WS-KEY (10).
MOVE "Entry Ten        " TO WS-DATA (10).


↪    *-------------------------------------------------------------
* Perform binary search using SEARCH ALL.
* The SEARCH ALL statement internally uses a binary
↪    search algorithm.
* Worst-case comparisons are bound by
↪    CEILING(LOG2(NUM-RECORDS)).

↪    *-------------------------------------------------------------
SEARCH ALL WS-RECORD
    AT END
        DISPLAY "TARGET KEY " TARGET-KEY " NOT FOUND."
    WHEN WS-KEY (WSINDEX) = TARGET-KEY
        MOVE WSINDEX TO FOUND-POS
        DISPLAY "TARGET KEY " TARGET-KEY
        DISPLAY " FOUND AT POSITION " FOUND-POS
END-SEARCH.


↪    *-------------------------------------------------------------
* Additional comments:
* Binary search leverages contiguous memory allocation.
```

```
      * For a table with NUM-RECORDS elements, the search cost
↪     is O(LOG n).
      * The midpoint decision is implicitly handled by SEARCH
↪     ALL.

↪     *----------------------------------------------------------
      STOP RUN.
```

Chapter 43

Sorting Records with the SORT Statement

Mechanics of File Sorting in COBOL

The SORT statement in COBOL serves as an interface to external file-sorting mechanisms that systematically reorders records based on explicitly defined key fields. The process is divided into distinct phases: reading unsorted records from an input file, executing the sort algorithm externally, and writing the sorted output to a designated file. This external sorting process typically employs a multipass technique analogous to an external merge-sort algorithm. For a dataset containing n records, the underlying sorting algorithm exhibits a performance characteristic on the order of $O(n \log n)$ comparisons in its most efficient implementations. The external sorter demarcates the phases of data ingestion, computational reordering, and eventual data output, ensuring that the final record sequence adheres strictly to the lexicographical order defined by the sort keys.

Syntactic and Declarative Elements of the SORT Statement

The syntactic structure of the SORT statement in COBOL is rigorously defined through a series of declarative clauses. These clauses identify not only the source file that contains the unsorted records but also the target file for the sorted output. Central to this syntax are the sort key definitions. One or more keys are specified, along with an indication of the desired order—either ascending or descending. The precise arrangement of these elements within the statement adheres to the language's formal grammar, ensuring unambiguous interpretation by the compiler. The internal semantics of the SORT statement leverage these declared keys to partition and subsequently reassemble the record set. The declarative nature of the syntax imposes a deterministic transformation from the unsorted to the sorted state, with the order of operations being explicitly governed by the key layout as stipulated in the source code.

Data Flow, Memory Architecture, and Operational Semantics

The operational efficacy of the SORT statement is markedly influenced by the interplay between data flow mechanisms and the underlying memory architecture. Records are initially read from the input file into a contiguous block of memory, a design choice that facilitates a direct mapping between logical record indices and their physical memory locations. This contiguous allocation underpins the efficiency of the sort process by enabling rapid, sequential access during the sorting phase. As the external sorting routine progresses, it systematically compares and exchanges records based on the designated key definitions. The deterministic ordering is achieved by iteratively subdividing the dataset and merging sorted subsequences, ensuring that the final output conforms to the prescribed criteria. The integration of well-defined memory access patterns, precise data flow controls, and stringent syntactic declarations contributes to an operational model that is both theory-driven and practically robust in reordering extensive record sets.

Cobol Code Snippet

```
       IDENTIFICATION DIVISION.
       PROGRAM-ID. SORTDEMO.
      *--------------------------------------------------*
      * This program demonstrates the use of the COBOL SORT
      ↪  *
```

189

```
* statement to reorder records using an external merge-sort
↪  *
* algorithm. The algorithm, with an efficiency of O(n log n)
↪  *
* comparisons, processes records in three phases: reading,
↪  *
* sorting (by partitioning and merging), and writing the
↪  output. *
*---------------------------------------------------*

ENVIRONMENT DIVISION.
INPUT-OUTPUT SECTION.
FILE-CONTROL.
    SELECT UNSORTED-FILE ASSIGN TO "unsorted.dat"
        ORGANIZATION IS SEQUENTIAL.
    SELECT SORTED-FILE   ASSIGN TO "sorted.dat"
        ORGANIZATION IS SEQUENTIAL.

DATA DIVISION.
FILE SECTION.
FD  UNSORTED-FILE.
01  UNSORTED-REC.
    05  SORT-KEY    PIC X(10).
    05  DATA-FIELD  PIC X(40).

FD  SORTED-FILE.
01  SORTED-REC.
    05  SORT-KEY    PIC X(10).
    05  DATA-FIELD  PIC X(40).

WORKING-STORAGE SECTION.
01  WS-MESSAGE.
    05  WS-INFO   PIC X(50)
        VALUE "Initiating external merge-sort process.".
01  WS-STATUS.
    05  WS-RESULT PIC X(50)
        VALUE "Sorting completed successfully.".

PROCEDURE DIVISION.
MAIN-PROCEDURE.
    DISPLAY WS-INFO.

    ↪  *----------------------------------------------------*
    * The SORT statement below executes the following steps:*
    * 1. Reads the unsorted records from UNSORTED-FILE.
    ↪  *
    * 2. Utilizes the specified SORT-KEY to partition the
    ↪  data  *
    *    and perform a multi-pass merge sort (O(n log n)
    ↪  behavior).*
    * 3. Writes the sorted records to SORTED-FILE.
    ↪  *
```

```
↩    *-------------------------------------------------------------*
SORT SORTED-FILE
     ON ASCENDING KEY SORT-KEY
     USING UNSORTED-FILE
     GIVING SORTED-FILE.
DISPLAY WS-RESULT.
STOP RUN.
```

Chapter 44

Merging Files with the MERGE Statement

Conceptual Foundations of File Merging

The MERGE statement represents a deterministic operation designed to consolidate two or more pre-sorted files into a single, ordered output. The underlying principle is predicated on the invariant that each input file is already arranged according to a common key structure. This precondition permits the merging process to operate with linear efficiency with respect to the cumulative number of records. In effect, the merge operation functions by concurrently scanning the sorted input files, comparing current records across all inputs, and sequentially appending the record that satisfies the predetermined order. This systematic interleaving of entries adheres to the lexicographical criteria imposed by the key definitions, thereby yielding an output that is globally ordered. The abstract model governing this process is congruent with the classical multiway merge algorithm employed in external sorting paradigms, in which the time complexity may be characterized by $O(N)$, where N denotes the total count of records being merged.

Syntactic Structure and Declarative Semantics

The declarative formulation of the MERGE statement is an embodiment of the language's commitment to explicit and formal specification of file manipulation semantics. Within the context of COBOL, the MERGE statement is constructed with precise syntactic elements that denote the source files and the resultant file. The statement leverages key clauses to explicitly state the ordering requirements and the connection between the input and output data structures. The language's grammar mandates that the identifiers corresponding to pre-sorted files be declared in the FILE SECTION of the DATA DIVISION prior to their integration within the MERGE operation. Furthermore, the declarative nature of the statement imposes a deterministic transformation; the logical sequence of merging is completely dictated by the configuration of the key fields and the ordered arrangement of the constituent files. This explicit syntax eliminates ambiguity, thereby ensuring that the runtime behavior aligns exactly with the statically defined intent.

Algorithmic Analysis and Memory Considerations

At an algorithmic level, the process of merging pre-sorted records can be examined through the lens of a multiway merge algorithm. When merging k pre-sorted files with a combined total of N records, a straightforward implementation exhibits a time complexity of $O(N)$, as each record is processed exactly once. More elaborate implementations, particularly when merging a larger number of files, might employ priority queues to manage current record references, resulting in a time complexity of $O(N \log k)$. Even though the MERGE statement abstracts these details from the programmer, the underlying runtime system exploits these algorithmic principles to maintain efficiency and correctness. Memory considerations play a critical role in this process. Typically, the runtime environment allocates a dedicated buffer space to temporarily hold portions of each input file. This buffering facilitates rapid access and minimizes the number of expensive I/O operations. The deterministic synchronization of memory accesses with file operations ensures a seamless and efficient merging process, despite the potential challenges imposed by limited memory resources in large-scale data environments.

Operational Semantics and Execution Model

The operational semantics of the MERGE statement are shaped by the rigorous coordination of file pointers, buffer management, and comparator functions within the COBOL runtime environment. Upon invocation of the MERGE operation, each input file is assigned an internal pointer that iterates over its records. The runtime system continuously selects the record with the smallest key value from among the current records across all files, transferring it to the output file and advancing the corresponding pointer. This selection process is inherently iterative and is maintained until all input files have been fully traversed. The execution model is underpinned by a series of conditional evaluations that are performed to ascertain the record ordering at every iteration. These evaluations leverage the intrinsic ordering characteristics of the pre-sorted files, thereby ensuring that the merged output preserves the overall order without necessitating an additional, post-hoc sorting phase. In this manner, the MERGE statement achieves a robust and efficient integration of multiple sorted data streams into a single, cohesive file.

Cobol Code Snippet

```
IDENTIFICATION DIVISION.
PROGRAM-ID. MERGEFILES.
AUTHOR. Maxwell_Vector.
DATE-WRITTEN. "2024-10-05".

ENVIRONMENT DIVISION.
INPUT-OUTPUT SECTION.
FILE-CONTROL.
    SELECT INFILE1    ASSIGN TO "INFILE1.DAT"
        ORGANIZATION IS SEQUENTIAL.
    SELECT INFILE2    ASSIGN TO "INFILE2.DAT"
        ORGANIZATION IS SEQUENTIAL.
    SELECT MERGEDFILE ASSIGN TO "MERGED.DAT"
        ORGANIZATION IS MERGE
        FILE STATUS IS WS-MERGED-STATUS.

DATA DIVISION.
```

```
FILE SECTION.
FD   INFILE1.
01   INREC-1.
     05  KEY-FIELD     PIC 9(4).
     05  DATA-VALUE    PIC X(20).


FD   INFILE2.
01   INREC-2.
     05  KEY-FIELD     PIC 9(4).
     05  DATA-VALUE    PIC X(20).


FD   MERGEDFILE.
01   MERGED-REC.
     05  KEY-FIELD     PIC 9(4).
     05  DATA-VALUE    PIC X(20).


WORKING-STORAGE SECTION.
01   WS-MERGED-STATUS    PIC XX.
01   WS-REC-COUNT        PIC 9(7)  VALUE ZERO.
01   WS-TIME-COMPLEXITY  PIC 9(7)  VALUE ZERO.
01   EOF-FLAG            PIC X     VALUE 'N'.
     88  EOF                 VALUE 'Y'.
     88  NOT-EOF             VALUE 'N'.


PROCEDURE DIVISION.
MAIN-PARA.
     DISPLAY "STARTING THE MERGE OPERATION...".

     OPEN INPUT INFILE1 INFILE2.
     OPEN OUTPUT MERGEDFILE.

     *>----------------------------------------------------
     *> The MERGE statement below consolidates two pre-sorted
     ↪  files
     *> into a single, ordered output file. The merge is based
     ↪  on
     *> the ascending order of the common KEY-FIELD.
     *>
     *> Algorithmic Insight:
     *> - Each record across the input files is processed
     ↪  exactly once,
     *>   demonstrating an O(N) time complexity (where N is
     ↪  the total
     *>   number of records).
     *> - The runtime system employs an internal multiway
     ↪  merge process,
     *>   buffering input records to minimize I/O overhead.
     *>----------------------------------------------------
     MERGE MERGEDFILE
          ON ASCENDING KEY KEY-FIELD
          USING INFILE1, INFILE2
     END-MERGE.
```

```
CLOSE INFILE1 INFILE2 MERGEDFILE.

DISPLAY "MERGE OPERATION COMPLETED.".
DISPLAY "COUNTING MERGED RECORDS FOR VALIDATION...".

OPEN INPUT MERGEDFILE.
PERFORM UNTIL EOF-FLAG = 'Y'
    READ MERGEDFILE
        AT END
            MOVE 'Y' TO EOF-FLAG
        NOT AT END
            ADD 1 TO WS-REC-COUNT
    END-READ
END-PERFORM.
CLOSE MERGEDFILE.

*>------------------------------------------------------
*> Illustrative Computation:
*> The following COMPUTE demonstrates a placeholder
↪  calculation
*> where the total number of merged records (N) is used
↪  to reflect
*> the linear, O(N), behavior of the merge algorithm.
*>------------------------------------------------------
COMPUTE WS-TIME-COMPLEXITY = WS-REC-COUNT.

DISPLAY "TOTAL RECORDS MERGED: " WS-REC-COUNT.
DISPLAY "COMPUTED TIME COMPLEXITY VALUE (O(N)): "
↪  WS-TIME-COMPLEXITY.

STOP RUN.
```

Chapter 45

Managing Table Indexes with the SET Statement

Conceptual Framework of Index Modification

Within COBOL's data management paradigm, OCCURS tables are employed to organize collections of homogeneous data items in a linear, array-like structure. The SET statement serves as a precise mechanism for altering index data items that reference individual occurrences within such tables. In this context, an index is an auxiliary variable that indicates the active position or current offset within the array. Modification of this index through the SET statement enables the program to adjust its focus dynamically, thereby facilitating targeted access to particular records without necessitating a complete traversal of the table. This deterministic update mechanism is of paramount importance in operations that require non-sequential access or when implementing search routines that depend on an accurately maintained pointer.

Syntactic Characteristics and Semantic Roles

The SET statement is defined with a syntax that explicitly identifies the target index and the value to which it is to be set. This operation is integrated within the language's procedural constructs and is closely associated with the structure imposed by the OCCURS clause. Syntactically, the statement isolates the assignment to the index data item, ensuring that modifications remain confined to the pointer mechanism without inadvertently altering the data stored in the table. Semantically, the SET statement performs an operation analogous to pointer arithmetic; it recalculates the current position within the table based on predefined rules and constraints. Such precision in syntax and semantics guarantees that the subsequent use of the table—whether in iterative processing or conditional evaluations—accurately reflects the newly assigned index, thus upholding the integrity of data access protocols.

Operational Dynamics and Algorithmic Integration

The runtime behavior associated with the SET statement represents a fundamental aspect of index management in table-driven processing. Upon execution, the SET statement instantaneously updates the index data item, an operation that is achieved in constant time, i.e., in $O(1)$ time complexity. This immediate update allows for the rapid repositioning of the active element pointer within an OCCURS table comprising N fixed records. In algorithmic applications, such as search and sort routines, the SET statement is critical in navigating the array structure. It allows the program to reposition the index to the desired occurrence in anticipation of, or in response to, control flow decisions. This capability is essential when implementing multi-pass algorithms or when coordinating complex, index-driven iterations. The deterministic nature of the SET operation ensures that the transformation of the index state is both efficient and predictable, thereby facilitating reliable integration into broader algorithmic constructs.

Memory and Data Integrity Considerations

From a memory management perspective, the employment of the SET statement demands stringent adherence to the invariants governing the OCCURS table structure. The data items corresponding to table elements are statically allocated in memory, and the index data items are maintained separately to provide a logical access pathway. When the SET statement is invoked, the update to the index variable must preserve the invariant linking the table's logical ordering with its physical layout in memory. This encapsulation is vital for maintaining consistency across operations that iterate over or reference different portions of the table. Buffer management mechanisms and the static memory allocation model together ensure that adjustments to the index data item via the SET statement are seamlessly integrated with overall data access patterns. Consequently, the operation supports both the efficiency of direct access and the reliability of controlled data manipulation, thereby ensuring that the table remains a consistent and coherent structure throughout its usage.

Cobol Code Snippet

```
IDENTIFICATION DIVISION.
PROGRAM-ID. TableIndexDemo.
ENVIRONMENT DIVISION.
CONFIGURATION SECTION.
      SOURCE-COMPUTER. IBM-370.
      OBJECT-COMPUTER. IBM-370.
DATA DIVISION.
WORKING-STORAGE SECTION.
* Define an OCCURS table with an index for managing table entries.
01 NUM-TABLE.
   05 NUM-ENTRY OCCURS 10 TIMES INDEXED BY TBL-INDX.
      10 NUM-VALUE PIC 9(4) VALUE ZEROS.
* Variables for search functionality and control.
01 SEARCH-KEY      PIC 9(4) VALUE 1234.
01 FOUND-FLAG      PIC X    VALUE 'N'.
01 FOUND-INDEX     PIC 9(2) VALUE 0.
01 I               PIC 9(2) VALUE 1.

PROCEDURE DIVISION.
MAIN-PARA.
   PERFORM INITIALIZE-TABLE.
   PERFORM DISPLAY-TABLE.
   PERFORM SEARCH-TABLE.
   IF FOUND-FLAG = 'Y'
       DISPLAY "Search key " SEARCH-KEY " found at index "
       ↪  FOUND-INDEX
   ELSE
       DISPLAY "Search key " SEARCH-KEY " not found in the table."
   END-IF.
   STOP RUN.
```

```
INITIALIZE-TABLE.
    MOVE 1000 TO NUM-VALUE (1).
    MOVE 1100 TO NUM-VALUE (2).
    MOVE 1200 TO NUM-VALUE (3).
    MOVE 1234 TO NUM-VALUE (4).
    MOVE 1300 TO NUM-VALUE (5).
    MOVE 1400 TO NUM-VALUE (6).
    MOVE 1500 TO NUM-VALUE (7).
    MOVE 1600 TO NUM-VALUE (8).
    MOVE 1700 TO NUM-VALUE (9).
    MOVE 1800 TO NUM-VALUE (10).
    .

DISPLAY-TABLE.
    PERFORM VARYING I FROM 1 BY 1 UNTIL I > 10
        * Set table index to the current occurrence in constant
        ↪  O(1) time.
        SET TBL-INDX TO NUM-ENTRY (I)
        DISPLAY "Table Entry " I ": " NUM-VALUE (TBL-INDX)
    END-PERFORM.
    .

SEARCH-TABLE.
    PERFORM VARYING I FROM 1 BY 1 UNTIL I > 10 OR FOUND-FLAG = 'Y'
        SET TBL-INDX TO NUM-ENTRY (I)
        IF NUM-VALUE (TBL-INDX) = SEARCH-KEY
            MOVE 'Y' TO FOUND-FLAG
            MOVE I TO FOUND-INDEX
        END-IF
    END-PERFORM.
    .

END PROGRAM TableIndexDemo.
```

Chapter 46

Declaratives: Handling Special Conditions

Conceptual Foundations of Declarative Sections

Declarative sections constitute a specialized mechanism within the programming paradigm that isolates the handling of exceptional processing conditions from the primary procedural logic. This construct is designed to encapsulate processing scenarios that fall outside the normal execution flow, such as error detection and special condition management. By segregating such routines into their own defined blocks, the architecture inherently supports modular design and enhances the clarity of the program's control structure. Declarative sections are defined with precise syntactic boundaries, ensuring that any processing associated with non-standard conditions remains isolated from routine operations. Such isolation reinforces robustness by preventing the inadvertent propagation of exceptional states into the core algorithmic pathways.

Syntactic and Semantic Characteristics

Within the language's formal specification, declarative sections are demarcated by reserved syntactic constructs that signal their distinct operational semantics. The syntax is purposefully designed to integrate seamlessly with the overall program structure while maintaining distinct boundaries. Semantically, declarative sections serve as dedicated handlers for special processing conditions, ensuring that upon detection of an exceptional event, control is transferred immediately to the appropriate block. This mechanism facilitates a deterministic and ordered approach to exception handling, analogous to pointer redirection in other contexts. Strict adherence to these syntactic and semantic rules guarantees that the overall system behavior remains predictable, and that exceptional situations are managed in a controlled fashion without interfering with routine execution flows.

Mechanisms for Special Processing Conditions

The runtime environment enforces the declarative paradigm by continually monitoring for conditions that necessitate deviation from standard processing. When an exceptional event is identified, the system initiates a control transfer to the corresponding declarative block based on pre-established selection criteria. This control transfer is executed with a defined order of precedence, ensuring that the handling of the special condition is resolved in an unambiguous and timely manner. The mechanism is designed to operate in constant time, guaranteeing that exceptional scenarios do not introduce undue complexity or latency into the processing sequence. Moreover, the isolation provided by declarative sections preserves the integrity of the system state and facilitates meticulous error recovery procedures. By rigorously delineating these processes, the system upholds both data integrity and operational stability under a wide range of exceptional conditions.

Cobol Code Snippet

```
IDENTIFICATION DIVISION.
PROGRAM-ID. SPECIAL-CALCULATION.
*-------------------------------------------------------------
* This program demonstrates handling a special arithmetic
* calculation and uses a declarative section to manage any
* exceptional conditions (e.g., division by zero) that may
* occur during computation.
* Equation: NUM-RESULT = (NUM-A + NUM-B) / NUM-DIVISOR
*-------------------------------------------------------------
```

```
ENVIRONMENT DIVISION.
* (No file operations are performed in this example)

DATA DIVISION.
WORKING-STORAGE SECTION.
    01  NUM-A.
        05  NUM-A-VALUE      PIC S9(4) COMP VALUE 100.
    01  NUM-B.
        05  NUM-B-VALUE      PIC S9(4) COMP VALUE 50.
    01  NUM-DIVISOR.
        05  DIVISOR-VALUE    PIC S9(4) COMP VALUE 0.
    01  NUM-RESULT.
        05  RESULT-VALUE     PIC S9(6) COMP.
    01  WS-ERROR-MSG         PIC X(50) VALUE "NO ERROR".
    01  WS-DISPLAY-TEXT      PIC X(80).

PROCEDURE DIVISION.
MAIN-PARA.
    DISPLAY "Starting Special Calculation.".
    PERFORM CALCULATE-RESULT.
    DISPLAY "Calculation complete.".
    STOP RUN.

CALCULATE-RESULT.
    *---------------------------------------------------------------
    * The following COMPUTE statement performs the arithmetic
    * operation using the formula: (NUM-A + NUM-B) / NUM-DIVISOR.
    * A division by zero in the denominator (DIVISOR-VALUE) will
    * trigger an exception, transferring control to the associated
    * declarative section.
    *---------------------------------------------------------------
    COMPUTE RESULT-VALUE = (NUM-A-VALUE + NUM-B-VALUE) /
    ↪  DIVISOR-VALUE.
    MOVE "Calculated Result: " TO WS-DISPLAY-TEXT.
    STRING WS-DISPLAY-TEXT DELIMITED BY SPACE
           RESULT-VALUE     DELIMITED BY SIZE
           INTO WS-DISPLAY-TEXT.
    DISPLAY WS-DISPLAY-TEXT.
    EXIT.

DECLARATIVES.
SPECIAL-ERROR-SECTION.
    *---------------------------------------------------------------
    * The following USE clause directs that any exception raised
    * during the COMPUTE statement in CALCULATE-RESULT (such as a
    * division by zero) will be handled in this section.
    *---------------------------------------------------------------
    USE AFTER EXCEPTION ON COMPUTE CALCULATE-RESULT.
        MOVE "Error: Division by zero encountered during
        ↪  calculation."
            TO WS-ERROR-MSG.
        DISPLAY WS-ERROR-MSG.
        GOBACK.
```

END DECLARATIVES.

Chapter 47

Exception Handling with USE in Declaratives

Declarative Paradigm in Exception Management

Within the broader scope of procedural programming, declarative sections serve as an architectural mechanism for isolating nonstandard execution flows from core algorithmic operations. The declarative paradigm establishes a clear demarcation between routine computational logic and exceptional processing events, thereby ensuring that the management of error conditions is both systematic and architecturally independent. This method of partitioning contributes to overall system stability by preventing the inadvertent propagation of exceptions into routine processes. In such an environment, exceptional events—whether they arise from arithmetic anomalies, data corruption, or invalid operations—are treated as discrete entities, requiring a deterministic response that is dissociated from the primary control logic.

Mechanics and Semantics of the USE Statement

The USE statement operates as a specialized directive within declarative sections to immediately redirect execution upon the occurrence of an exceptional event. Its syntax is incorporated into the declarative framework so that any runtime error triggered during the execution of primary procedures is caught and processed via an associated declarative block. The semantic model underlying the USE statement is predicated on the principle of immediate exception resolution, where the identification of an error condition, such as the presence of an invalid divisor (0) during an arithmetic operation, prompts a rapid transition to a designated handler. This mechanism ensures that the integrity of both data and system state is preserved. On a syntactic level, the USE clause is embedded within the declarative section, and its precise arrangement within the source code reflects both the modular design of the program and the commitment to robust exception semantics.

Operational Flow of Exception Handling

The operational dynamics of exception handling via the USE statement are characterized by the instantaneous transfer of control from the point of error detection to a structured handler within the declarative section. When an exceptional condition is encountered, the runtime environment triggers a preconfigured response that bypasses the usual sequential execution in favor of invoking the USE-based handler. Such an invocation occurs in a manner that is both inline with the predetermined control precedence and independent of the standard procedural flow. The process situates the USE statement as a critical nexus between error detection and error management, enabling the runtime system to address anomalies in a consistent and time-deterministic fashion. In this context, the theoretical underpinnings of declarative exception handling are realized by ensuring that exceptional events are managed exclusively within their designated scope, thereby maintaining a separation of concerns that enhances both the predictability and the maintainability of the system.

Cobol Code Snippet

```
IDENTIFICATION DIVISION.
PROGRAM-ID. EXCEPTION-HANDLING-DEMO.

ENVIRONMENT DIVISION.
INPUT-OUTPUT SECTION.

DATA DIVISION.
WORKING-STORAGE SECTION.
01  WS-DIVIDEND     PIC 9(8)V99 VALUE 12345678.90.
01  WS-DIVISOR      PIC 9(8)V99 VALUE 0.
01  WS-QUOTIENT     PIC 9(8)V99 VALUE ZERO.
01  WS-MESSAGE      PIC X(50).

PROCEDURE DIVISION.
MAIN-PARA.
    DISPLAY "**** COBOL Exception Handling Demo ****".
    DISPLAY "Enter Divisor (enter zero to trigger exception): " WITH
    ↪  NO ADVANCING.
    ACCEPT WS-DIVISOR.
    PERFORM COMPUTE-DIVISION.
    DISPLAY "Division Result: " WS-QUOTIENT.
    DISPLAY "Program Terminated Successfully.".
    STOP RUN.

COMPUTE-DIVISION.
    DIVIDE WS-DIVIDEND BY WS-DIVISOR GIVING WS-QUOTIENT
    END-DIVIDE.

DECLARATIVES.
DIVIDE-ERROR-SECTION.
    USE AFTER ERROR ON DIVIDE
        HANDLE-DIVIDE-ERROR.
HANDLE-DIVIDE-ERROR.
    DISPLAY "****** Exception Handler Invoked ******".
    DISPLAY "Error: Division by zero or invalid divisor
    ↪  encountered.".
    MOVE ZERO TO WS-QUOTIENT.
    STOP RUN.
END DECLARATIVES.
```

Chapter 48

Opening Files with the OPEN Statement

Formal Syntax and Structural Placement

The formal syntax of the $OPEN$ statement is defined by a rigid structure that reflects its pivotal role in initiating file access within COBOL programs. This statement is composed of the $OPEN$ keyword followed by a mode specifier that designates the nature of the file transaction. Typically, mode specifiers such as $INPUT$, $OUTPUT$, and $I-O$ are employed to indicate whether a file is to be read, written, or updated. Each file referenced by the $OPEN$ statement corresponds to an abstract file descriptor established in the DATA or ENVIRONMENT DIVISION, thereby ensuring that file management remains consistent with the overall program architecture. The syntax is further constrained by the fixed-format rules of COBOL, which impose predetermined column positions for specific elements and maintain the integrity of program semantics as enforced during the compilation process.

Mechanics of File Access Initiation

The invocation of the $OPEN$ statement marks the initiation of file access, transitioning control to the underlying runtime system that manages I/O operations. At the point of execution, the statement triggers a series of systematic checks, which include verification of access permissions, confirmation of file existence, and validation of the file's current state as reflected in preassigned status fields. Upon successful validation, the runtime environment establishes a binding between the program's file definition and the operating system's file control blocks. This binding process involves allocation of the necessary internal buffers and configuration of system-level parameters that govern subsequent file read or write operations. The operational semantics of the $OPEN$ statement are thus not confined to a simple directive but extend into a comprehensive procedure that encapsulates error detection, state synchronization, and preparatory steps that are essential for reliable file manipulation in a production environment.

Integration with System-Level File Management

The design of the $OPEN$ statement demonstrates a seamless integration with system-level file management mechanisms. Its implementation ensures that file descriptors, once activated, interact directly with operating system routines that monitor and control file accessibility. The statement is constructed to respond to both normal and anomalous conditions; when the expected preconditions for file access are met, the file is opened in the designated mode and becomes available for immediate use by the program. In contrast, should any inconsistencies or access violations be detected—such as conflicts in file modes or the absence of a required file—the operating system's error handling protocols are engaged, and appropriate status codes are relayed back to the program. This rigorous integration facilitates a robust and transparent mechanism whereby the state of file-based I/O operations is continuously monitored and maintained, thereby ensuring that all subsequent file operations inherit a consistent and controllable state.

Cobol Code Snippet

```
IDENTIFICATION DIVISION.
PROGRAM-ID. FILEIO-EXAMPLE.
AUTHOR. Maxwell_Vector.

ENVIRONMENT DIVISION.
INPUT-OUTPUT SECTION.
```

```
FILE-CONTROL.
    SELECT INFILE ASSIGN TO 'TESTFILE.DAT'
        ORGANIZATION IS SEQUENTIAL
        ACCESS MODE IS SEQUENTIAL
        FILE STATUS IS WS-FILE-STATUS.

DATA DIVISION.
FILE SECTION.
FD  INFILE.
01  FILE-RECORD       PIC X(80).

WORKING-STORAGE SECTION.
01  WS-FILE-STATUS    PIC XX.
01  WS-EOF            PIC X VALUE 'N'.
    88  END-OF-FILE   VALUE 'Y'.
01  WS-REC-COUNT      PIC 9(5) VALUE ZERO.
01  WS-ERROR-MESSAGE  PIC X(80).

PROCEDURE DIVISION.
MAIN-LOGIC.
    DISPLAY 'Starting file open process for TESTFILE.DAT...'.
    OPEN INPUT INFILE.
    IF WS-FILE-STATUS NOT = '00'
        DISPLAY 'Error: Unable to open file. File-status = '
        ↪  WS-FILE-STATUS
        GO TO FILE-ERROR
    END-IF.

    PERFORM UNTIL END-OF-FILE = 'Y'
        READ INFILE
            AT END
                MOVE 'Y' TO WS-EOF
            NOT AT END
                ADD 1 TO WS-REC-COUNT
                DISPLAY 'Record ' WS-REC-COUNT ': '
                ↪  FILE-RECORD
        END-READ
    END-PERFORM.

    CLOSE INFILE.
    DISPLAY 'File processed successfully. Total records read:
    ↪  ' WS-REC-COUNT.
    STOP RUN.

FILE-ERROR.
    DISPLAY 'File open error encountered. File-status = '
    ↪  WS-FILE-STATUS.
    STOP RUN.
```

Chapter 49

Closing Files with the CLOSE Statement

Formal Syntax and Operational Semantics

The $CLOSE$ statement is defined by a precise syntactical pattern within the COBOL language specification. This statement consists solely of the $CLOSE$ keyword followed by one or more file identifiers that have been previously declared in the DATA or ENVIRONMENT DIVISION. The formal grammar mandates that the statement appear at specific locations within the PROCEDURE DIVISION, adhering to the fixed-format rules that enforce columnar integrity and positional requirements. As an operation, the $CLOSE$ statement serves as a deterministic command that signals the termination of file-based input/output activities. When executed, it guarantees that all preceding file operations—such as buffered writes or read completions—are concluded in an orderly fashion. The execution of the $CLOSE$ statement thereby initiates a series of internal procedures within the runtime environment, including the flushing of internal buffers and the updating of file status indicators, ensuring that file handles are properly deallocated and that the program state is accurately synchronized with the underlying operating system.

Mechanisms for Data Integrity Assurance

Data integrity during and after the file closing process is paramount in ensuring that all intended changes to persistent storage are firmly established. The invocation of the $CLOSE$ statement plays a critical role in this verification process by compelling a final commit of any outstanding file operations. In systems where buffering mechanisms are employed to optimize performance, the proper termination of file access necessitates a complete and irreversible flush of these buffers. The operational semantics of the $CLOSE$ statement require that every record written during the session is accurately transferred from volatile storage to the permanency of disk or other secondary storage media. This atomic operation, performed as part of the file closure, prevents transient states where modifications could otherwise be lost due to unforeseen interruptions. The runtime protocol associated with the $CLOSE$ operation also checks for consistency and potential errors during the final file synchronization phase, updating system status codes accordingly to reflect either a successful closure or the detection of anomalies that might compromise data reliability.

System Integration and Resource Management

The process governed by the $CLOSE$ statement extends beyond mere syntactic termination and is deeply integrated with the operating system's I/O control mechanisms. Upon execution, the statement establishes a communication pathway between the language runtime and the host operating system, triggering a series of system-level routines dedicated to finalizing file transactions. These routines perform an array of tasks, such as the deallocation of file control blocks, the release of allocated internal buffers, and the reversion of system locks that were maintained during active file operations. The tightly coupled interaction ensures that the deactivation of the file descriptor is completed under strict consistency checks, thereby preserving the logical state of both the program and the underlying file system. This integration is crucial in environments where multiple file accesses occur concurrently, as it prevents resource contention and guarantees the availability of system resources for subsequent processes. The structured termination via the $CLOSE$ statement thereby reinforces the overall robustness and reliability of the file management subsystem within COBOL-based applications.

Cobol Code Snippet

```
IDENTIFICATION DIVISION.
PROGRAM-ID. CLOSEFILEPROGRAM.
AUTHOR. Maxwell_Vector.

ENVIRONMENT DIVISION.
INPUT-OUTPUT SECTION.
FILE-CONTROL.
    SELECT DATAFILE ASSIGN TO "DATAFILE.DAT"
        ORGANIZATION IS SEQUENTIAL
        FILE STATUS IS WS-FILE-STATUS.

DATA DIVISION.
FILE SECTION.
FD  DATAFILE.
01  DATA-RECORD.
    05  FIELD1          PIC X(50).

WORKING-STORAGE SECTION.
01  WS-FILE-STATUS      PIC XX.
01  WS-MSG              PIC X(80)
    VALUE "Operation completed successfully.".
01  WS-ERR-MSG          PIC X(80)
    VALUE "Operation failed with file status: ".
01  WS-FLUSH-COMMIT     PIC X(80)
    VALUE "Flushing buffers and committing changes.".
01  WS-VALUE1           PIC 9(4) VALUE 1000.
01  WS-VALUE2           PIC 9(4) VALUE 250.
01  WS-TOTAL            PIC 9(5).

PROCEDURE DIVISION.
MAIN-PARA.
    OPEN OUTPUT DATAFILE.
    IF WS-FILE-STATUS NOT = "00"
        DISPLAY "Error: Cannot open file. Status: "
        ↪  WS-FILE-STATUS
        STOP RUN
    END-IF.

    PERFORM WRITE-RECORDS.
    PERFORM ADDITION-EXAMPLE.
    PERFORM FLUSH-AND-CLOSE.
    PERFORM VERIFY-FILE-CLOSURE.

    STOP RUN.
```

```
WRITE-RECORDS.
    MOVE "This is record 1" TO FIELD1.
    WRITE DATA-RECORD.
    MOVE "This is record 2" TO FIELD1.
    WRITE DATA-RECORD.
    EXIT.

ADDITION-EXAMPLE.
    *------------------------------------------------------*
    * Demonstrates an important equation:
    *     WS-TOTAL = WS-VALUE1 + WS-VALUE2
    * This computation illustrates how numeric formulas can
    ↪  be
    * executed within the program logic.
    *------------------------------------------------------*
    COMPUTE WS-TOTAL = WS-VALUE1 + WS-VALUE2.
    DISPLAY "Equation: WS-TOTAL = WS-VALUE1 + WS-VALUE2".
    DISPLAY "Computed Total: " WS-TOTAL.
    EXIT.

FLUSH-AND-CLOSE.
    *------------------------------------------------------*
    * Simulate flushing of internal buffers and initiate the
    ↪  CLOSE
    * procedure to finalize file operations. This ensures
    ↪  that all
    * buffered writes are committed and file descriptors
    ↪  released.
    *------------------------------------------------------*
    DISPLAY WS-FLUSH-COMMIT.
    CLOSE DATAFILE.
    IF WS-FILE-STATUS = "00"
        DISPLAY "File closed successfully."
    ELSE
        DISPLAY WS-ERR-MSG WS-FILE-STATUS
    END-IF.
    EXIT.

VERIFY-FILE-CLOSURE.
    *------------------------------------------------------*
    * Final integrity check to verify atomically that the
    ↪  file has
    * been closed and that the internal state is correctly
    ↪  synchronized
    * with the operating system.
    *------------------------------------------------------*
    IF WS-FILE-STATUS = "00"
        DISPLAY "Integrity Check: File closure is complete
        ↪  and consistent."
    ELSE
        DISPLAY "Integrity Check: Anomalies detected in file
        ↪  closure."
    END-IF.
```

EXIT.

Chapter 50

Reading Files using the READ Statement

Syntactic Structure of the $READ$ Statement

The $READ$ statement is formally defined by the COBOL language specification as a directive that initiates the transfer of data from an external file into the program's internal memory structures. Its syntax mandates that the statement begin with the literal keyword $READ$, immediately followed by one or more file identifiers that correspond to files declared in the FILE SECTION. The statement may be augmented by optional clauses, such as $AT END$, which designate alternative processing pathways when the terminal condition of the file is reached. In this syntactic framework, the placement of each lexical element is governed by fixed-format requirements that ensure positional and structural consistency within the source code. This formal definition ensures that the mapping between the text of the statement and its operational effect is unambiguous and rigorously enforced by the compiler.

Operational Semantics and Clause Options

The operational semantics of the $READ$ statement encapsulate the deterministic and atomic nature of record retrieval in COBOL. Upon invocation, the runtime system processes the statement by

216

interacting with the designated file's input channel, retrieving the next available record in the aligned data stream. The processing environment guarantees that all internal buffering operations and file pointer adjustments occur prior to any subsequent program execution. Clause options, such as $AT END$, are syntactically coupled with the basic $READ$ directive and provide a conditional branch that is executed when the file has been completely traversed. Other optional clauses, for example those designed to handle invalid key conditions in indexed file access, further illustrate an integrated mechanism for managing exceptional states. These clause options collectively ensure that the status of the record retrieval process is accurately propagated through system-provided file status codes and that such outcomes are immediately available for conditional logic embedded within the program.

Techniques for Efficient Record Retrieval

The process of reading records is underpinned by a strategic alignment between the file's physical structure and the program's internal data layouts, as defined in the DATA DIVISION. During a $READ$ operation, the runtime system transposes the raw data from external storage into preallocated memory areas whose layout is rigorously specified by the record definitions. This mapping is essential for maintaining the integrity of data types and for ensuring that field boundaries are respected throughout the retrieval process. In many instances, buffering mechanisms inherent to the operating environment are leveraged to prefetch data, thereby optimizing the throughput of sequential file access. Additionally, when files are organized in indexed or relative formats, the $READ$ statement operates in conjunction with auxiliary routines that facilitate direct access to the desired record, thus minimizing latency and enhancing overall performance. The interplay between these techniques exemplifies the balance between deterministic I/O operations and performance optimization strategies within the COBOL paradigm.

Error Propagation, End-of-File, and Status Management

Robust error handling is an integral aspect of the $READ$ statement and is manifested through a systematic approach to status management. Immediately following the execution of a $READ$ operation, the runtime system assesses a set of file status indicators that reflect the outcome of the record retrieval. These indicators are instrumental in discerning between a successful read, the occurrence of an error, or the activation of the $AT END$ clause. In the event of an error, a nonzero file status code is generated and made available for subsequent conditional evaluation, thereby enabling the program to invoke appropriate remedial procedures. The mechanism for recognizing an end-of-file condition is explicitly tied to the presence of the $AT END$ clause, which directs the control flow to specialized handling routines designed to address the cessation of input. This rigorous approach to status management ensures that every read operation is accompanied by a precise recording of its outcome, thereby facilitating a coherent and reliable model of file-based data processing.

Cobol Code Snippet

```
        IDENTIFICATION DIVISION.
        PROGRAM-ID. FILE-READ-ALGO.
        AUTHOR. Maxwell_Vector.
        INSTALLATION. "Your Site".
        DATE-WRITTEN. 2024-10-09.

        ENVIRONMENT DIVISION.
        INPUT-OUTPUT SECTION.
        FILE-CONTROL.
            SELECT INPUT-FILE ASSIGN TO "INPUT.DAT"
                ORGANIZATION IS SEQUENTIAL
                ACCESS MODE IS SEQUENTIAL
                FILE STATUS IS WS-FILE-STATUS.

        DATA DIVISION.
        FILE SECTION.
        FD  INPUT-FILE.
        01  INPUT-RECORD.
            05 REC-NUM1        PIC 9(5).
            05 REC-NUM2        PIC 9(5).
            05 FILLER          PIC X(70).
```

```cobol
WORKING-STORAGE SECTION.
01 WS-FILE-STATUS      PIC XX.
   88  STATUS-OK                 VALUE "00".
01 WS-END-OF-FILE      PIC X VALUE "N".
   88  EOF-REACHED               VALUE "Y".
01 WS-REC-COUNT        PIC 9(5) VALUE 0.
01 WS-SUM              PIC 9(9) VALUE 0.
01 WS-AVERAGE          PIC 9(5)V99 VALUE 0.
01 WS-CALCULATION      PIC 9(9)V99 VALUE 0.
01 WS-MULTIPLIER       PIC 9(3) VALUE 2.
01 WS-DIVISOR          PIC 9(3) VALUE 3.
01 WS-DISPLAY-MSG      PIC X(80).


PROCEDURE DIVISION.
MAIN-PROGRAM.
    OPEN INPUT INPUT-FILE
    IF WS-FILE-STATUS NOT = "00"
        DISPLAY "Error opening file. Status: " WS-FILE-STATUS
        STOP RUN
    END-IF.

    PERFORM UNTIL WS-END-OF-FILE = "Y"
        READ INPUT-FILE
            AT END
                MOVE "Y" TO WS-END-OF-FILE
            NOT AT END
                ADD 1 TO WS-REC-COUNT
                PERFORM PROCESS-RECORD
        END-READ
    END-PERFORM.

    IF WS-REC-COUNT > 0
        COMPUTE WS-AVERAGE = WS-SUM / WS-REC-COUNT
    ELSE
        MOVE 0 TO WS-AVERAGE
    END-IF.

    MOVE "Total Records Processed: " TO WS-DISPLAY-MSG
    DISPLAY WS-DISPLAY-MSG WS-REC-COUNT.
    MOVE "Cumulative Sum of Calculated Values: " TO
    ↪  WS-DISPLAY-MSG
    DISPLAY WS-DISPLAY-MSG WS-SUM.
    MOVE "Average of Calculated Values: " TO WS-DISPLAY-MSG
    DISPLAY WS-DISPLAY-MSG WS-AVERAGE.

    CLOSE INPUT-FILE.
    STOP RUN.

PROCESS-RECORD.
    *--------------------------------------------------
    * This paragraph demonstrates an important calculation:
    * WS-CALCULATION = (REC-NUM1 * WS-MULTIPLIER) + (REC-NUM2
    ↪  / WS-DIVISOR)
```

```
* The computed value is then added to WS-SUM for summary
↪   statistics.
*--------------------------------------------------
COMPUTE WS-CALCULATION = (REC-NUM1 * WS-MULTIPLIER) +
↪   (REC-NUM2 / WS-DIVISOR)
ADD WS-CALCULATION TO WS-SUM.
DISPLAY "Record " WS-REC-COUNT " processed. Calculation =
↪   " WS-CALCULATION.
EXIT.
```

Chapter 51

Writing Files using the WRITE Statement

Syntactic Structure of the $WRITE$ Statement

The $WRITE$ statement is defined by the COBOL language standard as a directive to transfer data from internal working storage into an external file, conforming to a predefined record layout. In its formal syntax, the statement commences with the literal $WRITE$ keyword, immediately followed by a file identifier that corresponds to an entry declared in the FILE SECTION of the DATA DIVISION. The precise arrangement and positional requirements of each lexical element are dictated by COBOL's fixed-format conventions, which ensure that keywords, file names, and associated clauses reside in their mandated columns. This rigor in syntactic specification guarantees that every instance of the $WRITE$ statement is unambiguously interpretable by the compiler, thereby enforcing consistent behavior during both compilation and runtime digitization.

Operational Semantics and Execution Flow

Upon execution, the $WRITE$ statement initiates an atomic sequence of operations that culminates in the output and storage of a record. At runtime, the data stored in program-defined memory regions is marshaled into a temporary record structure matching the layout specified in the FILE SECTION. This procedural event guarantees that the record, once constructed and fully validated against its field definitions, is transmitted to the file's I/O subsystem. The operation is strand-synchronized such that any modification to file pointers or buffering mechanisms occurs prior to subsequent processing. Additionally, the COBOL runtime environment inspects the status of the write operation immediately after execution, thereby ensuring that any manifestation of an exception or deviation from the expected behavior is recorded through file status indicators.

Clause Options and Key Modifiers

The $WRITE$ statement may be accompanied by optional clause options that modulate its standard execution and provide enhanced control over output operations. For instance, modifiers intended for record-commitment and file-locking behaviors are incorporated to refine the interaction between program flow and external file management. These optional clauses, when present, allow the system to adapt the write operation to a variety of conditions, such as ensuring that the record is appended in a manner that respects the underlying file organization or that concurrent write attempts do not lead to data corruption. The syntax of these clauses is carefully interwoven into the primary statement such that each additional directive complements the predefined structure without compromising the overall formatting requirements dictated by the language standard.

File Integration, Data Consistency, and Status Management

The integration of the $WRITE$ statement with the file subsystem is a critical aspect of its operation. The statement transfers a meticulously defined record from internal memory into an external storage medium, ensuring that the record fields adhere to the predetermined layout described in the DATA DIVISION. This interaction is supported by internal buffering strategies that allow for the transient retention of output data until the commit phase is completed, thereby maintaining data consistency across variable system states. Concurrently, the propagation of file status codes immediately after the write operation provides an indispensable mechanism for error detection and monitoring of the file I/O process. These status codes serve as verifiable checkpoints, enabling the system to execute additional error-handling routines if a deviation from normal operation is observed.

Cobol Code Snippet

```
        IDENTIFICATION DIVISION.
        PROGRAM-ID. WRITEFILE.

        ENVIRONMENT DIVISION.
        INPUT-OUTPUT SECTION.
        FILE-CONTROL.
            SELECT OUTPUT-FILE ASSIGN TO "output.dat"
                ORGANIZATION IS SEQUENTIAL
                FILE STATUS IS WS-FILE-STATUS.

        DATA DIVISION.
        FILE SECTION.
        FD  OUTPUT-FILE.
        01  OUT-RECORD.
            05  OUT-LABEL      PIC X(15) VALUE "RECORD: ".
            05  NUM-1          PIC 9(4).
            05  PLUS-SIGN      PIC X VALUE "+".
            05  NUM-2          PIC 9(4).
            05  EQUALS-SIGN    PIC X VALUE "=".
            05  RESULT         PIC 9(6)V99.

        WORKING-STORAGE SECTION.
        01  WS-FILE-STATUS     PIC XX VALUE SPACES.
        01  WS-NUMBER1         PIC 9(4) VALUE 1000.
        01  WS-NUMBER2         PIC 9(4) VALUE 2500.
        01  WS-RESULT          PIC 9(6)V99 VALUE ZERO.
        01  WS-DISPLAY-MSG     PIC X(50) VALUE "File write
        ↪  operation completed successfully.".

        PROCEDURE DIVISION.
        MAIN-PARA.
            OPEN OUTPUT OUTPUT-FILE.
            IF WS-FILE-STATUS NOT = "00"
                DISPLAY "Error opening file. Status: " WS-FILE-STATUS
                STOP RUN
            END-IF.

            *-------------------------------------------------
            * Compute the average of two numbers as an example
            ↪  formula.
```

```
* The equation used is: WS-RESULT = (WS-NUMBER1 +
↪  WS-NUMBER2) / 2.
* This serves as a representative arithmetic algorithm.
*-------------------------------------------------
COMPUTE WS-RESULT = (WS-NUMBER1 + WS-NUMBER2) / 2.
MOVE WS-NUMBER1 TO NUM-1.
MOVE WS-NUMBER2 TO NUM-2.
MOVE WS-RESULT  TO RESULT.

* Write the constructed record to the external file.
WRITE OUT-RECORD.
IF WS-FILE-STATUS NOT = "00"
    DISPLAY "Error writing to file. Status: "
    ↪  WS-FILE-STATUS
    STOP RUN
END-IF.

CLOSE OUTPUT-FILE.
DISPLAY WS-DISPLAY-MSG.
STOP RUN.
```

Chapter 52

Updating Records with the REWRITE Statement

Lexical and Syntactic Analysis

The $REWRITE$ statement in COBOL constitutes an essential construct for effecting in-place modifications of existing file records. Its syntactic formulation is governed by the stringent fixed-format conventions intrinsic to the language, wherein the precise positioning of keywords, record identifiers, and any auxiliary clauses is mandated by the COBOL standard. This lexical structure ensures that the $REWRITE$ directive is parsed with unerring consistency, establishing an unequivocal correspondence between the in-memory representation of data and the physical record layout as defined in the FILE SECTION of the DATA DIVISION. The operation presupposes that the record structure, as previously delineated, is available and unambiguously identifiable, thereby obviating potential ambiguities during the update process.

Operational Semantics and Execution Characteristics

At runtime, the execution of the $REWRITE$ statement unfolds as an atomic operation that systematically replaces the pre-existing file record with the modified data resident in working storage. This process is characterized by a multi-phase execution flow that begins with the consolidation of the updated data into a temporary record buffer conforming to the file's defined structure. The subsequent traversal of the I/O subsystem ensures that the in-memory record is accurately mapped to and overwrites its persistent counterpart. Integral to this mechanism is the synchronization of file pointers, which maintains the logical sequence of file records and guarantees that the rewriting occurs without disrupting the overall file organization. Immediate post-operation evaluation via file status codes enables the runtime environment to detect and report any anomalies arising during the update, thereby providing a robust framework for error identification.

File Integration, Data Integrity, and Error Handling

The invocation of the $REWRITE$ statement is critically interwoven with the file integration subsystem, where the imperative of data integrity is paramount. Prior to the update, a rigorous validation mechanism verifies that the in-memory record adheres to the structural and format specifications prescribed in the FILE SECTION. This alignment is fundamental to preserving consistency between the transient and persistent representations of data. During the rewrite process, internal buffering schemes temporarily retain the updated record, ensuring that the commit phase is executed only upon successful reconciliation with the underlying file structure. Concurrently, file status indicators are meticulously monitored, furnishing immediate feedback regarding any deviations or errors encountered during the operation. Such vigilant error handling forms the cornerstone of reliable record updates, as it facilitates the prompt detection and resolution of discrepancies that might otherwise compromise data fidelity.

Cobol Code Snippet

```
IDENTIFICATION DIVISION.
PROGRAM-ID. UPDATE-RECORD.

ENVIRONMENT DIVISION.
INPUT-OUTPUT SECTION.
FILE-CONTROL.
    SELECT STUDENT-FILE ASSIGN TO 'student.dat'
        ORGANIZATION IS SEQUENTIAL
        ACCESS MODE IS SEQUENTIAL
        FILE STATUS IS WS-FILE-STATUS.

DATA DIVISION.
FILE SECTION.
FD  STUDENT-FILE.
01  STUDENT-REC.
    05  STUDENT-ID        PIC 9(4).
    05  STUDENT-NAME      PIC X(20).
    05  ORIGINAL-SCORE    PIC 9(3).
    05  UPDATED-SCORE     PIC 9(3).

WORKING-STORAGE SECTION.
01  WS-FILE-STATUS     PIC XX.
    88 WS-FILE-OK      VALUE "00".
01  WS-END-FILE        PIC X VALUE "N".
    88 END-OF-FILE     VALUE "Y".
01  WS-TOTAL-SCORE     PIC 9(5) VALUE 0.
01  WS-RECORD-COUNT    PIC 9(4) VALUE 0.
01  WS-AVERAGE-SCORE   PIC 9(3) VALUE 0.

PROCEDURE DIVISION.
MAIN-PROCEDURE.
    OPEN I-O STUDENT-FILE
    PERFORM UNTIL WS-END-FILE = "Y"
        READ STUDENT-FILE
            AT END
                MOVE "Y" TO WS-END-FILE
            NOT AT END
                PERFORM UPDATE-AND-CALCULATE
        END-READ
    END-PERFORM
    IF WS-RECORD-COUNT > 0
        COMPUTE WS-AVERAGE-SCORE = WS-TOTAL-SCORE /
        ↪   WS-RECORD-COUNT
    ELSE
        MOVE 0 TO WS-AVERAGE-SCORE
    END-IF
    CLOSE STUDENT-FILE
    DISPLAY "Total Records Processed: " WS-RECORD-COUNT
    DISPLAY "Average Score: " WS-AVERAGE-SCORE
    STOP RUN.
```

```
UPDATE-AND-CALCULATE.
    ADD 1 TO WS-RECORD-COUNT
    ADD ORIGINAL-SCORE TO WS-TOTAL-SCORE
    *----------------------------------------------------
    * Important Equation:
    *   UPDATED-SCORE = ORIGINAL-SCORE + 5
    * This formula represents a simple bonus mechanism being
    ↪  applied
    * to the original score before rewriting the record.
    *----------------------------------------------------
    COMPUTE UPDATED-SCORE = ORIGINAL-SCORE + 5
    REWRITE STUDENT-REC
    IF WS-FILE-STATUS NOT = "00"
        DISPLAY "Error: REWRITE of record " STUDENT-ID "
        ↪  failed. Status: " WS-FILE-STATUS
    END-IF.
```

Chapter 53

Deleting Records with the DELETE Statement

Lexical and Syntactic Considerations

The DELETE statement in COBOL is defined by a precise lexical structure that adheres strictly to the fixed-format rules of the language. The syntax mandates that the keyword DELETE appear in an exact columnar position within the source code, ensuring that the record deletion directive is unambiguously identified by the compiler. This syntactic rigidity is necessitated by the underlying design of COBOL, where every character position carries semantic significance. In the context of file operations, the DELETE statement is accompanied by explicit references to file identifiers and may include conditional clauses that interact with file status variables. The lexical parsing mechanism ensures that each token, from keywords to delimiters, is recognized in conformity with the predefined grammar, thereby permitting a seamless transition from source code to machine-level interpretation.

Operational Semantics and Execution Analyses

At execution, the DELETE statement is processed as an atomic operation within the COBOL runtime environment, ensuring that record deletion occurs in a discrete and indivisible step. During this phase, the system validates the current state of the indexed or sequential file against the criteria specified in the statement. The operation initiates by locating the target record using the file control metadata available in the DATA DIVISION's FILE SECTION. Once identified, the deletion operation engages internal buffering mechanisms which temporarily remove the record from the in-memory representation. This process is synchronized with the I/O subsystem such that the physical file is updated in a manner that reflects the removal instantaneously. The DELETE operation is accompanied by rigorous error checking, with file status indicators being updated to reflect success (typically denoted by a status code such as 00) or error conditions arising during the deletion attempt. The exhaustive evaluation of these status codes is essential for diagnosing potential anomalies, as the robustness of file manipulation hinges upon the accurate orchestration of this operational sequence.

File Management and Data Integrity Mechanisms

Record deletion using the DELETE statement is integrally tied to the underlying data integrity and file management protocols within COBOL. When a record is deleted, the system must ensure that the overall structure and coherence of the file remain intact. In cases where files are stored sequentially, deletion may result in the creation of a gap within the storage sequence; hence, subsequent procedures often involve file reorganization to eliminate such discontinuities. The deletion process is preconditioned on prior validation checks that confirm adherence to the schema defined in the FILE SECTION, thus preventing inadvertent removal of data that does not conform to expected formats. Additionally, the management of file pointers during the deletion process is critical in preserving the logical sequence of records, which is fundamental to both data retrieval and subsequent processing tasks. An intrinsic part of the DELETE operation is the continuous monitoring of file status codes, which provides real-time feedback regarding the success of the transaction. This meticulous approach to error handling ensures that any discrepancies between the in-memory state and the persistent storage are promptly identified and addressed, thereby upholding the overall integrity of the data repository.

Cobol Code Snippet

```
IDENTIFICATION DIVISION.
PROGRAM-ID. RECORD-DELETE.

ENVIRONMENT DIVISION.
CONFIGURATION SECTION.
SOURCE-COMPUTER. IBM-370.
OBJECT-COMPUTER. IBM-370.

INPUT-OUTPUT SECTION.
FILE-CONTROL.
    SELECT IN-FILE ASSIGN TO 'DATAFILE.DAT'
        ORGANIZATION IS INDEXED
        ACCESS MODE IS DYNAMIC
        RECORD KEY IS REC-ID
        FILE STATUS IS WS-FILE-STATUS.

DATA DIVISION.
FILE SECTION.
FD  IN-FILE.
01  RECORD-RECEIVE.
    05  REC-ID          PIC X(10).
    05  REC-DATA        PIC X(50).

WORKING-STORAGE SECTION.
01  WS-FILE-STATUS      PIC XX.
01  WS-EOF              PIC X VALUE 'N'.
    88  END-OF-FILE     VALUE 'Y'.
    88  NOT-END-OF-FILE VALUE 'N'.
01  WS-DELETE-KEY       PIC X(10) VALUE 'DELREC001'.
01  WS-MESSAGE          PIC X(30).

PROCEDURE DIVISION.
MAIN-PARA.
    OPEN I-O IN-FILE.
    PERFORM UNTIL END-OF-FILE

        READ IN-FILE
            AT END
                MOVE 'Y' TO WS-EOF
            NOT AT END
```

```
                IF REC-ID = WS-DELETE-KEY
                    DELETE IN-FILE
                        INVALID KEY
                            MOVE "ERROR: DELETE FAILED" TO
                            ↪  WS-MESSAGE
                            DISPLAY WS-MESSAGE
                        NOT INVALID KEY
                            MOVE "RECORD SUCCESSFULLY
                            ↪  DELETED" TO WS-MESSAGE
                            DISPLAY WS-MESSAGE
                    END-IF
                ELSE
                    DISPLAY "Record " REC-ID " retained."
                END-IF
        END-READ
    END-PERFORM.
    CLOSE IN-FILE.
    STOP RUN.
```

Chapter 54

Managing End-of-File Conditions

EOF Detection and Recognition

Within file processing architectures, the detection of the end-of-file condition is fundamental to maintaining the determinism and consistency of data access operations. The EOF condition is defined by the cessation of valid data retrieval, which is typically identified through a combination of system-level flags and explicit status codes. In many implementations, the file reading mechanism continuously monitors the returned data size or token and transitions to an EOF state when the underlying input stream yields no further records. This transition is governed by the precepts of formal language theory as applied to I/O systems, where the EOF marker serves as a sentinel, denoted abstractly as EOF, indicating that the data source has been completely exhausted. The lexical analysis of the file stream, therefore, incorporates systematic scanning for this marker, ensuring that all subsequent read operations are precluded once the terminal condition is confirmed.

Buffering and State Synchronization in File I/O

The management of the EOF condition is inextricably linked with the mechanisms of internal buffering and state maintenance inherent in file I/O systems. Buffers serve to mediate between high-speed memory operations and the relatively slower physical I/O, thereby necessitating a protocol for synchronizing the logical file pointer with the actual data stream. When the end-of-file marker is reached, the buffer management unit is designed to update the internal state, thereby preventing the accidental retrieval of spurious or residual data. This synchronization process is executed through a cascade of checks, where each read operation is cross-referenced with the buffer contents and the file system's metadata. The resulting state machine, which may be modeled by a finite automaton, ensures that the transition to the end-of-file state is both atomic and irreversible. Furthermore, the integration of these low-level operational details with the higher-level semantic constructs of the programming language guarantees that subsequent file operations are executed within a consistent and error-free context.

Error Propagation and Data Integrity Assurance

The robust handling of end-of-file conditions plays a crucial role in safeguarding data integrity across file operations. As the EOF condition is detected, the system's error-handling infrastructure is invoked to propagate status indicators that reflect either a benign termination of the data stream or an anomalous state that could potentially compromise subsequent processing. The file I/O subsystem employs rigorous error-checking protocols that compare the expected behavior—as dictated by the FILE SECTION definitions—with the actual state of the input stream. Any divergence, particularly in scenarios where the logical file pointer exceeds the boundary of available records, triggers an immediate update of the error status flags. These flags, often represented as two-digit codes, are then utilized by higher-level routines to implement conditional logic that precludes further file manipulation in the event of integrity violations. Such layered error propagation ensures that the system remains resilient, thereby upholding the overall coherence of both in-memory and persistent data representations.

System-Level Integration and Operational Semantics

The operational semantics governing end-of-file condition management are woven into the fabric of the I/O system's design, interfacing directly with both software and hardware components. At the hardware level, the physical medium's characteristics impose constraints on data retrieval speeds and error recovery techniques, while at the software level, detailed semantic models prescribe the precise sequences of operations to be executed upon reaching the EOF state. This integration ensures that any file operation that signals termination is seamlessly reconciled with ongoing processing tasks. In particular, the transition to, and recognition of, an EOF condition is synchronized with the internal buffering mechanisms and the corresponding update of file status registers. Such synchronization is critical; it guarantees that the state of the system is consistent with the current processing context and that no inadvertent read or write operations occur after the EOF has been reached. Through this seamless integration of hardware-level imperatives with high-level language constructs, file operations are rendered both reliable and free from processing errors.

Cobol Code Snippet

```
IDENTIFICATION DIVISION.
PROGRAM-ID. EOFHANDLER.

ENVIRONMENT DIVISION.
INPUT-OUTPUT SECTION.
FILE-CONTROL.
    SELECT INFILE ASSIGN TO 'input.dat'
        ORGANIZATION IS SEQUENTIAL.

DATA DIVISION.
FILE SECTION.
FD  INFILE.
01  INREC                   PIC X(80).

WORKING-STORAGE SECTION.
01  WS-END-OF-FILE          PIC X        VALUE 'N'.
01  WS-ERROR-CODE           PIC 99       VALUE ZERO.
01  WS-ERROR-STATUS         PIC X(2)     VALUE SPACES.
01  WS-CALC-VALUE           PIC 9(5)V99  VALUE 0.
01  WS-READ-VALUE           PIC 9(5)V99  VALUE 0.
```

```
01  WS-RECORD-COUNT            PIC 9(5)     VALUE 0.
01  WS-AVERAGE                 PIC 9(5)V99 VALUE 0.

PROCEDURE DIVISION.
MAIN-PARA.
    OPEN INPUT INFILE.
    PERFORM UNTIL WS-END-OF-FILE = 'Y'
        READ INFILE
            AT END
                MOVE 'Y' TO WS-END-OF-FILE
            NOT AT END
                PERFORM PROCESS-RECORD
        END-READ
    END-PERFORM.
    IF WS-RECORD-COUNT > 0
        COMPUTE WS-AVERAGE = WS-CALC-VALUE / WS-RECORD-COUNT
    ELSE
        MOVE 0 TO WS-AVERAGE
    END-IF.
    DISPLAY "Total Records Processed: " WS-RECORD-COUNT.
    DISPLAY "Cumulative Total Value : " WS-CALC-VALUE.
    DISPLAY "Average Value          : " WS-AVERAGE.
    CLOSE INFILE.
    STOP RUN.


PROCESS-RECORD.
    ADD 1 TO WS-RECORD-COUNT.
    *--------------------------------------------------
    * Convert a portion of the record (first 7 characters)
    * to a numeric value. This value represents a key
    * component in the overall computation algorithm.
    *--------------------------------------------------
    MOVE FUNCTION NUMVAL(INREC(1:7)) TO WS-READ-VALUE.
    COMPUTE WS-CALC-VALUE = WS-CALC-VALUE + WS-READ-VALUE.
    *--------------------------------------------------
    * Check for error condition: a zero value may indicate
    * an unexpected or missing data element. Set error code.
    *--------------------------------------------------
    IF WS-READ-VALUE = 0
        MOVE 99 TO WS-ERROR-CODE
        MOVE 'ER' TO WS-ERROR-STATUS
        DISPLAY "Error: Zero value encountered. Error Code: "
        ↪  WS-ERROR-CODE
    ELSE
        MOVE 0 TO WS-ERROR-CODE
        MOVE 'OK' TO WS-ERROR-STATUS
    END-IF.
    *--------------------------------------------------
    * Display the details of the processed record,
    * including a running total and the error status.
    *--------------------------------------------------
    DISPLAY "Processed Record " WS-RECORD-COUNT
            ": Value=" WS-READ-VALUE
```

236

```
          " Running Total=" WS-CALC-VALUE
          " Status=" WS-ERROR-STATUS.
```

Chapter 55

Structuring Modular Programs

Foundations of Modularity in COBOL

Modularity in COBOL is predicated on the classical principles of software decomposition, whereby a monolithic program is dissected into semantically coherent units. The elementary tenets involve the segregation of functionality into discrete subunits possessing well-defined responsibilities. Such segmentation facilitates a structured environment in which each module operates as an independent building block, enhancing clarity and reducing the complexity inherent in large-scale procedural code. A modular COBOL program is often characterized by the clear delineation among various divisions, wherein the procedural logic is partitioned into units that mirror the logical decomposition of tasks. This approach is underpinned by an adherence to the concepts of low coupling and high cohesion, ensuring that inter-module dependencies are minimized while each module maintains a concentrated focus on its designated computational domain.

Architectural Design and Code Decomposition

The architectural framework for modular programming in COBOL necessitates a disciplined method for decomposing the overall problem into manageable components. This is achieved by leveraging the inherent structure provided by the language's divisions, thereby facilitating the encapsulation of related procedures within self-contained modules. Within the procedural division, for example, a clear demarcation of paragraphs and sections serves to delineate logical groupings of operations that perform distinct tasks. When a program is dissected into modules, the resulting architecture allows each segment to be developed and verified independently, contributing to an overall structure in which the program P is conceptualized as a union of subprograms $M_1, M_2, \ldots, M_n$, with each module M_i handling a specific subset of the processing requirements. This methodical decomposition permits the isolation of functionalities that are conceptually and operationally distinct, thereby promoting the maintainability and scalability of the software.

Module Interfaces and Communication

The establishment of well-defined interfaces is a critical component of modular programming in COBOL. Each module must expose a controlled interface that delineates the parameters through which data is exchanged. In the COBOL environment, such interfaces are typically manifested via the LINKAGE Section and associated CALL statements, which govern the manner in which procedures invoke one another and transfer control. By carefully delineating these interfaces, the design ensures that any interaction between modules occurs through predetermined channels, thereby mitigating the risk of unintended side effects and promoting a clear contractual relationship among the individual program components. This explicit specification of inter-module communication protocols enables the enforcement of encapsulation boundaries, ensuring that the internal workings of a module remain insulated from external influences and that only the agreed-upon data representations are exchanged during routine operations.

Best Practices in Code Segmentation and Encapsulation

The systematic division of code into modules demands adherence to best practices that optimize both the readability and maintainability of the program. A primary practice is the rigorous application of naming conventions and documentation standards, which provide an intuitive mapping between a module's designated function and its implementation. Each module is expected to encapsulate a discrete slice of the overall problem domain, thereby minimizing redundant code and alleviating the cognitive load during program evolution. Structural encapsulation is further enhanced by ensuring that modules possess minimal overlapping functionality, with well-defined control pathways that streamline debugging and testing processes. The deliberate segregation of concerns permits an environment where modifications to one module incur minimal repercussions on others, thereby fostering a design in which the integrity of the program is preserved even as individual modules undergo iterative refinement. In this paradigm, the architectural emphasis is placed on the convergence of modular boundaries and the explicit declaration of module interfaces, thus ensuring that each segment contributes to a coherent and unified program structure.

Cobol Code Snippet

```
IDENTIFICATION DIVISION.
PROGRAM-ID. MODULAR-DEMO.
AUTHOR. Maxwell_Vector.
REMARKS. "This program demonstrates modular design in COBOL
  ↪ by dividing processing into discrete modules. It shows
  ↪ arithmetic operations, array processing, and inter-module
  ↪ communication using well-defined interfaces."

ENVIRONMENT DIVISION.
CONFIGURATION SECTION.
SOURCE-COMPUTER. IBM-370.
OBJECT-COMPUTER. IBM-370.

DATA DIVISION.
WORKING-STORAGE SECTION.
*---------------------------------------------------------------
* Declaration of numeric variables used for basic arithmetic.
*---------------------------------------------------------------
01  WS-NUMBER1      PIC 9(4) VALUE 0025.
01  WS-NUMBER2      PIC 9(4) VALUE 0015.
01  WS-SUM          PIC 9(5) VALUE ZERO.
01  WS-PRODUCT      PIC 9(7) VALUE ZERO.


*---------------------------------------------------------------
* Declarations for array processing module.
```

```
*----------------------------------------------------------------
01  WS-COUNT        PIC 9(2) VALUE 5.
01  WS-SUM-ARRAY    PIC 9(7) VALUE ZERO.
01  WS-AVG          PIC 9(5)V99 VALUE ZERO.
01  I               PIC 9(2) VALUE ZERO.
01  WS-ARRAY.
    05  WS-ARRAY-ELEM OCCURS 5 TIMES PIC 9(4) VALUE ZERO.


PROCEDURE DIVISION.
MAIN-PROGRAM.
    *----------------------------------------------------------------
    * Main program acting as a coordinator to call each
    ↪  module.
    *----------------------------------------------------------------
    PERFORM CALCULATION-MODULE
    PERFORM ARRAY-PROCESSING-MODULE
    PERFORM DISPLAY-MODULE
    STOP RUN.

CALCULATION-MODULE.
    *------------------------------------------------------------
    * Module: CALCULATION-MODULE
    * Purpose: Perform basic arithmetic operations.
    * Equations:
    *     WS-SUM = WS-NUMBER1 + WS-NUMBER2
    *     WS-PRODUCT = WS-NUMBER1 * WS-NUMBER2
    *------------------------------------------------------------
    ADD WS-NUMBER1 TO WS-NUMBER2 GIVING WS-SUM.
    MULTIPLY WS-NUMBER1 BY WS-NUMBER2 GIVING WS-PRODUCT.
    EXIT.

ARRAY-PROCESSING-MODULE.
    *------------------------------------------------------------
    * Module: ARRAY-PROCESSING-MODULE
    * Purpose: Populate an array using a formula and compute:
    *     For each element: WS-ARRAY-ELEM(I) = WS-NUMBER1 + (I
    ↪  * 2)
    *     Then, WS-SUM-ARRAY accumulates the sum of these
    ↪  elements.
    *     Finally, calculate average as WS-AVG = WS-SUM-ARRAY
    ↪  / WS-COUNT.
    *------------------------------------------------------------
    PERFORM VARYING I FROM 1 BY 1 UNTIL I > WS-COUNT
        COMPUTE WS-ARRAY-ELEM(I) = WS-NUMBER1 + (I * 2)
        ADD WS-ARRAY-ELEM(I) TO WS-SUM-ARRAY
    END-PERFORM.
    COMPUTE WS-AVG = WS-SUM-ARRAY / WS-COUNT.
    EXIT.

DISPLAY-MODULE.
    *------------------------------------------------------------
    * Module: DISPLAY-MODULE
```

```
* Purpose: Output the results from the arithmetic and
↪  array
* processing modules.
*---------------------------------------------------
DISPLAY "------- Modular Programming Demo -------".
DISPLAY "Sum (NUMBER1 + NUMBER2): " WS-SUM.
DISPLAY "Product (NUMBER1 * NUMBER2): " WS-PRODUCT.
DISPLAY "Sum of Array Elements: " WS-SUM-ARRAY.
DISPLAY "Average of Array Elements: " WS-AVG.
EXIT.
```

Chapter 56

Subprogram Creation and the CALL Statement

Theoretical Framework of Subprogram Creation

Modular design in procedural languages is predicated upon the isolation of algorithmically discrete tasks into self-contained units. The concept of a subprogram emerges as an abstraction that encapsulates a specific domain of functionality, thereby decoupling distinct operations from the monolithic structure of the overall application. In formal terms, the complete program can be represented as

$$P = \bigcup_{i=1}^{n} M_i,$$

where each M_i corresponds to a subprogram that embodies a coherent subset of operational logic. Such a formulation underscores the emphasis on minimizing interdependencies and promoting independent verification of each constituent module. The theoretical underpinnings of subprogram creation advocate for a partitioned design approach that enhances both the rigorous correctness of the implementation and the long-term maintainability of the system.

Architectural Considerations and Interface Specification

The architectural design of subprograms necessitates the articulation of clearly defined interfaces that serve as the conduit for data exchange between the calling program and the invoked module. In this context, the interface is characterized via an explicit declaration of parameter lists and data structures within the subprogram's environment. Such an interface ensures that parameters

$$p_1, p_2, \ldots, p_k$$

are transmitted reliably from the caller to the subprogram, thereby enforcing a stringent contractual relationship. The encapsulation achieved through designated interface sections mitigates inadvertent dependencies and reinforces the principle of high cohesion within each discrete module. This design paradigm is instrumental in establishing a robust modular architecture where internal implementation details remain insulated, and the permissible data interactions are confined to preestablished channels.

Operational Semantics of the CALL Statement

The mechanism by which control is transferred from a calling program to an external subprogram is instantiated through the CALL statement. This operation initiates a dynamic linkage process whereby the subprogram is identified through its unique identifier and its associated parameter list is aligned with the calling context. The semantics of the CALL statement are characterized by an immediate suspension of the current execution context, followed by the activation of the subprogram's entry point. Conceptually, this process can be modeled by a function

$$f : C \to S \to C',$$

where C represents the original calling context, S denotes the execution environment of the subprogram, and C' is the resulting context upon the subprogram's termination. The restoration of control upon completion guarantees that the state transitions and data modifications remain both deterministic and verifiable. This controlled handoff is central to the execution model in which subprograms are seamlessly integrated into a larger application framework.

Parameter Passing and Data Encapsulation

The parameter passing mechanism employed in subprogram invocations is fundamental to maintaining the integrity of data exchange between separate modules. In many implementations, parameters are passed by reference, ensuring that the subprogram operates directly on memory locations defined in the caller's environment. This approach is advantageous in that it obviates the necessity for data duplication and maintains synchronization between the modules. The parameters may be formally denoted as the tuple

$$P = (p_1, p_2, \ldots, p_k),$$

with each p_i serving as a direct handle to a specific data element. The explicit declaration of such parameters within the interface sections enforces a rigorous boundary for data encapsulation and minimizes the potential for unintended side effects. By precisely delineating the scope and semantics of each transmitted variable, the CALL statement facilitates an operational integrity that underpins both maintainability and modular reusability within the broader system architecture.

Cobol Code Snippet

```
*----------------------------------------------------------------
* Main Program: Demonstrates CALL of a subprogram that computes
* arithmetic operations (Sum, Product, Quotient) on two numbers.
* This illustrates the transfer of the calling context (C) into
* the subprogram's environment (S) and the resulting context (C')
* being returned.
*----------------------------------------------------------------
IDENTIFICATION DIVISION.
PROGRAM-ID. MAINPROGRAM.

ENVIRONMENT DIVISION.

DATA DIVISION.
WORKING-STORAGE SECTION.
```

```
* Define input numbers and storage for computed results
01  WS-NUM1      PIC 9(4) VALUE 15.
01  WS-NUM2      PIC 9(4) VALUE 5.
01  WS-SUM       PIC 9(4).
01  WS-PRODUCT   PIC 9(6).
01  WS-QUOTIENT  PIC 9(4).

PROCEDURE DIVISION.
    DISPLAY "Before CALL:".
    DISPLAY "Number 1 = " WS-NUM1.
    DISPLAY "Number 2 = " WS-NUM2.

    * Calling subprogram CALCULATE to perform arithmetic operations
    CALL "CALCULATE" USING WS-NUM1, WS-NUM2, WS-SUM, WS-PRODUCT,
    ↪  WS-QUOTIENT.

    DISPLAY "After CALL:".
    DISPLAY "Sum = " WS-SUM.
    DISPLAY "Product = " WS-PRODUCT.
    DISPLAY "Quotient = " WS-QUOTIENT.

    STOP RUN.

*---------------------------------------------------------------
* Subprogram: CALCULATE
* This subprogram receives two input numbers and computes:
*     LS-SUM      = LS-NUM1 + LS-NUM2
*     LS-PRODUCT  = LS-NUM1 * LS-NUM2
*     LS-QUOTIENT = LS-NUM1 / LS-NUM2  (if LS-NUM2 is non-zero)
* The parameter passing demonstrates the seamless transition
* of control as defined by f: C -> S -> C'.
*---------------------------------------------------------------
IDENTIFICATION DIVISION.
PROGRAM-ID. CALCULATE.

ENVIRONMENT DIVISION.

DATA DIVISION.
LINKAGE SECTION.
* Parameters received from the caller:
01  LS-NUM1      PIC 9(4).
01  LS-NUM2      PIC 9(4).
01  LS-SUM       PIC 9(4).
01  LS-PRODUCT   PIC 9(6).
01  LS-QUOTIENT  PIC 9(4).

PROCEDURE DIVISION USING LS-NUM1, LS-NUM2, LS-SUM, LS-PRODUCT,
↪  LS-QUOTIENT.
    * Compute the sum of LS-NUM1 and LS-NUM2
    COMPUTE LS-SUM = LS-NUM1 + LS-NUM2.

    * Compute the product of LS-NUM1 and LS-NUM2
    COMPUTE LS-PRODUCT = LS-NUM1 * LS-NUM2.
```

```
* Compute the quotient if LS-NUM2 is not zero, else set to zero
IF LS-NUM2 NOT = 0
    COMPUTE LS-QUOTIENT = LS-NUM1 / LS-NUM2
ELSE
    MOVE 0 TO LS-QUOTIENT
END-IF.

* Return control to the calling program
EXIT PROGRAM.
```

Chapter 57

Parameter Passing via the Linkage Section

Conceptual Foundations and Theoretical Underpinnings

Parameter passing in modular programming environments involves the systematic transfer of data between a calling program and a subordinate module. Within the context of COBOL, the LINKAGE Section serves as the designated structure for receiving parameters from the invoking routine. The theoretical model can be abstracted by considering a parameter tuple

$$P = (p_1, p_2, \ldots, p_k),$$

which encapsulates the discrete data elements transmitted during the invocation. This formulation emphasizes the importance of ensuring that the semantic properties of each parameter remain invariant under the transformation from the caller's environment to that of the callee. The abstraction delineates a clear boundary that separates the operational context of the main program from that of the subprogram, thereby facilitating rigor in both type-conformance and data integrity during the exchange.

Architectural Role of the LINKAGE Section

The architectural design of subprograms in COBOL mandates that data exchange be rigorously structured, and the LINKAGE Section embodies this principle. In this context, the LINKAGE Section defines the parameters that the subprogram anticipates receiving from external callers, thereby establishing a formal interface. The mechanism ensures that each parameter, when passed, is represented in memory with a clear correlation to its original declaration in the calling program. This association can be conceptualized through the mapping function

$$f : C \to S,$$

where C represents the calling environment and S denotes the subprogram's operating space. By declaring parameters in the LINKAGE Section, the subprogram effectively asserts a contract, dictating both the data types and the order of values expected from the invocation. This contract is fundamental to the operational semantics of the subprogram call, ensuring that the necessary data integrity and type safety are preserved across the boundary between program modules.

Implications for Encapsulation and Data Integrity

The use of the LINKAGE Section in parameter passing has significant ramifications for maintaining encapsulation and ensuring data integrity in modular applications. By confining the external parameters to a well-defined section, the subprogram delineates its interface from its internal procedural logic. This separation enforces high cohesion within each module and minimizes inadvertent side effects that may arise from uncontrolled access to the caller's data space. Formally, the invariant

$$I(p_i)$$

associated with each parameter p_i is upheld as the parameter flows from the calling context to the subprogram, such that any transformation

$$T : p_i \to p_i'$$

249

applied within the subprogram adheres to the constraints of this invariant. The clear demarcation provided by the LINKAGE Section thereby supports robust data encapsulation, ensuring that modifications to the transmitted data are both intentional and verifiable. This methodology contributes to a disciplined approach in the design of modular systems, where the integrity and consistency of data exchanges are paramount.

Cobol Code Snippet

```
* Main Program: Demonstrates invoking a subprogram with parameter
↪  passing.
        IDENTIFICATION DIVISION.
        PROGRAM-ID. MAINPROG.
        ENVIRONMENT DIVISION.
        DATA DIVISION.
        WORKING-STORAGE SECTION.
        * Declare parameters to be passed as a tuple P = (p1, p2)
        01 WS-NUM-PARAM   PIC 9(4)  VALUE 1234.
        01 WS-ALPHA-PARAM PIC A(10) VALUE 'COBOLMOD'.

        PROCEDURE DIVISION.
            DISPLAY 'MAINPROG: Before CALL, WS-NUM-PARAM = '
            ↪  WS-NUM-PARAM.
            DISPLAY 'MAINPROG: Before CALL, WS-ALPHA-PARAM = '
            ↪  WS-ALPHA-PARAM.
            * Invoke subprogram SUBP; mapping function f: C -> S is
            ↪  implicitly applied via USING clause.
            CALL 'SUBP' USING WS-NUM-PARAM, WS-ALPHA-PARAM.
            DISPLAY 'MAINPROG: After CALL, WS-NUM-PARAM = '
            ↪  WS-NUM-PARAM.
            DISPLAY 'MAINPROG: After CALL, WS-ALPHA-PARAM = '
            ↪  WS-ALPHA-PARAM.
            STOP RUN.

* Subprogram: Implements parameter passing via the LINKAGE SECTION.
* It receives parameters as a tuple and applies an integrity check
↪  (invariant I)
* and a transformation (T: p -> p') to demonstrate the algorithm.
        IDENTIFICATION DIVISION.
        PROGRAM-ID. SUBP.
        ENVIRONMENT DIVISION.
        DATA DIVISION.
        LINKAGE SECTION.
        * Received parameter tuple: P = (p1, p2)
        01 LS-NUM-PARAM   PIC 9(4).
        01 LS-ALPHA-PARAM PIC A(10).

        PROCEDURE DIVISION USING LS-NUM-PARAM, LS-ALPHA-PARAM.
```

```
DISPLAY 'SUBP: Received LS-NUM-PARAM = ' LS-NUM-PARAM.
DISPLAY 'SUBP: Received LS-ALPHA-PARAM = '
↪  LS-ALPHA-PARAM.

* Invariant Check: Ensure the numeric parameter adheres
↪  to invariant I(p) (non-negative).
IF LS-NUM-PARAM < 0
    DISPLAY 'SUBP Error: Numeric parameter invariant
    ↪  violated'
    STOP RUN
END-IF.

* Transformation T: Modify numeric parameter (e.g., add
↪  100) to obtain p' such that p' = p + 100.
ADD 100 TO LS-NUM-PARAM.

* Demonstrate modification of LS-ALPHA-PARAM by appending
↪  a suffix,
* symbolizing a transformation and confirming the
↪  contract.
STRING LS-ALPHA-PARAM DELIMITED BY SPACE,
       '-MOD'           DELIMITED BY SIZE
    INTO LS-ALPHA-PARAM.

DISPLAY 'SUBP: After transformation, LS-NUM-PARAM = '
↪  LS-NUM-PARAM.
DISPLAY 'SUBP: After transformation, LS-ALPHA-PARAM = '
↪  LS-ALPHA-PARAM.

EXIT PROGRAM.
```

Chapter 58

Using the COPY Statement for Code Reuse

Conceptual Framework of Code Reusability

In modular programming paradigms, code reusability represents a cornerstone principle that enables the systematic reduction of redundancy and promotes consistency across multiple program units. The COPY statement embodies a formal mechanism by which common code segments can be maintained in an external repository and integrated into programs during the compilation process. This approach conceptualizes a code segment as an abstract entity, denoted by S, whose replication into various contexts is governed by a transformation function T such that

$$T : S \to S',$$

where S' denotes the in situ instantiation of the copied code. Under this framework, the clear delineation between original code segments and their subsequent deployments underscores the importance of centralized maintenance; modifications in the master module propagate uniformly through every instance of the copied segment.

Mechanisms Underpinning the COPY Statement

The operation of the COPY statement is inherently tied to its role as a preprocessor directive within the compilation workflow. During this preliminary phase, the directive instructs the compiler to substitute the COPY statement with the full text of the referenced external file. This substitution is performed prior to the syntactic and semantic analysis of the program, ensuring that the integrated code adheres to the overarching language specifications and structural rules. The substitution process can be modeled as a mapping function

$$f : \mathcal{F} \times \mathcal{P} \to \mathcal{S},$$

where $\mathcal{F}$ represents the collection of external files containing common code segments, $\mathcal{P}$ is the set of potential parameterizations or contextual configurations, and $\mathcal{S}$ constitutes the resulting integrated code snippet. Such a formal description highlights that the integration process preserves both the syntactic integrity and the semantic invariants specified within the original code segment.

Simplification of Code Management Through COPY

The utility of the COPY statement extends beyond mere replication; it systematically simplifies the management of common code segments within complex software systems. By centralizing frequently used logic or data definitions in a single source file, the COPY mechanism minimizes inconsistencies that may arise from ad hoc code duplication. The approach allows for a unified update protocol, whereby changes implemented in the master file are inherently reflected in all dependent program modules. From the perspective of software engineering, this property is essential in maintaining a coherent and maintainable codebase, as it effectively reduces the cognitive overhead related to tracking and synchronizing multiple copies of similar code constructs.

Furthermore, the COPY statement contributes to a disciplined modular architecture by enabling the segregation of concerns. The segregation is achieved through the establishment of well-defined boundaries between common code segments and module-specific logic. This architectural choice engenders a more robust design, wherein the propagation of updates is both controlled and predictable, thereby fostering a software development environment characterized by maintainability and extensibility. The resulting system benefits from a reduction in the potential for defects associated with code inconsistency, as the centralized control of common components imposes a rigorous adherence to established invariants and design contracts.

Semantic Integration and Structural Consistency

The semantic integration facilitated by the COPY statement is predicated on the assumption that the externally maintained code segments are developed in isolation from the host program. Upon inclusion via the COPY mechanism, these segments are assimilated into the host code while preserving their internal structure and behavioral semantics. The consistency of this integration can be formally described by an invariant property

$$I : \forall s \in S, \ I(s) \text{ holds},$$

where $I(s)$ denotes the set of semantic and syntactic conditions associated with each code segment s. The maintenance of this invariant across all instantiations ensures that the replicated code not only retains its original functionality but also harmonizes with the contextual demands of the host environment.

In summary, the COPY statement for code reuse operates as an efficient mechanism for achieving modularity, reducing redundancy, and ensuring the structural and semantic consistency of common code segments within large-scale software systems.

Cobol Code Snippet

```
IDENTIFICATION DIVISION.
PROGRAM-ID. COPY-DEMO.
AUTHOR. Maxwell_Vector.
* Purpose: Demonstrates how the COPY statement enables code
↪   reuse.
*         It integrates common code segments, applying the
↪   transformation:
*             T: S -> S'
*             and simulates the mapping function:
```

```
*              f: (REUSABLE-COMMONS, context) -> Integrated
↪    Code Segment,
*              while maintaining the invariant I(s) for every
↪    copied element.

ENVIRONMENT DIVISION.
CONFIGURATION SECTION.
SOURCE-COMPUTER. IBM-370.
OBJECT-COMPUTER. IBM-370.

DATA DIVISION.
WORKING-STORAGE SECTION.
* The following COPY statement imports common definitions
↪    from an external file.
COPY REUSABLE-COMMONS.
*> The external file REUSABLE-COMMONS contains:
*>    01 MASTER-VALUE       PIC 9(4) VALUE 1000.
*>    01 PARAMETER-VALUE    PIC 9(4) VALUE 50.

01 TRANSFORMED-VALUE    PIC 9(4).
01 WS-DISPLAY-MESSAGE    PIC X(50).

PROCEDURE DIVISION.
MAIN-PROCEDURE.
    DISPLAY "Starting COPY Statement Demonstration...".

    *--------------------------------------------------
    * Transformation Section: T: S -> S'
    * Here, S is represented by MASTER-VALUE and S' by
    ↪    TRANSFORMED-VALUE.
    * The algorithm applies the simple arithmetic
    ↪    transformation:
    *        TRANSFORMED-VALUE = MASTER-VALUE +
    ↪    PARAMETER-VALUE
    * which corresponds to the formal expression: T(S) = S +
    ↪    P.
    *--------------------------------------------------
    ADD MASTER-VALUE, PARAMETER-VALUE GIVING
    ↪    TRANSFORMED-VALUE.

    MOVE "MASTER VALUE: " TO WS-DISPLAY-MESSAGE.
    DISPLAY WS-DISPLAY-MESSAGE, MASTER-VALUE.

    MOVE "PARAMETER VALUE: " TO WS-DISPLAY-MESSAGE.
    DISPLAY WS-DISPLAY-MESSAGE, PARAMETER-VALUE.

    MOVE "TRANSFORMED VALUE: " TO WS-DISPLAY-MESSAGE.
    DISPLAY WS-DISPLAY-MESSAGE, TRANSFORMED-VALUE.

    *--------------------------------------------------
    * Integration Simulation Section: f: F x P -> S
    * The COPY statement acts as a preprocessor directive
    ↪    that maps
```

255

```
      * an external file (F) and contextual parameters (P) into
      ↪   the host
      * code segment (S). In all instances, the invariant I(s)
      ↪   holds true,
      * ensuring that the copied segment retains its integrity.
      *--------------------------------------------------
      PERFORM DISPLAY-COPY-INTEGRATION.

      DISPLAY "End of COPY Statement Demonstration.".
      STOP RUN.

  DISPLAY-COPY-INTEGRATION.
      DISPLAY "Simulating integration of copied code
      ↪   segments:".
      DISPLAY "    --> Invariant I(s) maintained for all
      ↪   elements in REUSABLE-COMMONS.".
      DISPLAY "    --> Centralized updates via COPY propagate
      ↪   uniformly.".
      EXIT.

  END PROGRAM COPY-DEMO.
```

Chapter 59

Applying the REPLACE Clause

Conceptual Framework of the REPLACE Clause

The REPLACE clause serves as an advanced directive that enables the systematic modification of reused code segments during the preprocessing phase. In conjunction with the COPY statement, this clause permits a precise alteration of imported code without necessitating changes in the master file. The operation may be abstractly modeled as a transformation function

$$R : S \to S',$$

where S represents the original block of code extracted from an external repository and S' denotes the modified, context-specific instantiation. This function encapsulates both the substitution of designated tokens and the restructuring required to integrate the code seamlessly into the host program.

Mathematical Formalization of the Replacement Process

The mechanism of text substitution can be formalized by considering a code segment S as an ordered sequence of tokens $s_1, s_2, \ldots, s_n$.

257

Let the substitution set be defined as

$$\delta = \{(a, b) \mid a \to b\},$$

where each pair (a, b) specifies the replacement of token a with token b. The cumulative transformation induced by the REPLACE clause is given by

$$R(S, \delta) = S',$$

implying that every occurrence of a token $a \in S$ corresponding to a mapping in δ is substituted by b. The operation preserves formal invariants such that, for a predicate of syntactic and semantic correctness $I(s)$ defined over tokens,

$$\forall s \in S, \quad I(s) \implies I(R(s)).$$

This representation confirms that the REPLACE clause enforces a transformation that maintains the core properties of the original code while adapting it to the local context.

Interaction Between the REPLACE and COPY Mechanisms

Within the preprocessing phase, the COPY statement first imports the common code module from an external file. Following this, the REPLACE clause is applied, executing a sequence of substitution operations that customize the integrated code. The overall process can be viewed as the composition of two functions, where T_{copy} is the function representing the code importation and R is the replacement function. This can be expressed as

$$S' = R(T_{\text{copy}}(F), \delta),$$

with F denoting the external file that houses the commonly reused code segment. The composition of these functions ensures that the externally maintained module is incorporated in its entirety and thereafter tailored by the replacement rules defined in δ. This layered approach guarantees that centralized maintenance is preserved while allowing localized adaptations at compile time.

Semantic and Syntactic Implications of Replacement

The application of the REPLACE clause encompasses both semantic and syntactic dimensions. Syntactically, the operation must
yield a code segment S' that is fully compliant with the grammatical constraints of the programming language. Semantically, the
modifications effected by the replacement process must preserve
the intended behavior and logical structure of the original code.
Denote by $G(S)$ the predicate asserting grammatical correctness
and by $M(S)$ the predicate asserting semantic preservation. The
transformed segment S' satisfies the validity condition

$$G(S') \wedge M(S'),$$

thereby affirming that the substitution, though extensive, does not
compromise the operational integrity of the program. The design of
the substitution set δ is, therefore, subject to rigorous constraints
that ensure both syntactic fidelity and semantic robustness, culmi-
nating in a customized yet consistently integrated code module.

Cobol Code Snippet

```
        IDENTIFICATION DIVISION.
        PROGRAM-ID. REPLACEDEMO.

       *-----------------------------------------------------
       * This program demonstrates the use of the REPLACE clause in
       * COBOL to customize an imported code segment during the
       * preprocessing phase. The transformation can be conceptually
       * represented as:
       *
       *       R: S → S'
       *
       * where S is the original code block containing placeholder
       ↪   tokens,
       * and S' is the modified code after applying the substitution
       ↪   set:
       *
       *       = { (==OPERATIONS==, <Arithmetic Operations Code>) }
       *
       * The master copy file (MATH-OPS) includes a token
       ↪   '==OPERATIONS=='
       * which is replaced by the arithmetic operations that compute
       ↪   the sum
```

```
* and product of two numbers. This approach guarantees that
↪ the
* syntactic (G(S')) and semantic (M(S')) correctness of the
↪ code is maintained.
*----------------------------------------------------

ENVIRONMENT DIVISION.
CONFIGURATION SECTION.
SOURCE-COMPUTER. IBM-370.
OBJECT-COMPUTER. IBM-370.

DATA DIVISION.
WORKING-STORAGE SECTION.
01  WS-NUM1        PIC 9(4) VALUE 100.
01  WS-NUM2        PIC 9(4) VALUE  50.
01  WS-SUM         PIC 9(4).
01  WS-PRODUCT     PIC 9(6).

PROCEDURE DIVISION.
    DISPLAY "Starting REPLACE Clause Demonstration
    ↪ Program...".

    *----------------------------------------------------
    * The following COPY statement imports the common
    ↪ arithmetic
    * module from the external file "MATH-OPS". The REPLACE
    ↪ clause
    * customizes the imported code by substituting the token
    * '==OPERATIONS==' with the actual arithmetic operations.
    *----------------------------------------------------
    COPY MATH-OPS
        REPLACING ==OPERATIONS== BY
        "COMPUTE WS-SUM = WS-NUM1 + WS-NUM2.
         COMPUTE WS-PRODUCT = WS-NUM1 * WS-NUM2.
         DISPLAY 'Sum of Numbers    : ' WS-SUM.
         DISPLAY 'Product of Numbers: ' WS-PRODUCT.".

    DISPLAY "Arithmetic operations executed using REPLACE
    ↪ clause.".
    STOP RUN.
```

Chapter 60

Conditional Compilation Techniques

Theoretical Foundations of Conditional Compilation

Conditional compilation constitutes a preprocessing paradigm wherein segments of source code are either included or omitted based on compile-time predicates. This technique is predicated on the existence of compile-time expressions, here denoted by E, that evaluate to boolean values. The transformation can be conceptualized by introducing a function $F : S \rightarrow S'$, where S represents the original source code and S' denotes the modified version after conditional evaluation. In this formalism, each code block $B \subset S$ is subjected to a predicate $P(B)$, and its inclusion in S' is determined solely by whether $P(B)$ evaluates to true. This model ensures that the intrinsic semantics of the program are retained while permitting variability in the compiled output based on predetermined conditions.

Directive Syntax and Evaluation Process

The syntactical design of conditional compilation directives is integrated into the lexical analysis phase of the compiler. These directives are symbolized by specific tokens within the code, which serve as markers to delineate conditional blocks. The evaluation of the associated condition is performed by a boolean function $C : E \rightarrow \{0, 1\}$, where E represents the embedded conditional expression. Under this schema, a code block B is compiled if and only if $C(E) = 1$, otherwise the block is omitted. The precision in the directive syntax and its rigorous evaluation protocol affords a deterministic approach to include or exclude code segments, thereby enabling the compiler to process multiple configurations within the same source file.

Semantic Preservation under Conditional Directives

Ensuring semantic integrity is paramount in the implementation of conditional compilation. The transformation from S to S' must uphold a set of invariants, denoted by a predicate M, which encapsulates the semantic constraints of the code. Formally, for every token $s \in S$ that is retained in S', the invariant $M(s)$ must hold true. This requirement is essential to guarantee that the operation of conditional directives does not disrupt the logical behavior and intended side effects of the program. The careful structuring of conditions, therefore, not only influences syntactical inclusion but also assures that the functional semantics remain consistently preserved across all compiled configurations.

Operational and Structural Considerations

The application of conditional compilation techniques introduces a multi-layered processing framework within the compiler architecture. Initially, the preprocessor identifies and segregates conditional directives from the primary code body. Subsequently, an evaluation engine applies the boolean conditions to each marked code segment. Let $T : \{B_i\} \rightarrow \{B_i'\}$ denote the transformation mapping, where each block B_i is independently assessed and either propagated as B_i' in the final code or discarded based on the outcome of its respective evaluation function. This meticulous operation affords the compiler the flexibility to generate distinct executable forms from a single source file while ensuring that the compiled code adheres to both syntactical correctness and semantic robustness.

Cobol Code Snippet

```
IDENTIFICATION DIVISION.
PROGRAM-ID. CONDITIONAL-COMPILATION.
*$SET INCLUDE_EXTRA_FEATURE = TRUE

ENVIRONMENT DIVISION.
CONFIGURATION SECTION.
SOURCE-COMPUTER. IBM-AS.
OBJECT-COMPUTER. IBM-AS.

DATA DIVISION.
WORKING-STORAGE SECTION.
01 WS-STATUS            PIC X(10) VALUE "UNKNOWN".
01 WS-EVALUATION-E      PIC X(01) VALUE "1".
01 WS-TRANSFORM-RESULT  PIC X(30).

PROCEDURE DIVISION.
MAIN-ROUTINE.
    DISPLAY "Starting Conditional Compilation Demo".
    PERFORM EVALUATE-CONDITION.
    PERFORM FINAL-MESSAGE.
    STOP RUN.

EVALUATE-CONDITION.
    $IF INCLUDE_EXTRA_FEATURE = TRUE
        MOVE "ENABLED" TO WS-STATUS.
        DISPLAY "Extra features are enabled based on
        ↪   compile-time directive.".
        PERFORM EXTRA-FEATURES.
    $ELSE
        MOVE "DISABLED" TO WS-STATUS.
        DISPLAY "Extra features are disabled as per
        ↪   compile-time directive.".
    $END-IF.
    EXIT.

EXTRA-FEATURES.
    DISPLAY "Executing transformation algorithm F: S -> S'".
    * Simulate transformation applying function F and mapping
    ↪   T: {B_i} -> {B_i'}.
    PERFORM TRANSFORMATION-PROCESS.
    EXIT.

TRANSFORMATION-PROCESS.
    DISPLAY "Evaluating predicate P(B) using boolean function
    ↪   C(E)..." .
```

263

```
      IF WS-EVALUATION-E = "1"
          THEN DISPLAY "Predicate true: Block B is included
          ↪  (C(E)=1)."
          ELSE DISPLAY "Predicate false: Block B is omitted."
      END-IF.
      * Demonstrate semantic preservation: each token s must
      ↪  satisfy invariant M(s).
      DISPLAY "Ensuring semantic invariants M(s) hold for all
      ↪  retained tokens.".
      MOVE "Transformation Complete" TO WS-TRANSFORM-RESULT.
      DISPLAY "Transformation Result: " WS-TRANSFORM-RESULT.
      EXIT.

  FINAL-MESSAGE.
      DISPLAY "Conditional compilation and transformation
      ↪  demonstration complete.".
      DISPLAY "Current feature status: " WS-STATUS.
      EXIT.
```

Boolean and Logical Expressions

Foundations of Boolean Algebra in COBOL

Boolean algebra forms the mathematical foundation upon which COBOL's conditional constructs are built. In this framework, binary values, represented as 1 for truth and 0 for falsehood, serve to encode the status of conditions that govern program execution. The essential operations of conjunction, disjunction, and negation are employed to compose complex logical expressions in a precise and unambiguous manner. These operations adhere to the standard axioms of Boolean logic, where expressions such as $A \wedge B$, $A \vee B$, and $\neg A$ formalize the criteria under which conditional branches are activated. The abstraction of logical variables and operators into the syntactical elements of the language permits the rigorous definition of decision-making processes that are both predictable and analytically tractable.

Logical Operators in COBOL Expressions

COBOL integrates a distinct set of logical operators that facilitate the evaluation of Boolean expressions within conditional statements. The logical conjunction operator enforces the simultaneous satisfaction of multiple predicates, aligning with the formal definition that the compound condition $A \wedge B$ is true only if each of the atomic conditions A and B evaluates to true. Conversely, the logical disjunction operator, corresponding to the expression $A \vee B$, allows for the satisfaction of any one among several possible conditions, thereby introducing flexibility in decision logic. The logical negation operator, expressed mathematically as $\neg A$, inverts the truth value of a given condition. This suite of operators has been designed to integrate seamlessly into the COBOL language syntax, thereby ensuring that even intricate conditional statements are both syntactically coherent and semantically robust.

Evaluation Mechanics and Operator Precedence

In the context of COBOL, the evaluation of Boolean expressions is subject to a well-established hierarchy that guarantees deterministic execution. The logical operators are applied in accordance with operator precedence rules, which assign a higher evaluation order to the negation operator relative to conjunction and disjunction. Parentheses, denoted by (and), may be used to explicitly indicate the desired grouping of sub-expressions, thereby overriding the default precedence. This systematic mechanism ensures that a composite expression E, involving several atomic expressions E_i, is decomposed and recombined following an unambiguous mapping function. Such a function, here denoted as $\pi(E)$, partitions the expression into constituent segments that are subsequently evaluated in a prescribed order, thereby preserving the integrity of the logical conditions embedded within the program's control flow.

Implications for Program Flow Control

The strategic employment of Boolean and logical expressions exerts a significant influence on the control flow of COBOL programs. Conditional constructs utilize these expressions to determine the execution path, effectively transforming abstract logical relationships into concrete operational directives. When a composite Boolean condition evaluates to true, the corresponding branch of execution is activated, directing the program to execute a specific block of code. Conversely, a false evaluation results in the omission of that block. This operating principle enables the design of intricate control mechanisms wherein multiple conditional paths may coexist, and their interactions are governed by the pre-

cise rules of Boolean evaluation. The deterministic nature of this
process ensures that program behavior remains consistent, even in
the presence of complex logical conditions that govern branching
and iterative operations.

Cobol Code Snippet

```
IDENTIFICATION DIVISION.
PROGRAM-ID. BOOLEAN-LOGIC.
AUTHOR. Maxwell_Vector.

ENVIRONMENT DIVISION.
* This example does not require special file handling or devices.

DATA DIVISION.
WORKING-STORAGE SECTION.
    * Define Boolean values using numeric flags: 1 is TRUE, 0 is
    ↪ FALSE.
01  WS-A        PIC 9 VALUE 1.
01  WS-B        PIC 9 VALUE 0.
01  WS-C        PIC 9 VALUE 1.
01  WS-D        PIC 9 VALUE 0.
01  WS-EXPR-RES PIC 9 VALUE 0.
01  WS-MESSAGE  PIC X(50).

PROCEDURE DIVISION.
MAIN-PROCEDURE.
    DISPLAY "---- COBOL Boolean Logical Expression Evaluation ----".

    *-------------------------------------------------------
    * Example 1: Evaluate (A AND (NOT B)) OR (C AND D)
    * Explanation:
    *   - (WS-A = 1 AND WS-B = 0) is analogous to (A  ¬B)
    *   - (WS-C = 1 AND WS-D = 1) is analogous to (C  D)
    *   - The overall expression is (A  ¬B)  (C  D)
    *-------------------------------------------------------
    DISPLAY "Evaluating: (A AND (NOT B)) OR (C AND D)".
    IF (WS-A = 1 AND WS-B = 0)
        OR (WS-C = 1 AND WS-D = 1)
        MOVE 1 TO WS-EXPR-RES
    ELSE
        MOVE 0 TO WS-EXPR-RES
    END-IF.
    IF WS-EXPR-RES = 1
        MOVE "Expression 1 is TRUE" TO WS-MESSAGE
    ELSE
        MOVE "Expression 1 is FALSE" TO WS-MESSAGE
    END-IF.
    DISPLAY WS-MESSAGE.
```

```
*--------------------------------------------------------
* Example 2: Evaluate NOT (A OR B) AND C
* Explanation:
*    - Parentheses group (A OR B) before applying NOT.
*    - Evaluates to TRUE only if both A and B are FALSE and C is
↪    TRUE.
*--------------------------------------------------------
DISPLAY "Evaluating: NOT (A OR B) AND C".
IF (NOT (WS-A = 1 OR WS-B = 1)) AND (WS-C = 1)
    DISPLAY "Expression 2 is TRUE"
ELSE
    DISPLAY "Expression 2 is FALSE"
END-IF.


*--------------------------------------------------------
* Example 3: Evaluate a Nested Complex Expression
* Expression: (A AND (NOT B)) OR [C OR (D AND (NOT (A AND B)))]
* Explanation:
*    - The nested structure uses explicit grouping to override
*      default operator precedence.
*    - Part 1: (WS-A = 1 AND WS-B = 0)
*    - Part 2: WS-C = 1
*    - Part 3: (WS-D = 1 AND NOT (WS-A = 1 AND WS-B = 1))
*    - Overall: (Part 1) OR (Part 2 OR Part 3)
*--------------------------------------------------------
DISPLAY "Evaluating Nested Expression: (A AND (NOT B)) OR [C OR
↪    (D AND (NOT (A AND B)))]".
IF (WS-A = 1 AND WS-B = 0)
    OR (WS-C = 1
        OR (WS-D = 1 AND NOT (WS-A = 1 AND WS-B = 1)))
    DISPLAY "Nested Expression is TRUE"
ELSE
    DISPLAY "Nested Expression is FALSE"
END-IF.

STOP RUN.
```

Chapter 62

Data Conversion in COBOL

Conceptual Foundations of Data Representation

Data within COBOL is defined and structured in the DATA DIVISION through explicit declarations that dictate both the storage format and the interpretative constraints of individual data items. Numeric data is typically specified using a PIC clause that delineates the permissible range, precision, and, in some cases, the implied decimal point. Alphanumeric data, in contrast, is declared with a $PIC\ X$ format, which emphasizes fixed-length character representation. The process of data conversion involves the mapping of an item from its source domain, denoted by D, to a target domain R, which can be expressed by a transformation function $f : D \to R$. This mapping is governed by syntactic rules and semantic constraints embedded in the data definitions, ensuring that the transformation preserves the intrinsic properties of the original value while rendering it in a form suitable for subsequent operations.

Mechanisms for Data Type Transformation

COBOL employs a set of predetermined mechanisms to facilitate the conversion of data between disparate formats. These mechanisms are activated primarily through data movement operations, in which the compiler enforces a rigorous set of transformation rules. When an item defined under one PIC clause is moved to another data item with a different PIC definition, an implicit conversion process occurs. This process may involve several operations, including field alignment, zero-padding, truncation, and the reinterpretation of sign indicators. The transformation is not performed arbitrarily but follows a strict mapping dictated by the compile-time metadata associated with each data field. Accordingly, the conversion function can be analyzed mathematically as a deterministic operator that guarantees consistency, such that for any value $x \in D$, the transformed value $f(x) \in R$ adheres to the constraints imposed by the target field's definition.

1 Implicit and Explicit Conversion Paradigms

The conversion paradigms in COBOL can be classified into implicit and explicit strategies. Implicit conversion is executed automatically by the compiler during the MOVE operation whenever there is a discrepancy between the source and target data definitions. This automatic transformation respects the intrinsic formatting and alignment rules defined by the PIC and USAGE clauses. In situations where the conversion requires additional handling beyond the default behavior, explicit conversion strategies are employed through meticulous programming constructs. Explicit conversion entails the deliberate management of transformation nuances, ensuring that extraneous characters are handled, decimal points are correctly positioned, and sign conventions are maintained. The duality of these paradigms underscores a design philosophy that balances automation with programmer-directed precision, thereby mitigating errors that could arise from ambiguous data representations.

Techniques for Numerical and Alphanumeric Conversion

The translation of numerical values to an alphanumeric form, and the corresponding reconversion, involves several specialized techniques that preserve data integrity while accommodating format-specific constraints. For example, converting a numeric field specified as PIC $9(n)$ to an alphanumeric field declared as PIC $X(m)$ requires not only a change in representation but also an adjustment of the field width. This may involve the insertion of leading zeros or spaces, depending on the target specification. Conversely, when an alphanumeric field is interpreted as a numerical value, it is crucial to validate that non-numeric characters are absent or have been appropriately filtered. The conversion process, therefore, is characterized by a series of operations that include value normalization, padding or truncation based on field length, and the systematic application of formatting rules to enforce semantic consistency.

Memory Considerations in Data Conversion

The operational efficacy of data conversion routines is intrinsically linked to the memory layout and storage requirements prescribed by COBOL. Conversion operations are executed within the confines of statically allocated memory segments, where the dimensions of each data field are fixed by its PIC clause. The transformation of data between types with differing field widths necessitates careful attention to memory boundaries, to avoid overflow or underflow conditions. When converting from a compact numeric representation to an expanded alphanumeric format, the allocation of additional memory space may require compensatory measures such as the appending of padding characters. Similarly, the reverse conversion process must ensure that the extraction of numerical digits from an alphanumeric string is performed without violating the constraints of the original numerical format. This interplay between data conversion and memory management reinforces the need for precise adherence to format specifications, thereby ensuring that the conversion process is both reliable and predictable.

Cobol Code Snippet

```
IDENTIFICATION DIVISION.
PROGRAM-ID. DATA-CONVERSION-DEMO.
AUTHOR. Maxwell_Vector.
*--------------------------------------------------*
* This program demonstrates data conversion in COBOL by
↪  *
* applying both implicit and explicit conversion routines.
↪  *
* It also illustrates memory considerations using the
↪  *
* REDEFINES clause and exemplifies a transformation function
↪  *
* f: D -> R defined as f(x) = x * 2.
↪  *
*--------------------------------------------------*

ENVIRONMENT DIVISION.
CONFIGURATION SECTION.
SOURCE-COMPUTER. IBM-370.
OBJECT-COMPUTER. IBM-370.

DATA DIVISION.
WORKING-STORAGE SECTION.
* Numeric field defined with PIC 9(5)
77 WS-NUMERIC          PIC 9(5)      VALUE 12345.
* Alphanumeric field for implicit conversion (fixed width)
77 WS-ALPHA-ORIG       PIC X(5)      VALUE SPACES.
* Numeric field to hold the computed result using
↪  transformation f(x)=x*2
77 WS-COMPUTED         PIC 9(5)      VALUE ZERO.
* Alphanumeric field for explicit conversion of the computed
↪  value
77 WS-ALPHA-COMP       PIC X(5)      VALUE SPACES.
* Redefines WS-NUMERIC to offer an alternative alphanumeric
↪  view
77 WS-ALPHA-REDEF      PIC X(5)      REDEFINES WS-NUMERIC.

PROCEDURE DIVISION.
MAIN-PARA.
    PERFORM INITIALIZE-VALUES
    PERFORM DATA-CONVERSION
    PERFORM DISPLAY-RESULTS
    STOP RUN.

INITIALIZE-VALUES.
    MOVE 12345      TO WS-NUMERIC.
    MOVE SPACES     TO WS-ALPHA-ORIG.
    MOVE SPACES     TO WS-ALPHA-COMP.
    MOVE ZERO       TO WS-COMPUTED.
        .
```

```
DATA-CONVERSION.

    ↪    *-------------------------------------------------------------*
         * Implicit Conversion: MOVING numeric value to an
    ↪    *
         * alphanumeric field. The compiler automatically converts
    ↪    *
         * WS-NUMERIC to a character string in WS-ALPHA-ORIG.
    ↪    *

    ↪    *-------------------------------------------------------------*
         MOVE WS-NUMERIC     TO WS-ALPHA-ORIG.


    ↪    *-------------------------------------------------------------*
         * Explicit Conversion and Transformation:
    ↪    *
         * Apply the transformation function f(x) = x * 2 and then
    ↪    *
         * convert the resulting numeric value to an alphanumeric
    ↪    form. *

    ↪    *-------------------------------------------------------------*
         COMPUTE WS-COMPUTED = WS-NUMERIC * 2.
         MOVE WS-COMPUTED    TO WS-ALPHA-COMP.
             .

DISPLAY-RESULTS.
         DISPLAY "Original Numeric Value:         " WS-NUMERIC.
         DISPLAY "Implicit Conversion (PIC X):    "
    ↪    WS-ALPHA-ORIG.
         DISPLAY "Computed Numeric Result (x * 2):   "
    ↪    WS-COMPUTED.
         DISPLAY "Explicit Conversion to Alpha:    "
    ↪    WS-ALPHA-COMP.
         DISPLAY "Redefined Alphanumeric of Numeric:"
    ↪    WS-ALPHA-REDEF.
             .
```

Chapter 63

Formatting Numerical Data with PICTURE

Foundations of Numerical Field Format Specification

Within the data definitions of legacy and contemporary systems, the PICTURE clause functions as a declarative construct to precisely define the display characteristics of numerical values. This clause is composed of a sequence of symbolic characters that dictate both the structure and the internal constraints of a numeric field. Symbols such as 9 signify mandatory digit positions, while symbols like Z are used for zero suppression, replacing insignificant leading zeros with spaces. The character V is employed to indicate the assumed position of a decimal point, thereby separating the integer and fractional components without reserving an explicit space for the punctuation. Such formalism ensures that a numeric item is stored and subsequently rendered with consistency, establishing a strict correspondence between the physical representation in memory and its visual output.

Advanced Editing and Formatting Mechanisms

Beyond basic digit allocation, the advanced editing capabilities available through the PICTURE clause allow for sophisticated control over the appearance of numerical outputs. Editing symbols can be interwoven with the basic picture characters to perform nuanced operations such as conditional zero suppression, insertion of punctuation for grouping (as with commas or periods), and explicit sign indication. For example, when a format incorporates the Z symbol, leading zeros are replaced by blanks unless the numerical value occupies the entire field width, thereby enhancing readability. Modifiers that include sign indicators ensure that the polarity of a number is expressed unambiguously, while the integration of extraneous formatting characters allows for the display of numbers that conform to the aesthetic and regulatory demands of various domains. The combined effect of these editing tools is a transformation of the raw numeric value into a string representation that meets stringent formatting criteria.

Mathematical Modeling of Numeric Transformation

The operation of the PICTURE clause can be understood from a mathematical standpoint as a deterministic mapping between domains. Let the set D denote the range of raw, unformatted numerical data, and let the set R correspond to the range of formatted string representations. In this framework, the formatting process realized by the PICTURE clause is equivalent to a function $f : D \to R$ that applies a series of transformations—such as field alignment, padding, and the insertion of literal editing characters—to each element $x \in D$. The function f is constructed from a composition of sub-transformations that enforce fixed field widths, manage implicit decimal locations via the V symbol, and conditionally modify digit displays according to the embedded editing instructions. This algebraic perspective affirms that the conversion from a raw numerical value to its formatted output is governed by a well-defined and reproducible set of rules, ensuring consistency across all instances of numeric formatting.

Interactions Between Precision, Field Width, and Cultural Formats

The configuration of a numeric field using the PICTURE clause requires the careful coordination of precision and field width while also accommodating culturally specific formatting conventions. A design that stipulates strict decimal precision employs both explicit decimal markers and assumed positions (denoted by V) to segregate the integer and fractional parts of a number. At the same time, the fixed field width imposes a limit on the total number of displayed characters, necessitating deliberate decisions regarding padding, truncation, and the placement of grouping symbols. In some contexts, locale-sensitive punctuation is integrated into the format so that separators such as thousands delimiters adhere to regional standards. This synthesis of formatting specifications not only preserves the numerical integrity of the data but also ensures that the presentation conforms to both technical constraints and culturally informed norms.

Cobol Code Snippet

```
IDENTIFICATION DIVISION.
PROGRAM-ID. NUMFORMAT.
* This program demonstrates numeric formatting using the PICTURE
↪  clause.
* It shows how raw numerical data is transformed into a formatted
↪  string
* representation using a series of computations and the built-in
↪  editing features.

ENVIRONMENT DIVISION.
* No file operations are performed in this example.

DATA DIVISION.
WORKING-STORAGE SECTION.
    * Define a raw numeric value and a factor for transformation.
    01 WS-RAW-NUMBER      PIC S9(5)V99 VALUE 1234.56.
    01 WS-FACTOR          PIC 9(3)V9(2)   VALUE 1.23.
    01 WS-CALCULATED      PIC S9(7)V99.
    01 WS-FORMATTED       PIC $Z,ZZZ,ZZ9.99.

    * A loop index for table processing.
    01 INDEX-VAR          PIC 9(2)        VALUE 1.

    * Define a table of raw numbers and a corresponding table for
    ↪  formatted output.
    01 NUM-TABLE.
       05 WS-NUM-IN-TABLE OCCURS 3 TIMES PIC S9(5)V99.
    01 FORMATTED-TABLE.
       05 WS-FORM-ENTRY   OCCURS 3 TIMES PIC $Z,ZZZ,ZZ9.99.

PROCEDURE DIVISION.
```

276

```
MAIN-LOGIC.
    DISPLAY "COBOL PICTURE Clause Formatting Example".
    DISPLAY "----------------------------------------".
    DISPLAY "Initial Raw Number: " WS-RAW-NUMBER.

    * Compute a new value using a mathematical transformation.
    DISPLAY "Performing calculation: WS-CALCULATED = WS-RAW-NUMBER *
    ↪   WS-FACTOR".
    COMPUTE WS-CALCULATED = WS-RAW-NUMBER * WS-FACTOR.
    MOVE WS-CALCULATED TO WS-FORMATTED.
    DISPLAY "Numeric Calculation Result: " WS-CALCULATED.
    DISPLAY "Formatted Result: " WS-FORMATTED.
    DISPLAY " ".

    * Demonstrate processing a table of numeric values.
    DISPLAY "Iterating over a table of numbers:".
    PERFORM VARYING INDEX-VAR FROM 1 BY 1 UNTIL INDEX-VAR > 3
        COMPUTE WS-NUM-IN-TABLE(INDEX-VAR) = INDEX-VAR * 100.25
        MOVE WS-NUM-IN-TABLE(INDEX-VAR) TO WS-FORM-ENTRY(INDEX-VAR)
        DISPLAY "Table Entry " INDEX-VAR ": Raw = "
        ↪   WS-NUM-IN-TABLE(INDEX-VAR)
                " Formatted = " WS-FORM-ENTRY(INDEX-VAR)
    END-PERFORM.

    STOP RUN.
```

Chapter 64

Handling Signs in Numeric Fields

Fundamental Concepts in Sign Representation

A comprehensive treatment of numeric sign representation begins with the formal separation of a real number into its magnitude and polarity. Every numerical value x may be expressed in the form

$$x = s \cdot |x|,$$

where s is the sign factor that assumes the value 1 for non-negative quantities and -1 for negative quantities. In this formulation, the symbols $+$ and $-$ serve as the canonical indicators of positive and negative values, respectively. The encoding of these symbols within a numeric field, whether by direct insertion or inferred through structural conventions, is central to maintaining both computational precision and data integrity.

Implicit Sign Handling Mechanisms

Implicit sign handling integrates the representation of the sign into the overall numeric field without a dedicated sign character. In such configurations, the output field is structured in a manner that infers the sign from the disposition of digits and the absence of an overt sign indicator. Typically, this method leverages spacing conventions or predetermined placeholder positions. For example, a designated digit position may implicitly imply positivity when it lacks an alternative modifying marker and negativity when a particular formatting cue is activated. The transformation function associated with implicit sign handling, denoted as

$$f_{\text{imp}} : \mathbb{R} \to S,$$

maps a raw numeric value to a formatted string such that the sign is encoded within the layout of the field itself. This algebraic approach underlines the deterministic nature of implicit transformations, where the visual manifestation of a negative value arises from alterations in digit presentation rather than from an explicit symbol.

Explicit Sign Handling Techniques

Explicit sign handling, by contrast, mandates the unambiguous inclusion of a sign symbol within the formatted output. In this approach, the positive or negative indicator is deliberately prefixed (or suffixed) to the numeric data. Regardless of the value's magnitude, the resultant string is constructed to begin with a character that explicitly conveys its polarity, namely + for non-negative and − for negative numbers. The corresponding transformation function, expressed as

$$f_{\text{exp}} : \mathbb{R} \to S,$$

ensures that every numeric value is accompanied by an overt sign character. This technique not only facilitates immediate recognition of a number's sign for automated parsing systems but also enhances interpretability in domains that demand rigorous data validation. The explicit method separates the concern of sign representation from magnitude formatting, thereby allowing each element of the transformation to be independently verified for correctness.

Comparative Analysis of Sign Formatting Techniques

The operational distinctions between implicit and explicit sign handling methods yield notable differences in both efficiency and clarity. Implicit techniques economize on field width by forgoing an explicit sign character, relying instead on field structure and digit modification rules to convey polarity. Such an approach can lead to more compact representations, yet it necessitates a precise interpretation of layout conventions. Conversely, explicit sign handling introduces a direct and unambiguous signal by embedding the sign indicator within the formatted output. This inclusion, while increasing the overall character count, provides a robust means of ensuring that polarity information is immediately accessible for both human inspection and automated processing. The rigorous mathematical frameworks underlying these operations—embodied by the functions f_{imp} and f_{exp}—offer a systematic basis for understanding and implementing sign formatting in numeric fields according to well-defined computational principles.

Cobol Code Snippet

```
IDENTIFICATION DIVISION.
PROGRAM-ID. HANDLE-SIGN.
AUTHOR. MaxwellVector.

ENVIRONMENT DIVISION.
CONFIGURATION SECTION.

DATA DIVISION.
WORKING-STORAGE SECTION.
    *-----------------------------------------------------------
    * The following variables illustrate the key concepts:
    * x = s * |x|, where WS-NUMBER is the raw signed value.
    * WS-ABS-NUMBER holds the computed absolute value |x|.
    * WS-SIGN stores the sign factor ('+' or '-').
    * WS-EXPLICIT demonstrates explicit sign handling (f_exp):
    *    The formatted output always shows the sign.
    * WS-IMPLICIT demonstrates implicit sign handling (f_imp):
    *    Only the absolute number is displayed (the sign is
    ↪    embedded).
    *-----------------------------------------------------------
    01 WS-NUMBER        PIC S9(5)V99 VALUE -00123.45.
    01 WS-ABS-NUMBER    PIC 9(5)V99 VALUE ZERO.
    01 WS-SIGN          PIC X        VALUE '+'.
    01 WS-EXPLICIT      PIC +9(5).99.
    01 WS-IMPLICIT      PIC 9(5).99.

PROCEDURE DIVISION.
MAIN-LOGIC.
    * Determine absolute value and sign factor.
    IF WS-NUMBER < 0
        COMPUTE WS-ABS-NUMBER = WS-NUMBER * -1
```

```
        MOVE '-' TO WS-SIGN
ELSE
    COMPUTE WS-ABS-NUMBER = WS-NUMBER
    MOVE '+' TO WS-SIGN
END-IF.

* f_exp: Explicit sign transformation.
MOVE WS-NUMBER TO WS-EXPLICIT.

* f_imp: Implicit sign transformation - the sign is not shown.
MOVE WS-ABS-NUMBER TO WS-IMPLICIT.

* Display outputs.
DISPLAY "Original Number (Raw): " WS-NUMBER.
DISPLAY "Computed Absolute Value: " WS-ABS-NUMBER.
DISPLAY "Sign Factor: " WS-SIGN.
DISPLAY "Formatted with Explicit Sign (f_exp): " WS-EXPLICIT.
DISPLAY "Formatted with Implicit Sign (f_imp): " WS-IMPLICIT.

STOP RUN.
```

Chapter 65

Output Formatting and Data Masking

Strategies for Output Formatting

Output formatting in data reporting is a disciplined process that involves the systematic transformation of raw data into a structured representation suitable for display. The process is characterized by the establishment of fixed field widths, the precise positioning of numeric symbols, and the controlled insertion of delimiters, thus ensuring that each output element conforms to predetermined aesthetic and operational constraints. Formally, one may consider a transformation function

$$f : D \to F,$$

where D represents the set of unformatted data elements and F is the corresponding set of formatted outputs. Within this framework, considerations such as field padding, alignment, and rounding are incorporated to balance readability with the rigor required by reporting standards.

1   Field Specification and Alignment

The construction of output fields necessitates a careful definition of numerical and textual parameters. In many reporting systems, numeric values are aligned by adherence to a fixed schema that dictates the location of both significant digits and decimal markers.

This often involves the application of padding techniques—such as space or zero filling—to guarantee that data aligns uniformly across multiple records. Such methods allow for the reliable parsing of output by automated systems, as well as by human auditors, especially in contexts where precision is paramount. Mathematically, a formatting function g may be defined as

$$g : \mathbb{N} \cup \mathbb{R} \to F,$$

where the domain comprises both integer and real-number representations, and F embodies the space of fields conforming to required presentation rules.

2 Transformation Functions in Output Representation

The conversion of raw data into a readable output involves a series of composable transformation functions which collectively produce the final displayed field. Denote this composite transformation by

$$f = f_k \circ f_{k-1} \circ \cdots \circ f_1,$$

where each function f_i corresponds to a distinct formatting stage, such as rounding, truncation, or character rearrangement. The sequential composition of these operations allows for modular adjustments to the data presentation pipeline, thereby accommodating the variability of reporting requirements. This rigorous formulation ensures that output formatting remains both systematic and adaptable, capable of addressing the multifaceted constraints imposed by institutional and regulatory frameworks.

Methodologies for Data Masking in Sensitive Data Reporting

Data masking is employed to transform sensitive information prior to its inclusion in reports, thereby mitigating the risk of unauthorized data exposure. This process involves the deliberate substitution of specific data segments with obfuscatory symbols that maintain field structure without revealing the underlying content. The masking operation can be formally represented by a function

$$m : E \to E',$$

where E is the set of original data elements, and E' denotes the set of sanitized outputs designed to preserve confidentiality while retaining the overall format.

1 Foundations of Data Masking Techniques

At its core, data masking centers on the need to balance utility with security. The methodology often involves partitioning data elements into segments that are either exposed or concealed, based on their sensitivity. In contexts where the data includes personally identifiable information or confidential numeric sequences, specific portions of the field are substituted with predetermined placeholder characters. Such substitution is designed to preserve the overall character count and format, thereby ensuring compatibility with downstream processing systems. The mathematical underpinning of this approach is rooted in the concept of a masking function that selectively transforms parts of an element according to a well-defined schema.

2 Techniques for Mask Pattern Design

The design of a mask pattern requires both syntactic precision and semantic awareness. Mask patterns are typically derived from a set of rules that specify which portions of a data element are to be replaced and by which characters. In the case of numeric sequences, a common strategy involves the replacement of trailing digits while leaving leading digits intact, thereby retaining a semblance of the original value without disclosing sensitive details. For textual data, a mask may partially obscure characters using invariant symbols that serve as proxies for the concealed information. This operation can be modeled by a function

$$p : T \to T',$$

where T represents the original data template and T' is the corresponding template after application of the masking rules. Such an approach allows for the customization of masking strategies to meet varying levels of security and compliance requirements.

3 Integrative Considerations in Reporting Systems

Within robust reporting architectures, output formatting and data masking often coexist as interdependent processes. The sequential application of a formatting function f and a masking function m is captured by the composite function

$$h = m \circ f,$$

which ensures that data is first transformed into a structured format and subsequently sanitized. This integrative model supports a high degree of modularity, enabling independent refinement of formatting and masking procedures in response to changes in regulatory or operational standards. The systematic coordination of these techniques not only enhances the clarity and consistency of the presented data but also fortifies the report against potential breaches of confidentiality.

Cobol Code Snippet

```
IDENTIFICATION DIVISION.
PROGRAM-ID. FORMATMASK.

ENVIRONMENT DIVISION.
* No external files are required for this demonstration.

DATA DIVISION.
WORKING-STORAGE SECTION.
* Raw numeric data to be formatted (transformation function
↪  f: D → F).
77  WS-RAW-NUM        PIC 9(6)V99     VALUE 12345.67.
77  WS-FORMATTED-NUM  PIC ZZZZZ9.99   VALUE ZERO.

* Raw sensitive data to be masked (transformation function m:
↪  E → E').
77  WS-RAW-DATA       PIC X(12)       VALUE "123456789012".
77  WS-MASKED-DATA    PIC X(12)       VALUE SPACES.

* Working variables.
77  WS-INDEX          PIC 99          VALUE ZERO.
77  WS-DISPLAY        PIC X(80)       VALUE SPACES.

PROCEDURE DIVISION.
MAIN-PARA.
    * Apply the formatting transformation.
    PERFORM FORMAT-DATA.
```

```
    * Apply the data masking transformation.
    PERFORM MASK-DATA.
    * Compose and display the final output using h = m  f.
    PERFORM DISPLAY-RESULT.
    STOP RUN.

FORMAT-DATA.
    * This paragraph simulates the transformation function f:
    ↪  D → F.
    MOVE WS-RAW-NUM TO WS-FORMATTED-NUM.
    DISPLAY "Formatted Number (f): " WS-FORMATTED-NUM.
    EXIT.

MASK-DATA.
    * This paragraph simulates the masking function m: E →
    ↪  E'.
    MOVE WS-RAW-DATA TO WS-MASKED-DATA.
    * Mask characters in positions 5 through 8 (e.g.,
    ↪  applying mask pattern p: T → T').
    PERFORM VARYING WS-INDEX FROM 5 BY 1 UNTIL WS-INDEX > 8
        MOVE "*" TO WS-MASKED-DATA (WS-INDEX:1)
    END-PERFORM.
    DISPLAY "Masked Data (m): " WS-MASKED-DATA.
    EXIT.

DISPLAY-RESULT.
    * Composite the formatted and masked outputs (h = m  f).
    STRING "Final Composite Output: " DELIMITED BY SIZE,
           "Formatted: "              DELIMITED BY SIZE,
           WS-FORMATTED-NUM           DELIMITED BY SIZE,
           " | Masked: "              DELIMITED BY SIZE,
           WS-MASKED-DATA             DELIMITED BY SIZE
           INTO WS-DISPLAY.
    DISPLAY WS-DISPLAY.
    EXIT.
```

Chapter 66

Basic Debugging with DISPLAY Statements

Conceptual Underpinnings

The technique of embedding output instructions within a program has been formalized as a diagnostic mechanism to project internal computational states into an observable medium. When considering the program state as an element of a set S, each invocation of a DISPLAY statement may be conceived as a mapping

$$d : S \to O,$$

where O represents the set of observable outputs. This paradigm encapsulates the methodology of tracing variable assignments and system behavior by making explicit the otherwise implicit state transitions. The approach, while elementary in its construct, fosters a systematic insight into the logical progression of execution steps.

1   Functional Mapping from Program State to Output

A schematic representation of the observable process is achieved by isolating the key variables and parameters at specific execution points. The DISPLAY statement functions as an operator that extracts a subset of the program state, denoted by $\sigma \subset S$, and renders it visible in a predetermined format. This abstraction, viewed from the perspective of functional programming, enables the assignment of a diagnostic value $o \in O$ as

$$o = d(\sigma).$$

The selective projection offered by the DISPLAY command creates a layer of transparency that is crucial for pinpointing anomalies and verifying the integrity of computational logic.

Execution Tracing and Temporal Analysis

Execution tracing via discrete output statements constitutes a temporal dissection of the computational process. A program may be modeled as a sequence of state transitions, $s_0, s_1, s_2, \ldots$, where each transition embodies a transformation under some function $\tau : S \to S$. Strategic placement of DISPLAY instructions allows the chronological capture of essential state information, permitting an examination of the evolution of variable values over time.

1 Temporal Profiling of Execution Flow

The act of recording program state at successive intervals provides a temporal profile that illuminates the progression of control flow. This profile is instrumental in establishing the correspondence between expected and actual progression through the algorithmic steps. Analysis of such profiles involves comparing the observed sequence

$$\{o_0, o_1, o_2, \ldots\} \quad \text{with} \quad \{d(s_0), d(s_1), d(s_2), \ldots\},$$

thereby facilitating the identification of discrepancies that may suggest a deviation from the designed control paths.

2 Spatial Localization of Anomalous States

In addition to temporal sequencing, the spatial context of variable assignments further refines the debugging process. The judicious placement of DISPLAY statements provides a means to localize the origin of errors by correlating the output messages with precise positions in the source code. The spatial aspect of debugging, when coupled with sequential state observations, supports a comprehensive analysis of data flow and operational integrity.

Analytical Refinements in Display-Based Debugging

The methodological utility of DISPLAY-driven debugging extends into the quantitative assessment of program behavior. By delineating the program state into observable components, it becomes feasible to aggregate diagnostic outputs for a rigorous examination of the computational process. The aggregation function

$$a : O^* \to M,$$

where O^* represents the sequence of outputs and M denotes a set of measurable debugging metrics, affords a structured approach to error analysis.

1 Diagnostic Clarity through Explicit Output

The utility of explicit state outputs is further enhanced when the debugging process is imbued with descriptive and unambiguous output formatting. Establishing a well-defined output convention permits the extraction of invariant properties of the program state, thereby yielding enhanced diagnostic clarity. The deterministic nature of the DISPLAY operation ensures that each output encapsulates a faithful representation of the associated state parameters, an aspect that is fundamental to the subsequent extraction of debugging insights.

2 Integration with Program Analysis Paradigms

The incorporation of DISPLAY statements into the debugging framework facilitates a seamless integration with both static and dynamic analysis techniques. The recorded outputs serve as a basis for formulating hypotheses regarding program behavior and identifying potential deviations from theoretical models. This integration supports a dual-layer approach wherein dynamic outputs are juxtaposed with the rigorously derived static expectations, thereby advancing the overall analytical acumen in debugging practices.

Cobol Code Snippet

```
IDENTIFICATION DIVISION.
PROGRAM-ID. DEBUGGING-DEMO.
```

```
AUTHOR. MaxwellVector.

*----------------------------------------------------
* This program demonstrates the debugging concept using
* DISPLAY statements to trace state transitions. The
↪  conceptual
* mapping "d: S -> O" (where S is the program state and O is
↪  the
* observable output) is mimicked by showing state information
↪  at
* each computation step. Additionally, the aggregation
↪  function
* "a: O* -> M" is simulated by combining debug messages.
*----------------------------------------------------

ENVIRONMENT DIVISION.
* No external file processing is required for this
↪  demonstration.

DATA DIVISION.
WORKING-STORAGE SECTION.

* The program state S is defined below:
01 WS-STATE.
    05 WS-VAR1          PIC 9(4) VALUE 100.
    05 WS-VAR2          PIC 9(4) VALUE  50.
    05 WS-RESULT        PIC 9(4) VALUE   0.
    05 WS-STEP          PIC 9(4) VALUE   0.

* Variable for aggregated debug messages (for analysis
↪  metrics).
01 WS-DEBUG-MESSAGE     PIC X(80).

PROCEDURE DIVISION.
MAIN-PROGRAM.
    PERFORM INITIALIZE.
    PERFORM DEBUG-TRACE.
    PERFORM FINALIZE.
    STOP RUN.

INITIALIZE.
    DISPLAY "----- Debugging Initialization -----".
    * At this point, the initial state s0 is:
    *   WS-VAR1 = 100, WS-VAR2 = 50, WS-RESULT = 0.
    * Conceptually, this is our d(s0): S -> O.
    DISPLAY "Initial State: WS-VAR1=" WS-VAR1
            " WS-VAR2=" WS-VAR2 " WS-RESULT=" WS-RESULT.
    EXIT.

DEBUG-TRACE.
    * This section simulates state transitions:
    *   s0, s1, s2, ... where each transition is : S -> S.
    * Debug outputs mimic the mapping: o = d() with   S.
```

290

```
      PERFORM VARY-STATE VARYING WS-STEP FROM 1 BY 1 UNTIL
      ↪    WS-STEP > 5
      END-PERFORM.
      EXIT.

VARY-STATE.
      * Compute new state: WS-RESULT = WS-VAR1 + WS-VAR2.
      COMPUTE WS-RESULT = WS-VAR1 + WS-VAR2.

      * Display current state - a diagnostic snapshot.
      DISPLAY "Step " WS-STEP ": WS-VAR1=" WS-VAR1
             ", WS-VAR2=" WS-VAR2 ", WS-RESULT=" WS-RESULT.

      * Aggregate debug information for further analysis.
      MOVE "Debug Step " TO WS-DEBUG-MESSAGE.
      STRING WS-DEBUG-MESSAGE WS-STEP " => V1:" WS-VAR1
             " V2:" WS-VAR2 " RES:" WS-RESULT DELIMITED BY SIZE
             INTO WS-DEBUG-MESSAGE.
      DISPLAY WS-DEBUG-MESSAGE.

      * Update the state to simulate temporal evolution.
      ADD 10 TO WS-VAR1.
      EXIT.

FINALIZE.
      DISPLAY "----- Debugging Finalization -----".
      * Output the final observed state.
      DISPLAY "Final State: WS-VAR1=" WS-VAR1
             " WS-VAR2=" WS-VAR2 " WS-RESULT=" WS-RESULT.
      DISPLAY "End of Debugging Process.".
      EXIT.
```